SEASON OF THE
LONG GRASS

It is said that mid-wives in the Valleys of South Wales never slapped a baby's bottom...they merely stamped them 'Valleys born', thus ensuring a life-long, fierce loyalty to the region, a well honed Welsh emotional sensitivity and a vibrant awareness of belonging and 'sense of place'. Norma Lloyd-Nesling must surely have such a stamp about her person, for she displays all those attributes admirably in her mind's return to Abercynon and Mountain Ash in the 1950s. It is an evocative journey to a time and place that so many of us recognise, meeting characters we all know and re-living experiences that were ours too, but perhaps in other valleys. Her childhood world is viewed from Table Rock, where the grass grew long, high above the lower Cynon Valley. We can all relate to her early school days in the Clock School Abercynon, then Mountain Ash Grammar School, housed in Lord Aberdare's lovely Duffryn House and the trials of 'The Scholarship' exam that was the bridge into academia. Her rich broth of offerings include childhood adventures in the valley, trips to Barry Island, London, carnivals, Carpanini's Knickerbocker Glories, street names like Cemetery Road, Doctor's Hill and Granville Terrace and nicknamed characters common to all valleys. There is a sweet richness in Norma's tale telling, but it is mixed to the savoury of the common touch that clearly marks her as 'one of us'. Be honest, we have all known 'Seasons of the Long Grass' and Norma, wonderfully, does us all a favour, in reminding us of how we too, long ago,viewed life from our own Table Rock.

Roy Noble OBE . DL
BBC Wales Broadcaster

NORMA LLOYD-NESLING

SEASON OF THE LONG GRASS

Matador
9 De Montfort Mews
Leicester LE1 7FW, UK
Tel: (+44) 116 255 9311 / 9312
Email: books@troubador.co.uk
Web: www.troubador.co.uk/matador

ISBN 978-1906221-027

Typeset in 11.5pt Bembo by Troubador Publishing Ltd, Leicester, UK
Printed in the UK by The Cromwell Press Ltd, Trowbridge, Wilts, UK

Matador is an imprint of Troubador Publishing Ltd

For my mother Elizabeth Doreen
and
In memory of my father Douglas and my grandparents Henry,
Beatrice, Margaret and Edrice

AUTHOR'S NOTE TO THE READER

The characters in this book are real people and the events depicted actually took place. In retrospect, one forgets the ordinary, uneventful days of childhood. What sticks in the memory are those times that were funny, poignant, tragic or hilariously catastrophic.

To make the events more colourful I have tried to bring the characters alive by employing the local dialect prevalent at the time. The dialogue is composed of remembered conversations, snatches of banter between the characters during a lively tête à tête and various discussions that took place in the community.

There are a variety of accents in Wales: North Walian, West Walian, South Walian and Cardiffian. Accents also vary within villages, some being much more pronounced than others, or diluted after living or being educated outside Wales. Whatever the degree of Welshness one element they all have in common is the lilting, musical expressiveness of the dialect that is rarely lost.

Apart from family members, names that were in the public domain during the period depicted in this book and the multitude who have long since passed away, all other names have been changed to allow anonymity. Time lines, place names, geographic references, names of companies, references to wireless programmes and songs are as accurate as memory allows.

Nicknames were prevalent in Wales in the 1950s and the majority of them in this book are authentic. There was a Little Dai, Long Dai, Big John, Little John and Little Billy in almost every town and village in Wales. There were at least three small boys named David, otherwise known as Little Dai, living in the Abercynon area.

However, the Little Dai referred to in this book is a pseudonym for another person. It does not refer to anybody who was known as Little Dai who was actually living in Abercynon during the period this book covers. In this instance the nickname is entirely fictitious in order to preserve the identity of the person concerned.

I have attempted to recapture an often nostalgic picture of life living in a small mining village where the local people served as the glue that bonded the community. In those days families lived closer together; life for children and adolescents was altogether more innocent than today and there was a strong sense of community and duty. Help was always at hand for the lonely and those in need of a friend.

In conclusion, I would like to thank those who jogged my memory about village life and schooldays. In particular, to my family and friends with whom I shared those very special memories; memories that will stay with me forever.

'I am dreaming of the mountains of my home.
Of the mountains where in child-hood I did roam;
I have dwelt 'neath Southern skies,
Where the summer never dies,
But my heart is in the mountains of my home.'

'My Little Welsh Home'
Written by W S Williams
Published by Chappell Recorded Music Library

PROLOGUE

The sights, the sounds and the smells assaulted my senses. Vivid memories of a golden mist of long grass swam before my eyes as I scrambled over the loose stones to reach the top of the hill to find the secret place of my childhood bathed in the summer sun. This place that we had made our own. This place where the grass had magical properties that could sweep us on a journey of discovery so exciting that we would talk in whispers for fear of breaking the spell with the sound of a human voice. This place where I knew I would one day return, but for now one more dream on Table Rock before my journey to another land and another life.

The clearing near the old weather-beaten wall was overgrown with a tangle of purple foxgloves and nettles; the rugged, flat stone we had christened Table Rock, covered in moss and lichen, smoothed in places where the wind and rain had lashed at it mercilessly over the years. Wild flowers peppered the ground courting the ferns. Wind berry bushes hung purple with lush fruit amongst the 'long grass'. The sound of horses' hooves clattering against stone receded into the distance as the riders ambled up the winding farm road, then complete silence.

No sound save for the occasional faint rustle of some animal foraging for food. I watched a butterfly settle delicately and precariously on a wild strawberry plant and let the atmosphere envelop my whole being like warm snowflakes. Pressing my body against its hard surface I lay face down and ran my hands over the cracks and indentations and felt the years seeping through my thin shirt. The feeling was profoundly sensual suffusing my entire being with an almost physical yearning as I drifted over the precipice of the past to journey through my childhood.

1

CLOCK SCHOOL

The grey, flag-stoned side lobby that led into the infants' classroom at Abercynon 'Clock' school felt cold and smelled of disinfectant. Flaky, sickly-looking cream paint sat atop dark, dull-green, lower walls that reminded me of a hospital. Through the open classroom door on the left I could see children sitting on little wooden chairs. A teacher stood at the inner door waiting for her new charges.

"This is Mrs Nicholas, your teacher," said my mother comfortingly. "She'll look after yew until I pick yew up for lunch."

Whimpering, I clung on to her coat while she tried to prise my hands away to push me gently towards the classroom.

"No, I dwn't want to go to school!" I cried, hot tears rolling down my cheeks.

I couldn't understand why my mother wanted me to go into this awful place without her.

"Yew have to go to school. There'll be other children to play with. Yew'll love it," she said her voice querulous with anxiety.

Mrs Nicholas, dressed in a floral smock, closed the heavy, wooden door and dropped the latch before ushering me gently to the cloakroom.

"Come on now, yew can put your coat on this hook. Look, it has a coloured picture of a fish."

Tremulously, I took her hand as she guided me back into the classroom. Children were sitting in a semi-circle on the floor; some looking frightened others, whose older siblings peeped around the classroom door, sat with mischievous grins unconcerned at being abandoned in a strange place. Through my tears I saw Dobbin, the huge rocking horse, with a child on its back laughing down at me. One of the teachers was opening a window with a long pole with a hook on the end of it. Outside mothers, some in tears, were peering through the windows, on tip-toe, to catch sight of their little ones or tapping the window to catch their attention mouthing,

"Dwn't worry I'll be coming to fetch yew later. Be good!"

Catching sight of my mother's anxious face at the window I started to cry again until I caught sight of some colourful books.

"Yew like books, do yew?" Mrs Nicholas asked.

"Ye-es, I do. I can read a little bit."

"Well then, let's see if we can find a nice one for yew, shall we?"

Still snivelling, I glanced through the pages stopping when anything caught my attention. I loved books; just holding them filled me with anticipation. Mrs Nicholas left me in the book corner until I was urged to stop reading to join the other children for break.

Morning break brought a new torture. Standing patiently waiting for my small bottle of milk I was dismayed to find Mrs Nicholas handing me an egg-cup filled with orange juice with a blob of some foul-smelling, noxious-looking liquid floating on top. Screwing up my nose I pushed it away declaring,

"Yuk, looks awful! I'd rather some milk please."

This greasy stuff was the same as my mother tried to persuade me to drink in the mornings.

"Yew have lots of milk at home. Your mother wanted yew to have cod-liver oil instead. Drink it up. It's *lovely* mixed with orange-juice."

Holding the egg-cup to my mouth she urged me to pinch my nose and drink it quickly. "Swallow it!" she ordered watching me holding the vile mixture in my mouth.

Still refusing to drink I gagged holding my hand over my mouth. Finally, she took me off to the cloakroom where I obediently spat it into the sink. This ritual was repeated, day after day, until one morning she reached down into the crate sighing,

"Oh, very well," and thrust a bottle of milk at me.

In the afternoons we rested on little camp beds erected by the teachers. Each child had a blanket with a picture in the corner that matched their coat hook. Sleep never came to me as I lay studying the embroidered fish on my blanket and the colourful pictures on the classroom walls. How I wished 'rest hour' would end so that I could get back to reading my book.

Soulfully, Old Dobbin, the big rocking horse gazed back at me as restricted as I was by his hooves that were stuck to the wooden rockers. I imagined climbing up onto his back and galloping straight through the open window across the yard and into the green fields. Bright-eyed and snorting with pleasure his mane flying in the wind; eyes bright with excitement and the exhilaration of his new-found freedom.

Reality interrupted with Mrs Lewis, the Governess, hovering over my bed, gently tucking the blanket under my chin and whispering in a chiding tone;

"Shwsh now, there's a good girl. Close your eyes."

Silence except for the turning of a page or the quiet steps of Mrs Lewis as she walked between the beds. Yawning with boredom rather than tiredness; restlessly fidgeting and screwing up my eyes in a desperate attempt to will myself to sleep inevitably failed. My imagination ran riot until I heard the welcome words,

"Time to wake up and fold your blankets."

The year passed in feigned, restless sleep. Every afternoon I spent time inside my head sailing on rough seas, climbing mountains until I reached the clouds, tramping through snow-covered forests; journeying on and on until Mrs Nicholas finally folded away my little bed, smiled brightly and declared,

"Come along children," as she led us into Miss Edwards' classroom.

AN ANGEL OF THE LORD

Miss Edwards, a tall, dark-haired woman with rosy cheeks and a kindly face, was my favourite teacher. Without her heavy-framed glasses, with their thick lenses, she had white patches around her eyes where her face had been protected from the elements. Small, red, pressure grooves sat either side of her nose. Squinting short-sightedly, as she cleaned her glasses, her smile radiated warmth and concern for her 'children'. She showed interest in every child and never raised her voice even to those who were badly behaved.

When she asked,

"Who'd like to help me tidy up the books?" every hand in the class shot up in unison.

At the end of term we vied to be allowed to clean out her cupboards. Diligent pupils received a small chocolate bar for their efforts with the promise that it would be someone else's turn next time.

As Christmas approached excitement mounted especially when Miss Edwards asked with a knowing smile,

"Who'd like to be in the Christmas concert?"

"Me, me miss!" cried the children almost jumping out of their seats so that she could see their raised hands.

I hung back fervently hoping I wouldn't be chosen to take part. My shyness made performing in public a huge hurdle for me, because I hated being the centre of attention. Every smile and gesture from the audience found me staring at the floor red-faced and near to tears.

Whenever there was a concert my part was always a fairy or an angel. A gypsy, or any other character, would have been more exciting, but my lot was to be the tallest fairy in the history of the school. In one concert I played one of six fairies who pranced about a make-believe forest touching flowers and small creatures with the tips of their magic wands. My mother spent hours making a dress out of white tulle with silver stars sewn all over the bodice.

"It's absolutely gorgeous!" she cried proudly.

"But, I've got to have wings as well. I can't be a fairy without wings, can I?"

"I'll make yew some wings," declared Terry, my uncle. "The best wings yew've ever seen!"

My mother's youngest brother, just six years my senior, was more like an older brother. Enthusiastically, he set about making a pair of wings out of chicken wire and white tissue paper.

"Let's get these on to see if they fit," he said tying the string attached to the wings around my waist. "That looks great, but yew need a wand as well."

He worked for hours cutting out and discarding various designs. Finally, he produced a long, slim wand with a huge, silver star at the top decorated with silver tinsel wound round the handle.

"I'll have the best outfit in the class," I sighed contentedly.

The dress was very delicate so I was only allowed to take the wings and wand to school in readiness for the afternoon concert.

It snowed heavily that morning so unknown to some of the parents the concert was brought forward. Mothers, who had been worried about flimsy dresses being damaged, arrived furious to discover the concert had already started. My navy, pleated skirt and long, grey, woollen socks contrasted ludicrously with the flimsy, gauze wings and sparkling wand. Squirming with embarrassment I was pushed forward to dance with the more exquisite fairies, delicate wings stuck on the back of my red jersey.

At Christmas every child was given a part in the nativity play. As usual I was to be an Angel of the Lord dressed in shimmering white. This time my chief wing-maker made bigger, more elaborate creations covered with shiny, silver paper sprinkled with glittering, silver dust while my wand was decorated with sparkling streamers. The ensemble was completed with a silver halo that hovered over my head. At bed time my hair was wound round strips of cloth to ensure that I would emerge with the perfect, fat ringlets my mother favoured.

Walking to school next morning I held my breath with excitement and trepidation as we scurried down Doctor's Hill and through the school gates. At the last moment I hung back as fear took over my legs and they began to tremble. I decided I didn't want to be an angel but my mother had other ideas. There was no way I was going to get out of it. She led me firmly into the cloakroom, took off my coat, fastened the wings to my back and placed the halo gingerly over my ringlets.

Pulling at them furiously I stamped my foot.

"I don't want be an angel!" I pouted as my mother gently pushed me into the classroom towards the teacher who was lining up the children into their designated places.

"I don't want to be a soddin' angel either," screamed Phillip as his mother, face red and angry, looked sheepishly around to see if the other parents had heard.

"Little scamp," she said lovingly between her teeth grabbing him by the arm and shoving him forward. "I can't imagine where he heard such language. Tsk! Tsk! Wait until yewer father gets home my boy, then yew'll cop it in no uncertain terms!"

Some of the other little angels started to cry while shepherds fidgeted with the tea towels over their heads. Mary grabbed hold of the baby Jesus doll and swung it around by one arm. Joseph just stared ahead unblinkingly, with his thumb stuck in his mouth, apparently unconcerned with the behaviour of his wife.

My father's sister, Valerie, was also just six years my senior. She had a huge, baby doll with a smiling, celluloid face. I coveted that doll until she finally handed it over dressed completely in full-size baby clothes. With great difficulty I carried it from Caegarw to the 'bus stop in the centre of Mountain Ash resolutely refusing any help from my mother.

"It's bigger than yew!" the conductor of the Red & White 'bus laughed.

After struggling aboard I sat with the doll on my lap looking at the rosy-cheeked face lovingly. Now she was mine I determined that this was to be my baby in the forthcoming Christmas Concert. We had practised a lullaby for weeks. Holding hands a boy and girl sat on the floor facing each other, a make-believe baby in the middle. With my partner, a pale, fair-haired boy called Malcolm, we swayed to and fro in unison as we sang Brahms' 'Lullaby'.

I couldn't wait to take the doll to school the next day. Pushing his cycle with one hand Terry walked me to Williams' shop at the top of West Street. As soon as we were out of sight he mounted his bike, sat me and the doll on the crossbar and rode off towards North Street. As the road began to descend I held on tightly but lost my grip of the doll. My beautiful baby fell off the bike and into the road her face shattering into a dozen pieces. Screaming at Terry I sobbed,

"My baby's broken now, she's dead! It's your fault!"

"Stop being a silly idiot, it's a doll!" he said looking increasingly worried.

He knew he was going to be in trouble for putting me on the crossbar so he tried to soothe me as best he could.

"Dwn't tell Nana and Dad or I'll really be in trouble," he groaned. "We'll just say yew dropped it. Yew must have got another doll for the concert!"

After delivering me to school he rushed up the hill to get another doll. Fifteen minutes later he returned with a black doll that he had borrowed from a friend. I had never seen any black people. Pushing it away I dragged my feet as I was pulled, snivelling, into the hall to play my part.

"I dwn't want it!" I sobbed. "It's not my special doll, is it?"

Silent tears coursed down my cheeks all through the concert as Malcolm and I swayed to the music of the piano. The little doll stared up at me; bright red lips and white, toothy grin on its shiny, dark face. It looked happier than I did. I was too young to realise that there were others in the world who were different from me or that humiliation was not an isolated event and would strike again when the daffodils were in bloom.

PAPER DAFFODILS

On St. David's Day little boys in knee-britches and flat caps, scowls on their faces, hung their heads and dragged their feet to school. Girls dressed in white, lacy pinafores over their skirts, shoulders draped with Welsh shawls surmounted by the traditional tall, black hat, skipped down Doctor's Hill hand in hand. Costumed children in the concert had lines to quote as they joined hands and danced amongst the daffodils that were 'growing' in blobs of pale, grey clay stuck on to small, rectangular, wooden boards. Some girls had individually designed dresses based on wood nymphs or fairies, but my mother wanted something different.

Inspirational patriotism stirred her soul. Our Saint's day called for something unique.

"It'll be perfect for the day. There won't be another dress like it!" she beamed.

Night after night she sat making a dress out of sheets of crêpe paper covering it with a froth of delicate, yellow, tissue paper. My head-dress was a giant daffodil complete with bright, green stem. A pair of white, cotton socks were hand-dyed a garish yellow. Large paper daffodils were glued on the front of my shoes and trimmed with cut-out green leaves. To complete the ensemble I carried a bunch of real daffodils in a basket to hand out to staff as I 'flew' around the classroom.

Puffed up with pride she was convinced that no other child would have such a wonderful creation. After depositing me in the classroom she simpered off towards the other parents pausing to admire her handiwork. Once seated she chatted amiably with the other mothers all of whom were cooing away at the sight of their children dressed up.

"Oh, they do look lovely, dwn't they?" said Megan's mother. "Not quite as good as mine but nice mind just the same."

Needled, the other mothers sniffed disdainfully turning away to make some barbed comment. My daffodil dress was admired by Mrs Lewis, the Governess, poked and prodded by the other children while I hung my head in simultaneous embarrassment and pride.

The old adage about pride coming before a fall visited me with a vengeance that day. Pandemonium as children chattered excitedly while teachers helped to do up shoelaces, button up coats and wrap scarves around their small charges. Clamorous greetings as mothers came to collect their children who were tightly clutching the single daffodil they had been given after the concert.

"Mam! Mam! Look what I've got for yew!" they chorused.

"Thank yew love, it's beautiful innit!"

Exclamations of delight when the flower was presented and promises that it would be pressed into a book to be remembered in future years. There was a celebratory atmosphere as mothers and children thronged to the school gates to enjoy the half day holiday.

The cold, white sun of an end of winter day battled for dominance with one or two black, heavy-looking clouds hanging ominously overhead. Basking in our parents' and teachers' approbation we climbed up Doctor's Hill and turned into North Street with the other families. My nose in the air, still floating on a cloud of admiration, the heavens opened. It didn't just drizzle, it came in torrents while the wind whipped up to a howling gale.

First the hat, with its giant daffodil, was plucked from my head and whizzed like a Catherine wheel over Mrs Maddox' garden wall. Grasping fingers of wind tore at my dress until it was just strips of torn yellow clinging to my body below my cardigan. The paper wrapped itself around my legs and left huge, yellow stains. By the time we had run the last few yards home my dress had all but disappeared revealing my knickers which were also soaking wet with rain. Howling as loudly as the wind I looked in the mirror and saw my mother's creation limply draping my shoulders beneath the sodden ringlets plastered to my face. It was the first and last time my mother attempted haute couture in paper.

"My dress is all wet and floppy," I grizzled as I ran towards my grandparents. "Everybody was laughing at me."

"Never mind, it's not the end of the world now, is it?" Dad Smith soothed. "Yew be a good girl now and I'll take yew to see Topper next week.

THE CHESNUT STALLION

Dad Smith came from a long line of horse lovers and had ridden to hunt from a small boy. Emrys, the only one of his sons who had the same enthusiasm, was given a beautiful, sleek, chestnut stallion for his eighteenth birthday. Topper was a magnificent steed, highly strung with racing blood. Emrys loved him with a passion. Lifting me up to stroke his main simultaneously fascinated and terrified me, especially when he sat me on to the huge animal's back.

"Up yew come," Emrys said.

"I'll fall off!" I exclaimed.

"No yew won't, just hang on to his mane and keep your legs pressed against him."

I looked down at the ground feeling a thrill of fear, but also elated at the thought of riding this beautiful horse. Sitting so high in the air, the breeze rippling Topper's mane, my chest swelled with pride as I looked over the garden walls; the envy of every child in the neighbourhood. Emrys walked slowly down the lane until I was used to the movement.

"We'll go for a proper ride now," he said getting up behind me.

When Topper began to trot I was lost in my imagination. One minute charging into battle, the next galloping across the prairie with Red Indians in close pursuit as Topper snorted and neighed his approval. We cantered back up the lane at the back of the houses where Emrys lowered me to the ground.

"Let me feed him, please!" I begged.

"All right, we'll feed him later, but dwn't ever go near this horse unless I'm with yew," Emrys called over his shoulder as he rode off. "He's very highly strung."

Later that day, spying Topper tethered to a post that led into the lane behind the house contentedly munching at some hay, I went out to give him a handful hoping that I wouldn't be spotted. As I held out the hay, cradled in both arms, he suddenly lunged to grab a mouthful but his jaws enclosed my arm. I screamed;

"My arm, he's bitten my arm."

Startled, he pulled back his head as Dad Smith rushed out of the back door, caught the reins, and pushed him away.

"Let me see!"

A bruise was already forming where Topper's teeth marks had imprinted the skin of my upper arm.

"What did I tell yew about playing with him. Yew could have been badly injured."

Poor old Topper had only wanted to get at the straw but my arm had got in the way.

"Well, it doesn't look too bad but we'd better take yew to casualty just in case."

"What's wrong?" Nana Smith asked when I went indoors wincing with pain.

"Topper bit her on the arm," Emrys said.

"Bit her on the arm? Where were yew when this was going on?"

"I only turned my back for a minute then I heard her screaming like a banshee."

After the wound was declared superficial Nana bundled me into the car before laying down the law.

She glared at Emrys and Dad Smith,

"Dwn't ever go near that horse again on your own. Do yew hear me?"

"Yes Nana," I snivelled loudly.

She 'cwtched' me up to her saying sympathetically,

"The marks are fading already. I expect it'll be almost gone by tomorrow."

Her eyes showed concern, but her face warned me that if I disobeyed again there would be dire consequences.

Emrys and his friend kept their horses in a stable in a small clearing opposite the demolished shack of 'Brown the Slaughterer' halfway up the hill that led on to Cemetery Road. One morning he came back after going to feed the horses in a frenzy of distress.

"It's Topper," he cried, "somebody's been beating him. We've had to call the vet out."

Blindly, he rushed out and raced back up to the stables where Dad Smith was waiting for the vet to arrive.

"I'd better go and see what's happened," Nana Smith said as she descended the front steps. "Yew'd better go home now. Off yew go."

Taking my arm she hurriedly ushered me across the road calling to my mother who, completely oblivious, was in the kitchen singing along to some operatic aria on the wireless.

"I'll come with yew," I pleaded.

"No, yew go in and *stay* there," she said firmly.

I watched as she walked swiftly down the road and disappeared round the bend then trailed her at a safe distance. When she got to the stables Dad Smith barred her way keeping her out on the road away from the clearing.

"Yew'd better not come any closer; yew stay out here," he said firmly. "This is no place for yew either my girl. Yew'd better go back home with your nana."

Suddenly, realising I was behind her, Nana Smith looked over her shoulder,

"I thought I told yew to go home yew *naughty* girl," she said in a worried voice.

During the night the stable had been broken into and Topper had been badly beaten with a chain that was found nearby in the bushes. The beautiful animal had fallen to the ground soaked in his own blood, his body covered with deep wounds. Through a gap in the trees I saw him lying on the grass writhing with pain; his eyes glassy, whitish, grey foam seeping from the sides of his mouth. When the vet arrived he examined Topper and shook his head sadly.

"I'm sorry Harry but I'll have to put him down to prevent his suffering. He'll die within a few hours anyway. Such a beautiful horse. What kind of people would do such a thing to a defenceless animal?"

"They're the animals!" Emrys exclaimed.

Eyes misty Nana Smith relaxed her grip on my shoulder and covered her mouth with her hands.

Looking at her stricken face Dad Smith said gently,

"It's for the best. Yew wouldn't want him to suffer now would yew, not with such awful wounds?"

"Now yew two, off yew go," he continued casting Nana Smith a knowing, sorrowful glance.

In silent acknowledgment she grabbed me by the hand and led me down the hill towards the houses. A heavy feeling in my chest, that I did not fully understand, warned me of impending tragedy. Topper was suffering immense pain but everything looked so normal. Golden daffodils swayed in the breeze, birds chirruped in the trees at the edges of the road. A passing walker called a morning greeting as he passed with his dog, bounding joyfully ahead, yapping excitedly as the man threw a stick for it to catch. Muted voices drifted up the hill as people went about their usual business.

As we rounded the corner strains of music from '*Housewives' Choice*' temporarily lifted my gloom.

"Why couldn't we stay with Topper?" I asked.

"Well, he needs to be kept quiet for a bit to calm him down. He'll be all right," Nana Smith declared reassuringly."

"I saw him when I peeked through the trees," I replied sadly.

"I wish yew hadn't followed me. Yew shouldn't see things like that." Nana sighed shaking her head.

As we rounded the bend a loud, sharp crack filled the air bringing her to a sudden stop.

"What was that noise?" I queried feeling a tug of unaccountable fear.

"Oh, it's probably coming from the forestry. I think they've been felling trees," she whispered to comfort me.

She knew Topper was dead, shot by the vet at point blank range.

An aura of gloom settled over the house for weeks. Emrys rarely showed his emotions, but the sight of his beloved chestnut-gold horse, and the circumstances of his death, stayed with him for many long months. Summer arrived and brought a new horse for Emrys. For me it heralded release from school and the promise of long, sunny days in Milton Villa.

A LESSON LEARNED

Being the first grandchild for my maternal and paternal grandparents gave me ample scope for coercion when I wanted my own way. As a small child I loved staying in Milton Villa and shopping down the 'Mount' with Nana Howells and the girls. Pugh's was my favourite shop.

"Yew mustn't go behind the counter," Rita chided as I tugged at the knob of one of the wooden drawers behind the polished counter.

"But I want to see what's in the drawers," I insisted as she pulled me back to her side.

Always curious every visit saw me foraging in their contents: skeins of brightly-coloured silks, red, gold, green and blue: reels of cotton in a variety of hues, thimbles, bias binding and lengths of shiny, satin ribbon were investigated with enthusiasm.

"She's very active," Nana Howells apologised pulling me away with embarrassment. Innate curiosity always got the better of me. As one draw was firmly closed I pulled out another.

"We'll just close that one shall we?" the shop assistant smiled tightly tidying up the disarranged contents.

"She's very quiet usually. I dwn't know what's got into yew today." Nana Howells tutted with frustration as she retreated in as dignified a manner as possible.

The final humiliation came after a visit to the cinema to see a Walt Disney production. Squinting as we emerged into the bright light of a warm summer's evening we headed up Oxford Street. Families were making their way home or having a welcome, cold drink in the café opposite. Clutching Nana Howells' hand we strolled leisurely through town. Halfway across 'Mount' bridge Valerie, my twelve year old aunt, sniffed,

"I can smell chips. Let's go to Marshall's for some fish and chips. Please!"

"It's too hot. I thought we'd have a light meal tonight. I've prepared it ready."

"Please, we never have chips from the fish shop and I really fancy some," Valerie said peevishly.

"Oh, all right," nana agreed. "Yew come with me."

"I want to come as well," I bawled clinging to her skirt while she tried to extricate herself from my grip.

"It's better if yew go home and help to lay the table by the time we get back." She looked imploringly at my grandfather.

As he took my hand I started to cry and pulled away from him.

"Dwn't leave me! Dwn't leave me!" I screamed.

Appalled, Nana Howells watched in consternation as I threw myself down onto the pavement in the middle of 'Mount' Bridge while my grandfather made feeble attempts to pick me up and cart me off home. Livid with embarrassment she cautioned me,

"That's *enough* of that behaviour. Bed for yew my girl as soon as yew get back!" she said voice sharp with annoyance.

She kept walking over the bridge then back again to shush my wailing.

"Edrice, grab hold of her and take her home otherwise we'll be ages. We won't be two minutes. Yew can play with the button tin," she soothed.

Reluctantly, I went home with the promise of the button tin foremost in my mind.

I loved the button tin; an old container that had held National Dried Milk baby powder. Whenever Nana Howells, or the girls, discarded a garment they cut off the more ornate buttons and put them in the tin. Some of them were quite beautiful; gilt, black-lacquered, bright red, turquoise-blue and chequered: square-shaped, giant-sized or diamond-shaped. Toggles, pearl buttons and little, delicate creations encrusted with diamantes. The feel and texture of them fascinated me. Lovingly, I sorted them into sets, counted them or arranged them in a colourful, abstract mosaic.

"I dwn't understand it, you're so quiet in the house. Dwn't yew ever behave like that again, yew naughty girl!" Nana Howells chided when she arrived with the chips. "I've never been so embarrassed in my life."

"Sorry nana," I said contritely. "I promise I won't be bad again."

"No, yew certainly won't!"

"But, I thought yew were leaving me behind," I said tearfully. Her voice softened,

"Oh, dwn't be so silly," she replied lifting me up. "Anyway, Rita's taking yew out for the afternoon soon. Yew'll enjoy that."

Suitably chastened I 'cwtched' in Nana's lap, but my days as a 'wild child' were numbered.

Rita, blonde and blue-eyed like my grandmother, had the same high, cheek bones and finely-drawn features as her sisters. Unlike the mischievous, artistic Margaret, who was often in hot water because of her pranks, Rita was more reserved and didn't suffer fools gladly. After attending private school in Cardiff she had secured an excellent position with a big company in the city.

"I'm off now," she called.

"Slow down a bit, for goodness sake!" Dad Howells said as she hurtled towards the door to catch the train.

"Last day before the holidays," she called up to me. " Tomorrow we can go for that walk I promised yew."

Bright light pierced my eyelids as I lay in that dreamlike state between sleep and full consciousness. Giving a long yawn I rubbed at my gritty eyes with my fists. Voices babbled unintelligibly from a distance. From downstairs the smell of bacon and toasted bread wafted up the stairs.

"Breakfast!" Nana Howells called. "Yew'd better come down now or the bacon will be all gone."

"Not if I can help it." I thought throwing back the satin eiderdown and rushing downstairs still in my pyjamas.

"Oh no yew dwn't." Nana Howells grabbed me before I had a chance to sit down. "Get washed and dressed first."

"But yew said there'll be no breakfast left," I said in a pleading tone.

"Go on, I'll put it in the oven to keep warm."

In minutes I was back at the table tucking into bacon, eggs and fried bread with a huge plum tomato on the side. Anxious to be outside in the fresh air I slurped noisily at the last of my tea. Nana Howells clucked her tongue with distaste.

"Do yew have to make that noise when you're drinking? It's not nice yew know, and stop encouraging her Valerie," she said tartly. "You're old enough to know better."

"Sorry, may I leave the table now?"

"Yes, and dwn't forget Rita's taking yew out this afternoon."

Feeling deliciously cool in our light, cotton frocks Rita and I strolled languorously down Granville Terrace skirting the hospital entrance before entering the cool greenness of Duffryn Woods.

"What are those stones?" I asked quizzically gazing down into a hollow under the monument.

"Druid stones."

"Why are they all in a circle?"

"I dwn't know, but some people say they used to sacrifice animals on the flat stone in the middle."

"What's a sacrifice?"

"It's when they kill something and offer it up to the gods."

"Why?"

"Oh, I dwn't know, to pray for good fortune or something."

"What's that for up there?" I pointed to a statue.

"That's the war memorial."

"What's a war mem-mem-omrium then?"

"Memorial, it's to remember the servicemen who died in the two world wars."

"What's a..."

"Oh, come on!" Rita urged taking my hand or we'll *never* get over to Peace Park.

Two couples were playing tennis on the courts next to the grammar school as we passed the great, iron gates closed for the holidays.

"That's a big garden, isn't it Rita?" I remarked admiring the well-manicured lawns, flowering cherry trees and shrubs. "Look there's a little bridge!"

"There's a big house down over the other side. It used to belong to Lord Aberdare but it's been a school for years now."

"P'raps I'll go there one day?" I replied unaware of my destiny.

"P'raps yew will."

We ambled down Mill Lane and crossed over new Cardiff Road into Peace Park emerging at Glenboi near the grammar school 'tuck shop'.

"We'll start at the bottom, have a look round the shops, then work our way back," Rita said walking towards the town centre.

To the left loomed the imposing grey, stone façade of Mountain Ash Town Hall, its clock tower facing the bridge that spanned the River Cynon. Right at the bottom of town the Workman's Hall and Palace cinema dominated the street; a replica of almost every miner's hall in South Wales.

"Ooh, look there's kittens in the window and rabbits," I cried heading for the pet shop.

The kittens mewed and padded at the enclosure rubbing their little heads against the glass in the hope of some contact.

"Poor little mites. It's cruel to keep them in cages especially in this weather!" Rita exclaimed. "They must be boiling behind all that glass."

Taking a last look she dragged me across the road to the gown shop to admire the latest creation hugging the mannequin in the window.

"Right, let's go for an ice cream before we go back. It'll cool us down."

We wandered past the bank and the Co-operative stores just below the school that had been bombed during the Second World War. Another stray bomb had reputedly landed on a train in Penrhiwceiber. Stories had circulated about the tender being blown all the way up the track to Mountain Ash. Opposite the Co-op was an Italian café which was where Rita and I were headed. It was blissfully cool inside after walking in the searing heat.

"I want a North Pole!" I demanded.

"Well, you can't have one! I only have enough for two strawberry ices," Rita said eyeing me warily.

"Whata would yewa lika?" asked the waitress as she arrived at our table. Before Rita could stop me I said in a loud voice,

"A North Pole please."

Rita sat and glowered at me when the ice-cream arrived. I tucked in, enjoying every mouthful, while she looked on longingly. Stopping with the spoon halfway to my mouth I suddenly realised that she really didn't have enough money left to buy ice-cream for herself. She bent forward and said in a menacing whisper,

"You're a spoiled brat! Just wait until yew get home and I tell nana what you've done."

"Yew can have some of this," I said hopefully.

"You've got it now so eat it!" she said. "And yew'd better eat every bit of it too!"

Feeling slightly guilty I said confidently,

"Easy peasy!" as I eyed the enormous, luscious ice-cream covered with a generous helping of cream.

Halfway through it I started to feel queasy and pushed it away from me.

"I think I've had enough, I'm full," I said, not daring to meet Rita's eyes that were boring into me like ice-blue swords.

She was not going to let me leave a scrap even if I did feel sick. Mouth set in a determined line, eyes steely and devoid of the warmth they had emanated before the appearance of the ice-cream, it became a battle of wills. We just sat while I played with the ice-cream tasting a spoonful between protests.

"Eat it!" she said through clenched teeth. "Perhaps it'll teach you a lesson about being greedy."

"I feel a bit sick. I've got a funny stomach now because of yew."

"Well, serves yew right then for being so greedy."

"I'm going to tell nana about yew," I wailed.

"What's the matter?" Nana Howells queried when we returned. "Yew look a bit pale."

"Nothing, just a bit tired," I moaned heading for my bedroom.

For the rest of the afternoon I lay on the bed contemplating the injustice of it all. My stomach felt painful and bloated as if I'd eaten sour apples.

"And I've got to go to the hospital tomorrow." I whimpered to myself.

By the following morning, after a sleepless night clutching my distended, tender stomach, I was full of remorse for my selfish act. Suitably chastened, I hung around Rita the following morning waiting to be pardoned and the promise of another outing.

STREAM OF FLOWERS

The first day of the holidays delivered a murky, grey sky that hung like a pall over the village.

"It's started to rain," my mother called up the stairs. "Yew'd better come down and put on your Burberry."

I felt depressed and anxious knowing that we were going to the hospital for my routine check-up.

"Do we have to go?" I moaned as I descended the stairs. "I hate the hospital: it smells funny."

"Yes, but it won't take long then we can go straight up to Mountain Ash."

Mollified by the thought of a another visit to my paternal grandparents I buttoned my coat, pulled the hood tightly round my face, and stepped out into the chilling rain.

It lashed the pavements sending a Woodbines' cigarette packet careering down the gutter into the drain. People passed, umbrellas concealing their identities, as we huddled in Henley's shop doorway at the top of Doctor's Hill waiting for the 'bus. A small boy, dragging behind his mother, kicked at the puddles then jumped up and down splashing her legs with dirty water. An elderly man, Dai cap pulled firmly down over his eyes, coat collar turned up, scurried along eyes fixed on the pavement ahead. From round the bend a woman emerged, puffing and blowing, as she pushed a pram with one hand and grasped the reins of a little girl effortlessly scampering up the hill. Two boys raced by in hot pursuit of their tiny boats, constructed from paper and lollipop sticks, following them as they hurtled round the bend and down the hill.

"I'd rather be sailing a boat with the boys," I thought miserably, "than going to the hospital."

My fear of hospitals stemmed from very early childhood. After being called up for war service it was discovered that my father had contracted tuberculosis so I had to have regular check-ups in Cardiff Infirmary. The final months of his short life were confined to Pontsarn Sanatorium set in an isolated village a few miles outside Merthyr Tydfil. Contact with the outside world was minimal confined mainly to family visitors for fear of transmitting infection. As I was only a few months old I was not allowed inside so my mother would hold me up to the window so that he could see me.

Neither Nana Howells nor old Dr. Pierce, his family physician, could understand how such a fit, rugby-playing young man, from a healthy family, could have contracted the disease as it was not prevalent in the neighbourhood.

Finally, it was discovered that he had taken refreshments on one of the damaged wartime ships he had boarded in Cardiff docks during an assessment inspection as part of his work. Dr. Pierce was convinced he had consumed tubercular infected milk.

His illness made my mother very fastidious about my habits, warning,

"Dwn't yew dare lick that!" if another child proffered a lollipop or ice-cream cornet.

As I grew older she reminded me constantly,

"What have I told yew about eating or drinking after anyone else. It's dirty!" she'd chastise if I dipped into someone else's fish and chips.

"If yew want chips I'll buy some for yew. Yew remember what I said my girl!"

The risks of drinking from someone else's cup, or eating from another's plate or spoon, were ingrained by constant reinforcement.

The men in white coats became the enemy who talked to my mother over the top of my head and enquired about symptoms such as coughs and chest pains.

Drifting along the tunnel of time I can still see the tiled walls, smell the odour of disinfectant and antiseptic that hit my nostrils; the thrill of fear that fluttered in my chest like the wings of a bird.

"Smells awful in here," I complained sniffing the air as we sat in the outpatients' department.

"We won't be long here. It's our turn next then we can go and have a nice cup of tea," my mother said soothingly.

Suddenly, a uniformed nurse wearing a starched, white cap came into the corridor and called my name.

"But I dwn't want to see the doctor. I want to go home," I wailed resisting my mother's attempts to get me off the seat.

"Now, come on, dwn't be silly. There's nothing to be afraid of, is there?" she cajoled looking at the nurse for support.

"Come on lovely girl, yew'll be in and out in no time at all," the nurse assured as she grabbed my hand and ushered me into the doctor.

Feelings of apprehension and vulnerability as I spotted the strange implements on the trolley and watched the doctor squint as he thrust X-ray plates in the light box on the wall. Standing in liberty bodice and pink knickers, elasticated at the legs, I watched the nurse adjust the weights and felt the cold, hard metal of the weighing scales under my feet.

"I dwn't like it on here; my feet are cold. I want to get off!" I cried.

"Just stay there a minute while they see how heavy yew are."

"There, there, come on now; dwn't be afraid," the white coat said reassuringly. "She's tall for her age, isn't she?" he said observing my mother's petite figure.

"Yes, she takes after her father's side. They're all tall; her father was six feet four," she said with a mixture of pride and anxiety.

The warm, clammy hand of the doctor on my arm as he held me still to check my breathing with his stethoscope; the laundered smell of his white coat as he leaned forward and said gently,

"Breathe in, breathe out;" tapping my chest with his fingers.

Questions and answers exchanged with nodding heads and smiles. My mother's eyes fluttering with anxiety, voice cracking with uncertainty until the doctor declared that all was well.

"That wasn't so bad, was it?" white coat said. "So, back to school this afternoon, is it?

"No, I'm on school holidays so I'm going up to stay with my Nana Howells."

The photograph of my father that stared out at me from the wall of my grandmother's living room was of an exceptionally, good-looking man.

"That's for yew when you're older," Nana Howells said sadly.

Dark, wavy hair in contrast with my mother's petite blondeness. An enigmatic face tinged with a haunting sadness in the deep fathoms of magnetic, soulful, blue eyes. Finely-cut features, a deep cleft in his chin and high cheekbones inherited from my paternal grandmother by all her children. Tall and graceful they walked with the same dignified bearing that gave each of them undeniable presence: completely unaware of their haughtiness of appearance that belied the sensitivity, quick wit and dry humour that always lurked mischievously just beneath the surface.

When I looked in the mirror my father's eyes and expression gazed back at me. Villagers, who had known him briefly, often stopped to pass the time of day and lament over the unfairness of life. Old Mrs Wiltshire, who frequented the 'Jug and Bottle' in the Thorn Hotel, wizened face and world-weary eyes, gazed at me sorrowfully and exclaimed,

"Oh, yew look just like yewer father! Such a gentleman 'e was and 'e spoke very quiet as well."

"Duw, duw, such a shame, dyin' so young like that. Awful, innit? Dwn't make any sense at all, do it?" her companion lamented.

"So 'andsome 'e was. But d'yew know what I noticed about 'im most; 'is 'ands. Very smooth like, delicate 'ands 'e 'ad. I always knew he wasn't a long liver," Old Bopa chimed in shaking her head with sadness. "Too 'andsome to live long."

"Aye, there's no fairness in this world is there? Such a young man too. Still, they say the good die young, dwn't they?"

Their nostalgic meanderings filled my head with images of my father; images that pervaded my dream-filled sleep as he came to life in vivid scenes where he lived and breathed. Bitter-sweet sensations as he took my hand and we glided in slow motion in a soft, protective mist: his smooth, white hand holding mine protectively. Painful feelings of loss as his fingers slipped from mine; disappearing in the swirling, white mist as he held out his arms to me before he was pulled back into the darkness of oblivion, his face inscrutable like the photograph on the wall.

"We're going to the cemetery," Nana Howells said as she headed for the door with my mother.

"I'll come," I chimed in.

"Oh, I dwn't know," my mother replied uncertainly looking at Nana Howells for support. "Yew stay here with the girls."

"It's a lovely day for a walk. Let her come if she wants to. I doubt she'll understand what it's all about anyway."

"Let me carry some flowers," I pleaded reaching up for the colourful blooms.

We walked leisurely down Mill Lane across Peace Park into Maesyrarian Cemetery to visit my father's grave that lay next to that of a young man killed whilst serving in the Royal Air Force during the Second World War.

"Ironic, isn't it?" remarked Nana Howells sadly. "I was so afraid when he was called up for war service. I didn't want him to go. It's strange how things work out in the end."

"It just seems unreal, doesn't it?" my mother added quietly.

"Aye, it's a good job we dwn't know what's for us," sighed the man tending the flyer's grave.

They fell silent lost in their different memories, eyes misty with the pain of remembrance.

A warm, golden sun shone fiercely in a cornflower blue sky. Fluffy, white clouds scudded across the heavens shepherded by a gentle wind. Brilliant greenness and colourful flowers streamed down amongst the hilly avalanche of graves. Silently, I watched the red, white and blue ribbons on the young airman's headstone fluttering forlornly in the breeze; the colours intermingling and separating with every gentle breath of wind as they touched the grieving woman crying soundlessly over the grave. I knew that in this place I was meant to be quiet. Without knowing why I felt the atmosphere; the desperate sense of despair and waste. I wondered how a place could look so beautiful and yet create such tears.

ALIAS MR CATHTREE

The doorbell chimed merrily sending Margaret, my father's sister, scurrying off to see who it was. Long, dark, luxuriant hair, brown eyes, finely cut features and high cheek bones, her mischievous humour sometimes landed her in trouble. Mr. Castree, a local businessman, blessed with protruding teeth and thick glasses, gave her ample scope for trying out her skills as an impressionist. His teeth affected his speech giving anyone close to him a generous spray of saliva. She emerged into the living room bottom lip tucked under her top teeth, gums exposed as much as possible.

"We have a vithitor. It'th Mr. Cathtree. He athed me to tell you that he wanths to thsee yew."

"Yes Margaret, thank yew," said Nana Howells in a shocked voice.

"But he wanths to thsee yew now."

Unknown to Margaret Mr. Castree had followed her in and was standing indignantly right behind her. Nana Howells flushed with embarrassment while Rita and Valerie squirmed with discomfort pretending to cough into their handkerchiefs to disguise their laughter.

"Margaret!" said my grandmother sharply.

At this point she sensed that all was not well. Glancing over her shoulder her face blanched as she saw Mr. Castree standing behind her. Colour started to rise up her neck and face as she stuttered an apology.

"I'm really thorry Mr. Cathtree. It wath a thilly thing to do." In her confusion she did not realise she was still doing a perfect imitation of the poor man. Nana Howells looked at her furiously.

"I'll deal with you later!" she said as she guided the stunned Mr.

Castree to a chair. Margaret sat with a half-smirk, half-chastened expression as he sprayed his way through a detailed discussion blissfully unaware of the effect he was having on us.

As Nana placated Mr. Castree Margaret leaned over and said conspiratorially,

"I've got a glass eye. I take it out every night before going to sleep."

"Let me see," I said staring hard at her eyes.

Pointing at her left eye she said, "This one's false."

"How can it be false? It looks too real to me," I countered.

"Well, it isn't. When I go to bed I take it out and plop it into the little glass bowl on my dressing table."

"Dwn't believe yew," I answered uncertainly.

"I've got to wear a wig as well 'cause I'm bald underneath like dad."

"Well take it off then!"

"Can't, it's stuck on with glue," she replied. "Look!" as she pulled at her hair

For the rest of the evening I watched her carefully for any signs of the wig shifting on her head marvelling at how realistic her false eye looked.

"Stop it for goodness sake! You're frightening the girl. Dwn't worry she's only teasing yew. Of course her eye is real," Nana Howells said laughing at the look on my face.

Not entirely convinced I was determined to find out one way or the other. A few nights later, when everyone had gone to bed and the house was completely quiet, I made my move. Quietly, I got out of bed, eased the door open gently, and crept across the dark landing. A floorboard suddenly creaked under my weight. Heart beating rapidly I moved hesitantly forward expecting a light to come on with every footstep, but everything remained quiet and still.

"Margaret, Rita, are yew awake?" I whispered from the landing.

Not a sound except for the regular breathing of my grandfather coming from the next bedroom.

"They must be all asleep by now," I breathed.

Edging forward I quietly pushed open the door and stepped silently down the stair into the bedroom. Margaret tossed restlessly. I froze waiting with baited breath until the thrashing of arms and legs settled down. Vague shapes of furniture came into view as my eyes became accustomed to the darkness. Inching my way closer and closer to the dressing table I peered short-sightedly at the surface, but it was impossible to see anything in the gloom. Reaching out I explored the contents of the cut-glass dressing table set.

As I started to draw my hand away it passed over something familiar. Tentatively, I moved my hand back and rested it on a hard, round object that lay gleaming dully in the half light. Recoiling in terror I cried out,

"It's an eye! Nana, nana, it's an eye!" as I stumbled towards the door.

Margaret's eye was lying in the glass tray. Panicking, I hurtled past the bed and tripped grabbing at the bulky shadow above Margaret's head to steady myself. I screamed again.

"Oh, nana, nana, Margaret's hair's on the bed!"

Just as she had told me her wig was hanging from the headboard.

Suddenly lights came on in every room. Nana Howells came out on to the landing looking startled and fearful. I ran to her and told her, between sobs, that I had touched Margaret's false eye.

Rubbing her eyes Margaret emerged from her room, half asleep, wanting to know what was going on. Nana Howells glared at her.

"What have yew been doing?" she demanded.

"Nothing! I haven't been doing anything!" Margaret declared looking slightly confused. "What's the matter?"

"What's the matter! What do yew think's the matter? All these stories about false eyes and wigs have frightened the child silly. Yew've been up to something again!"

"It was just a pop alley marble, that's all. I knew she'd have a look, but I didn't think she'd come sneaking in during the middle of the night, did I?"

"Well what about the wig she was crying about? The one hanging from your headboard."

"That's not a wig! That's my shoulder bag!"

After touching the 'eye' my imagination had run riot. I had convinced myself that the shadowy object had been Margaret's false hair.

"Sorry," said Margaret with a mischievous grin, "it was just a bit of fun."

My grandmother's look was icy.

"I'll give you fun if anything like this happens again! Do yew hear me!" she said as Margaret slunk off to bed looking suitably ashamed of her self – again.

SMELLY WELLIES

Forced awake by shafts of late, summer sun piercing the gaps of the curtained windows I squinted as the light penetrated my closed eyelids. Rubbing my eyes sleepily I listened to wood pigeons cooing gently amongst the chirruping of birds in the street trees. Tempting breakfast smells wafted across my nostrils making it impossible to stay in bed especially with the promise of a glorious day ahead.

"Morning nana," I said cheerfully.

The kitchen was bathed in morning light; rays of sun streamed from the conservatory through the window shimmering on china casting dancing, mottled patterns of sunlight over the tablecloth.

"It's a smashing day! Let's go for a walk through Duffryn Woods," I remarked enthusiastically.

"I've got a bit of shopping then some business to attend to down the 'Mount'. Stay here until I get back and no nonsense yew two. Did yew here me now?" Nana Howells shot a warning glance at Valerie who was now a tall, shapely fifteen year old.

"We could have an 'elevenses' tea party," I suggested.

"Oh, all right get your tea set out."

Biscuits and fruit cake, cut into small portions, were laid on little red and yellow plates along with pieces of apple and plum.

"This tastes terrible; makes me feel sick!" Valerie gagged as we sipped tea from tiny celluloid cups. Right, we'd better clear away 'cause Eira is coming round later on this morning."

Struck with dismay I whined,

"Oh no, not her! Yew promised we'd go out!"

Valerie's school friend, Eira, was a pale, dark-haired girl with elongated, well-defined features. Her long, plaited hair, scraped back from a high forehead, reached to her waist. She seemed to have an aversion to getting her feet wet. The slightest suggestion of rain saw Eira wearing black, Wellington boots while carrying her shoes in a bag just in case it rained. Even in summer, when light showers turned the sky to a temporary leaden grey, her pretty, cotton dress was marred by ugly wellies.

"Eira's feet smell when she takes off her wellies," I cried in disgust.

"That's not true and yew know it," said Valerie with exasperation. "You're just being silly. Well, if yew dwn't like it yew'd better go upstairs and read when she's here then hadn't yew?"

When Eira arrived I bolted upstairs, but after half an hour I started to get restless. Feeling bored I wandered downstairs and found the girls in close conversation. Attempts to get them to play games with me fell on deaf ears. Frustrated, I grabbed my tennis racket and went outside to hit a few balls against the pine end, thumping it harder and harder against the wall.

Just as I was getting into my stride Valerie dashed out and yelled,

"Yew know you're not supposed to play against the wall. Nana's dinner service is shaking all over the place. If it smashes yew'll cop it in no uncertain terms!"

Grabbing me by the arm she marched me indoors to be greeted by a smirking Eira.

"Smelly wellies!" I jibed and darted up the stairs with Valerie close on my heels.

"Right, yew can get into your pyjamas. I'm going to do nana a favour and wash all the clothes yew brought with yew. Then I'm going to put your hair in 'rags' so yew'll have lovely ringlets by the time she gets back. Yew won't be able to come down and aggravate us then will yew?"

Struggling and issuing threats about Nana Howells' wrath when she found out failed to work. Eira held me down while Valerie made a botched job of putting 'rags' in my hair, winding them so tightly that they pulled uncomfortably at my scalp. Reluctantly, I dragged myself up to my bedroom deciding that it was in my best interests to stay there and read.

"I'll get them back for this," I grizzled pulling at the tight 'rags'. "Wait until nana comes home."

Feeling sorry for myself I gazed through the bedroom window that faced the back door onto Granville Terrace watching my clothes fluttering merrily on the line. Suddenly, Nana's blonde head came into view bobbing above the garden wall.

"Nana, nana, I'm a prisoner!" I shouted. " Let me out!"

Startled, she looked towards the window eyes wide with shock. Valerie and Eira came running out from the kitchen door gawping up at the bedroom window.

"What on earth's going on?" she demanded.

"Dwn't listen to her. I made her go upstairs 'cause she was naughty. I thought I'd wash her clothes and do her hair as a surprise."

"It's a surprise all right!"

This was my chance for revenge. Gathering some magazines I waited until the girls walked under the window and showered them with copies of 'Woman's Own' and 'Vogue'.

They dodged the flow of paper as the magazines rippled to the ground pages flying open and fluttering like the wings of a bird.

"What have yew been up to?" Nana said sharply.

"They took all my clothes and look what they've done to my hair!" I yowled.

"It was just a bit of fun, wasn't it Eira?"

"They've got no right to keep me prisoner, have they nana?"

"What do yew think you're up to? You're old enough to know better and yew," she said eyeing me angrily, "can stay upstairs until yew learn how to behave in a civilised manner!"

Beseechingly, I looked at her for support, but she was bristling with a mixture of annoyance and bewilderment. Worst of all was the hurt expression that silenced me completely, because I knew I was the cause.

"Oh drat!" she expostulated glaring up at me.

Chastened, I stayed in my room for the rest of the afternoon without a murmur of protest. Eventually, nana came up with a glass of milk and said I could come down for dinner. I hung my head in shame.

"I'm sorry nana. It wouldn't have happened if yew'd taken me with yew, would it?"

But this time I had learned my lesson. Never again did I want to see that look of hurt and disappointment on her face.

"Well, yew'd better make the most of the holiday. Yew'll be back in school next week."

MENTAL ARITHMETIC

Standing at the foot of the steps I eyed the grey, stone building of Carnetown Juniors, little tentacles of fear clutching at my chest. Apprehensively, I climbed the steps, crossed the yard and peeped around the door of the girls' cloakroom. Finding it empty I hesitated until I heard the sounds of low voices from above. Bounding up the stone stairs I found myself in a central hall surrounded by classrooms with half-glass doors. It was my first day and I was to jump Standard Two and move straight into Standard Three away from my friends.

The whole school was assembled in the main hall waiting for Mr. Bevan to appear. Like most of the new children I sang the morning hymn while looking round apprehensively at the unfamiliar surroundings and the strange sight of male teachers.

Finally, it was time to go into our allotted classrooms. Hanging behind the others I murmured quietly,

"Please Miss Thomas, I'd rather go with my friends." I had heard about F.F., the teacher of 3b.

"No, yew can't do that, you're to go in Standard Three," she directed as she shooed me unceremoniously next door.

3b was housed in an old-fashioned room painted institutional, dark-green and cream with high ceilings and large, vertically rectangular windows. The classroom rose up in platforms like a lecture theatre. Rows of double desks, with seats attached, stood like a battery of soldiers below which stood the teacher's high desk. The elevated position of the desks, as they receded to the back of the room, meant that it was futile for disruptive pupils to sit at the rear as they were even more noticeable at that angle.

The epicentre of this gloomy room was occupied by a morose,

dark-haired man known by some pupils as F.F., because they had not yet discovered the silent 'P' in his name. His face was hard and lined with a thin, mean mouth that curved into a sneer when he spoke to the children. Harsh treatment kept most of us quiet for fear of being the butt of his anger.

The school year dragged, the dreariness lifted only by the thought of forthcoming holidays. F.F., ruled with a coldness that rendered him unapproachable often punctuated by what he described as "disciplinary problems" with his charges.

The week before Easter bank holiday brought clear, blue skies. After weeks of heavy rain a white, watery sun forced its way into our classroom lifting our spirits. I squinted as its rays shone into the classroom soaking everything in a silvery glow. It made children restless to be outside in the fresh air. Something outside caught the eye of a quiet, delicate-looking boy sitting in the front row. He leaned over, barely perceptibly, to whisper to the lad next to him. Suddenly F.F., sprang forward and positioned himself in front of the boy.

"Turn round boy!" he hissed menacingly through his teeth. "What are yew looking at?"

"Nothing," said Jackie.

Red-faced and angry F.F., grabbed Jackie his hard eyes boring into the boy.

"Nothing! What do yew mean by nothing? Yew mean nothing, sir!"

"Nothing sir," whimpered Jackie hot tears coursing down his cheeks mixing with the snot from his nose.

"Louder boy!" shouted F.F., shaking Jackie so hard that his head rocked to and fro.

"Nothing sir!"

F.F., lifted Jackie out of his seat then threw him back with a violent push. Terrified, Jackie slumped in his seat burying his head in his arms.

"Get your head off the desk! Lift your head up boy!" screamed F.F., as he paced up and down between the desks.

Every time F.F., passed his desk, tapping his cane against his leg,

Jackie cringed bringing up his arm in a protective gesture. The class, hushed with fright, sat silently for the rest of the lesson listening to Jackie's muffled sobbing.

As soon as we were released into the hall for morning break Jackie ran as though being pursued by demons. I chased after him as he raced through the cloakroom, across the yard and down the stone steps of the main entrance. In his haste he tripped up and fell headlong down the last few steps landing with a thump on the pavement. It was weeks before we saw him again.

When he returned F.F., stared stonily at the boy during every lesson completely ignoring him if he put up his hand to ask a question, but he never laid hands on him again or on anyone else. We had all witnessed F.F., sadistically slamming a desk lid down on top of another boy's hands. Rumour was that his father had threatened F.F., with his life if he touched the boy again. In retrospect every day spent in 3b seemed dark and miserable. We breathed a corporate sigh of relief when, on the first day of the new school term, we moved up into 3a.

Snowy, the teacher of 3a, was a florid-faced, thick-set man with coarse, white hair. He was strict to the point of harshness and did not tolerate indiscipline. I was afraid of this big, brash man but the devil himself would not have let me admit it. Every morning, before break, we had a mental arithmetic lesson. Each pupil was asked a question; nobody escaped. This was the most hated part of the day, especially for slower-witted children who waited in trepidation for their turn. It was painful to watch the agonised expressions. One lad always blushed profusely, the flush rising from below the collar of his grey jersey and gradually creeping up his face to stain his ears blood-red: eyes screwed up tightly in concentration until beads of perspiration stood out on his forehead. A garbled, incorrect answer brought forth hot tears of shame; embarrassment springing to his eyes while the others giggled surreptitiously behind their hands.

One morning, in early spring, we waited breathlessly for the dreaded test. It was the turn of Susan, a scrawny, adenoidal girl with watery, blue eyes and dirty, blonde hair that hung in limp strands into her eyes and mouth along with the candles of fluid which ran down from her nose whenever she became stressed. After a valiant struggle with her unyielding brain she failed to answer the problem.

Snowy threw it open to the class to answer. A dozen or so hands shot up all eager to show their mental agility. Snowy glared at us and bellowed,

"What's the correct answer David?"

"Thra'pence Sir," said Little Dai, a smug look on his face. He was called 'little' Dai because he was much smaller than other boys of his age; even smaller than those in the class below.

"How many of yew think the answer is thra'pence?" roared Snowy. Anxiously, we watched as the mottled red appearing on his collar-line crept up to his cheeks. We squirmed uncomfortably in our seats knowing what was coming next. All hands remained stretched high to the sky.

"Stand on your seats yew idiots!" he shouted in scathing tones.

We did as we were told. Slowly, he walked among us armed with a wooden ruler. Sharply, he smacked the calves of each one of us with the ruler and then asked again,

"Well, come on then! What's the answer? Those of yew who think you're wrong sit down. Those of yew who think the answer is thra'pence remain standing on your seats!"

Half the group sat down rubbing the wheals on the backs of their legs.

"Now then yew little 'sionies'," said Snowy, "tell me again. Yew girl, what is the answer?"

"Thra'pence," I said face red and legs hot with pain.

Another stinging swipe with the ruler and a thump between the shoulder blades set my heart racing.

"Those of yew who think it's thra'pence stay on your seats. The rest of yew can sit down."

Only two of us remained stubbornly standing on the shiny, wooden, bench seats. For the next five minutes we flinched as the ruler was raised then swiftly thwacked against our legs. The sturdy boy on my right gasped with pain and sat down heavily in his seat.

I was alone now. Mental arithmetic was not my strongest point, but I was convinced that I was right. Swiftly turning the problem over and over in my mind I waited in fevered anticipation of another smarting blow.

For another few minutes he stalked to and fro swinging the ruler, bringing it down across my calves with painful regularity. Tears were rolling down my cheeks and I could hardly speak for the sobs caught in my throat. Taking a deep breath I forced myself to stop crying.

"I'm right, I know I am!" I thought feverishly. "I'll never give in!"

I stared in front of me the room a blur through my discomfort and tears.

"Are yew still convinced the answer is thra'pence?" he said in a milder tone.

"Yes sir!" I spluttered.

"Sit down," he said more gently. "Now, yew others. Let this be a lesson to yew. She's the only one who's right. The rest of you were afraid to stick to your guns. Remember this – if *yew* are convinced you're right never swerve from your beliefs. Do what *yew* know to be right whatever the consequences."

He looked at me with a smile on his face. From that moment on I could do nothing wrong in his eyes. It is a lesson I have carried with me throughout my life, but it was a harsh, cruel lesson to learn for an eight year old girl.

My mother had never had cause to complain to the school, because as I grew older I became a quiet, withdrawn child spending most of my time reading. Usually, if I complained about a teacher she would say,

"Oh yes, and what were yew doing? Not listening, had your nose in a book again oblivious to everything."

But not this time. When she saw the marks on my legs I thought she would explode with anger. Dad Smith, face red with fury, charged towards the front door when he found out what Snowy had done.

"Just wait until I get hold of him!" he spluttered. "Nobody, and I mean *nobody*, lays their hands on my grandchild; not while I'm breathing!"

Grabbing his arm my mother insisted that the matter be left for her to resolve.

The following morning she went to see the headmaster who disappeared to consult with Snowy. When he returned to his office other parents were waiting to complain about the harsh, sadistic treatment meted out to their children. Squirming with embarrassment I begged my mother not to do anything about it, but my entreaties fell on deaf ears. Snowy suffered the most embarrassing dressing down of his life as my outraged mother threatened him with legal action if he ever touched me again. One of the fathers had to be restrained threatening an 'eye for an eye' if he ever again resorted to physical abuse on his children.

Months later Mr. Bevan, the head teacher, came into out classroom looking very serious. Children watched him warily anxiety showing in their eyes. He rarely came into our classroom. What had we done to warrant a visit so early in the morning? He looked sightlessly up beyond the tiers of desks to the back of the room, gazed at his feet, shifted uncomfortably and said,

"Unfortunately, I have some rather bad news for yew."

A heavy silence fell over the children followed by a corporate gasp as Mr Bevan told us, in hushed tones, that Snowy had died.

Snatches of overheard, whispered conversations between staff created rumours that circulated and re-circulated regarding the circumstances of his death; one that he had been found dead in his bath. Nobody in Standard 3a mourned his passing, but we all remembered the harsh treatment and fear he had instilled in us.

Snowy's untimely demise was soon forgotten when other exciting news reached our ears.

"Mr. Bevan told us they're going to build a pool in the park," chattered a group of excited children, "but not for another twelve months at least."

Gloomily, I thought of a whole year stretching out before me until I could swim in the new pool. When I arrived home I rushed in to the kitchen to tell my mother, but she had even more exciting news to impart.

"Margaret is getting married next Valentine's Day."

TAFFETA AND TULLE

Christmas came in a blur of activity that increased after the new year as preparations for Margaret's wedding gathered momentum. Valentine's Day dawned murky and grey. A feeble sun attempted to take hold of a leaden sky, failed and finally retreated behind unbroken cloud. Bridesmaids for Margaret and Roy's wedding sat chattering and giggling amongst themselves waiting for the car to arrive to take them to St. Margaret's.

"The car will be here shortly," commented Nana Howells as the girls pirouetted and flounced in their pale swathes of blue taffeta covered with froths of tulle.

"Yew look really lovely," remarked Trevor my father's younger brother. "Give us a twirl then."

Shyly, accepting the compliment, they twirled their dresses ballooning out in what seemed to me an overcrowded room full of chattering women.

I wandered from room to room taking in the ripples of excitement and sense of anticipation. Snatches of conversations floated above my head,

"Oh, they all look lovely, dwn't they?" remarked a distant relative I'd never seen before.

But Dad Howells wasn't listening. His eyes were on an elegant, blonde woman, draped in a fox fur, who was just about to lower herself onto a chair. Her son, dark hair slicked down flat on his head, sat grinning quietly waiting for the disaster to happen.

"Mind my bowler!" said Dad Howells snatching it up before she could sit down.

"Yew and that hat!" Nana Howells tutted.

"Well, it's my favourite isn't it."

He brushed bits of imaginary lint from the brim and placed it on his head.

"I've had this bowler for years. It'll last me for a few more weddings yet," he observed, determined that it would go back in its box in pristine condition.

A jabber of voices competed with myriad other sounds; the rattle of cups and saucers, the rustling of dresses being smoothed and straightened. A little girl yawning with boredom impatiently tapping her feet against the chair legs. A captive boy, tired of sitting still, alternately tugging at his tie pretending to choke or pulling at his socks.

"Can I go out into the garden for a bit?" he queried starting to move towards the door.

"No, yew can't. Yew'll get dirty, and stop fidgeting with those socks. Yew won't be satisfied until the tops are all stretched!" cried his mother in an exasperated tone.

The cat, dignified and superior, wandered from room to room meowing plaintively amongst the bustle. Nana delicately dabbed at her finely-sculptured nose with a powder puff.

Unexpectedly, a new, harsher sound; an anguished scream came from the direction of the bridesmaids' room. Startled, nana's powder box jumped from her hand creating a cloud of pinky-cream powder that drifted across the room to land on the little trifles already prepared for the children. Her eyes widened with fright as her hand came up to cover her mouth.

For a fraction of time everything stopped. Silent figures frozen into a tableau of expectation. Suddenly, Trevor lunged from the living room towards the direction of the sound.

"What was that? Who screamed?" Nana cried running behind Trevor.

The rest followed into the hall nudging me to the rear of the group as they stared in horror at one of the bridesmaids. Her floating gown had touched the electric fire as she twirled; flames greedily devouring the fabric while she screamed in terror.

Like a silent, surreal film in slow motion Nana Howells stared helplessly at the licking flames, one hand covering her mouth. Dad

Howells, eyes wide with shock, gripped her arm to hold her back. Another held on to the door jamb staring into the room. Trevor took off the jacket of his new suit, moved towards the girl in a single stride, and threw it over her damping out the flames with his bare hands. What seemed an eternity of terror was over in seconds.

"Are yew all right?" Nana Howells' voice wavered with uncertainty as she put her arms round the quivering girl.

Now the room was a cacophony of voices.

"Ring for an ambulance!" ordered Dad Howells.

"I'm fine, just a bit shaken up that's all," she assured him

"Fetch a blanket; somebody get her a cup of sweet tea. The poor girl's in shock!" Nana Howells exclaimed.

"I'm fine, really, but a cup of tea would be nice. Trevor's hands look worse."

"Well, yew'd better go to casualty just in case. I'll get the car," Dad Howells declared firmly.

"*Yew* can't come; not the father of the bride. Go on ahead to the church," Trevor called looking at nana's troubled expression. "Dwn't worry, everything will be fine."

There were sighs of relief when they were whisked the hundred yards or so to Mountain Ash General Hospital.

Nana Howells fussed and worried when the bridesmaids' car arrived to take them to St. Margaret's.

"I've rung the vicar," Dad Howells declared breathlessly. "He can only hold on for about fifteen minutes 'cause he's got another wedding straight after."

"Well, we can't go until they get back," she said. "I won't feel happy until I know they're all right."

"I'll pop up to the hospital and find out what's happening. It won't take long."

Ten minutes later he burst through the door,

"They've just seen the doctor; the poor girl's a bit shocked otherwise she's all right, but Trevor's hands are quite nasty. They're putting on some dressings now then they can come to the wedding as long as they dwn't overdo it. He said he'll follow us to the church as soon as they've finished.

"Thank God!" Nana said with relief as she heard the church bells ringing out across the town.

Finally, the bridesmaids were bundled into the car gathering their beautiful dresses around them. The driver tucked in the last bits of errant taffeta and whisked them round the corner to the church where the vicar greeted them with a smile of relief.

Miraculously, the traumatised bridesmaid had suffered some minor burns to her legs, but Trevor's swift reactions had saved her from serious injury. Later, he arrived at the wedding reception his hands swathed in bandages. The reluctant hero of the day he was more concerned about his appearance than his injuries. Outside the day was still grey, but inside it was bright with happiness and laughter.

SWIMMERS AND SLIDERS

A pall of murky, grey cloud hung over Abercynon as the small crowd of onlookers gathered to witness the opening of the children's bathing pool in Abercynon Park. Fine rain misted the atmosphere seeping insidiously through thin, spring frocks to chill the bones. Firmly separated by spiked, iron railings from the councillors and their wives, adorned in their best costumes and hats, they huddled under umbrellas to witness the proceedings. Watched over by two burly policemen Council Chairman Lil Watts smiled broadly and piped,

"I declare this bathing pool opened on 31st May 1952."

Children dutifully cheered pushing their way forward to get a better view. Two little boys pressed against the railings eager to get inside.

"Can we go for a swim now mam?"

"No, not today, we've got to wait for them to fill the pool first. Anyway it's raining."

"Won't be long now. It'll be ready to swim in by next weekend," shouted one of the councillors over the fence.

"Well, at least we won't have to go all the way to Ponty now," said Mrs Cadwaladr.

"Aye, and about time too, I reckon," agreed the lads' father with a surly grunt.

"Aye, they can learn to swim by 'ere now instead."

Throughout the summer whole families flocked to the park to watch their children revel in the cool waters.

"I dwn't know whether to go round Pontcynon or round River Row," my mother dithered as Mrs Cadwaladr passed with her brood of girls.

"Let's go round Pontcynon with the Cadwaladr's then we can

come back the other way and call in Caparnini's for ice-cream," I said hopefully running to catch up with Anwen who had disappeared round the corner into Abercynon Road.

We sauntered past the woods across Quarter Mile bridge, that spanned the railway line, down Park Road grateful for the coolness of the tree-lined avenue.

The sound of children's laughter and splashing water reached us as we neared the park gates. All round the pool families sat on the grass chatting with friends and neighbours; on brightly-coloured beach towels, cardigans or khaki-coloured army blankets, relics of the war. Old ladies sat primly, in wide-brimmed hats, rocking prams or gently admonishing their grandchildren to take care as they rushed in and out of the water. Granddads cast off their jackets, loosened their ties and dropped their braces down over their shoulders grateful for the rejuvenating warmth of the sun.

Lying on the lush grass I squinted up at the shimmering sun shading my eyes against its glare. Interspersed with bright daisies, buttercups threaded the ground in little bursts of golden colour. Anwen picked a few and held them under my chin.

"Yew like butter," she said.

"That's just an old wives' tale. Look yew can see it anywhere," I mocked holding the tiny bunch against my leg.

Lethargically, we rolled onto our stomachs, legs in the air, content to whisper secrets that drifted off on summer's breath. At intervals we sat on the creamy wall of the pool dangling our feet in the water before jumping in to cool off.

Toddlers paddled excitedly in the enclosed 'baby' pool dipping their heads under the little fountain.

"He loves it dwn't 'e?" cried Mrs Williams as she held her gurgling, infant grandson firmly under his arms to dangle his tiny feet in the 'blue' water.

"Marvellous for the kids mind innit?" she remarked to my mother who was sitting on the grass watching Roger and Michael lying on their stomachs, pretending to swim in the shallow water.

"It's so safe 'ere. Yew can keep an eye on the older ones on the swings as well."

"Yes, but it's a long walk round Quarter Mile. It's about time the council built a bridge over the railway line before there's an accident."

"I 'eard a couple of boys nearly got it last week runnin' over the track to get to the park didn't they Sam?" continued Mrs Williams looking to her husband for confirmation.

"Aye, my old man was standin' on the 'Tump' shoutin' at 'em and wavin' 'is walkin' stick. Nearly gave 'im a stroke. *Stupid* little buggars!" declared Sam under his breath as he lay contentedly puffing at his pipe.

"Well, I'd better not catch yew going on that line!" my mother called after me as I ran towards the slide.

From the top the slide seemed to be a long way from the ground. Summoning up my courage I sat down on the shiny surface.

"Aw come on mun. We'll be 'ere all day at this rate," complained a ginger-haired boy shoving me in the back.

I gripped the sides tightly and let myself down a few inches knowing that as soon as I let go I would hurtle faster and faster until I reached the bottom. Suddenly, Ginger forced his way in behind me and pushed us forward.

Fortunately for me the previous slider had ignored the 'Parkee's' warnings about wearing a wet swimsuit on the slide which impeded my velocity. We jolted down the slide in stops and starts as my legs caught against the damp metal much to Ginger's disgust.

"Aw, they've been on 'ere in wet bathers again," he fumed. "We'll 'ave to shine it up again now."

When the 'Parkee' was out of sight older children slid down sitting on the yellow, waxed wrapper from a packet of sliced bread. Clutching the worn wrapper they clambered up the steps, shot off the top then raced around for another go. With every turn the slide became more and more slippery until it shone like glass sending them hurtling at speed to the bottom where friends were ready to catch them before they hit solid concrete. The sliders ruled until the 'Parkee' got wind of it and confiscated the bread wrappings.

"Try this," Anwen urged pushing a wrapper at me. "It's great!"

I placed the bread wrapper on the slide then sat down very carefully.

"Stop it!" I cried as Ginger pushed with all his might sending me careering downwards at break-neck speed.

"I can't stop!" I screamed frantically grabbing at the sides of the slide to slow myself down.

Too late, I shot over the end of the slide and hit the concrete landing with a bone-jarring thud on my coccyx.

"You're supposed to catch me!" I exclaimed indignantly glaring at Anwen.

"Are yew all right?" she asked in a concerned voice.

"Fine," I grinned through gritted teeth.

My back felt numb but, as life slowly returned, I felt a hot knife of burning pain jabbing in my lower back.

"What's wrong?" my mother asked as I limped over to the grass and lowered myself very carefully to the ground.

"I fell off the end of the slide and hit the bone near my bottom," I said gritting my teeth.

"How did yew do that?" she demanded.

"Ginger Roberts pushed in behind me and we came down too fast, that's all," I said blithely.

"Oh, did he now. Well, he'll get the sharp end of my tongue."

But before she could reprimand Ginger we saw the park keeper striding angrily towards him.

"What 'ave I told yew kids about those wrappers?" the 'Parkee' yelled as he spotted the culprits. "Now gerroff that slide before I warm yewer backsides."

"Aw, we weren't doin' any 'arm mun. Just a bit of fun tha's all," complained Ginger.

"Any more cheek from yew and yew're banned from this park. Do yew 'ear me boy? Now gerroff with yew."

Ginger slunk off shooting furious glances at the 'Parkee'. As he reached the gate he turned round, stuck out his tongue and shouted,

"The 'Parkee's' narkeed!"

Enraged the 'Parkee' raced towards the gate yelling,

"Stop that boy!" as Ginger hared down Park Road towards the allotments.

"I won't forget this Clarence Roberts," he blustered using the name he hated. "I'll be speakin' to yewer father tonight!"

Ginger stuck out his tongue again in a last show of diminishing bravado then disappeared, still laughing, through the tall privet hedge into the safety of the allotments.

"I'll be watchin' for yew boy. Yew'd better not come near 'ere for the carnival or I'll 'ave yew I will," the Parkee screeched with frustration.

CARNIVAL CAPERS

People jostled for prime positions up the length of Margaret Street waiting for the parade to begin.

"Stop pushin' will yew?" complained a flushed matron desperately trying to keep her balance as the crowd leaned forward to catch a glimpse of the first float.

"Well, if yew take yewer 'at off we might be able to see somethin' mun," retaliated a diminutive, pallid-faced youth.

"What was that? Dwn't yew dare give me any of yewer cheek Tudor Vaughan or yew'll be sorry!" she glared the flush deepening to a darker shade of crimson.

She tottered forward as a skinny lad forced himself through the forest of legs to the edge of the pavement grinning jubilantly.

"Oi, over by 'ere Jonesy! I'm right in front!" he shouted to the back of the crowd.

"Now then, now then, keep on the pavement," P.C. Coles ordered as the lad lost his footing and stepped onto the road.

"They're on the way! I can 'ear the music!" he exclaimed excitedly as the beat of drums reached our ears.

Sounds of clapping, cheering and marching feet filled the air as the parade reached the 'The Clock' and turned into Walter Street. As the lead band came into sight adults and children pressed forward. Waving at the gaily decorated floats a mother craned her neck and cried,

"Look Des, *there's* our Meryl. Dwn't she look smart?"

"Oh, aye, she's definitely the best marcher *and* the prettiest," declared Des eyes misty with paternal pride.

"Yoo hoo! We're over 'ere love!" but Meryl's eyes were firmly focussed on the drum majorette and her twirling baton.

Along the pavement similar declarations from parents convinced that their offspring were the stars of the show.

Proudly the youngsters piped their way up Margaret Street to the sound of their 'kazoos', resplendent in their uniforms. Bright green and gold, red, white and blue with old-fashioned, military-style, peaked helmets held with braided chin-straps.

"Oi, look at this float then boys!" exclaimed Jonesy his face aglow with admiration. "It's the Carnival Queen!"

Dark-haired and radiant Val Horseman waved regally from her elaborately decorated 'throne' as the float rolled past.

As the last marchers rounded the corner into Edwards Street the crowd followed at a more leisurely pace. Up the steepness of Doctor's Hill along Mountain Ash Road onto the flat stretch of Abercynon Road to Quarter Mile bridge. All along the route people stood at their front doors: mothers with babes in arms, toddlers tugging at their skirts. Older children their voices shrill with excitement yelled,

"Come on, let's tag on behind!" as they swaggered along Park Road emulating the marchers.

"Left, right, left, right!"

Through the park gates they marched, over the little bridge spanning the river, into the cricket field where the cheering crowds dispersed to try their luck at the 'coconut shies' or knocking down carefully constructed tins to win a goldfish. Children nagged for ice-cream and pop.

"Ooh, there's an ice-cream stall!" exclaimed Michael and Roger almost in unison.

"Can we have ice-cream and some orangeade?" they pleaded.

"And what comes after orangeade?" my mother rebuked.

Blank stares creased their brows quickly followed by comprehension.

"Can we have ice-cream and orangeade *please!*"

"That's better," she said tartly as she dipped her hand into her purse to produce a shiny sixpence.

"Let's sit on the grass," she gestured spreading out a blanket. "We'll have a nice glass of cordial and a Welsh cake while we watch the jazz band competition, is it?" She looked enquiringly at Nana Smith.

"I'm going over to see your father first. Save some until I come back," Nana Smith called as she headed towards a small knot of bystanders.

Dad Smith and Emrys were walking their horses across the far end of the field while parents queued with impatient children. The ponies ambled leisurely in the warmth of the midday sun with coaxing words and endearments.

"Whose a good girl then, Molly?" soothed Dad Smith as he patted the mare's rump.

"Up yew get then," said a tall, fresh-faced man as he hoisted his reluctant son into the saddle.

Nervously, the boy, trousers pressed to perfection, hair parted showing a concise channel of pink scalp, snow-white socks and crisp shirt, sat astride gentle Molly. As she ambled off, shaking her mane to deter the gnats, he started to cry,

"Gemme off! Gemme off dad!"

Embarrassed, his father tried to soothe him as he walked alongside holding him firmly on the saddle.

"Now dwn't be silly, she won't hurt yew will she Mr. Smith?"

"Gentle as a lamb she is. Steady now Molly," he urged as the boy's fear connected.

"I want to get off!"

"Aw, for goodness sake, yew've been naggin' for a ride all mornin'!"

"I dwn't care dad, gemme off!" the boy screamed now trembling with fear.

Looking at the toddler laughing with delight on the back of Emrys' chesnut gelding he retorted,

"Well that's the last time yew're goin' on a horse my boy, showin' me up like that." He dragged the blubbering lad to the comfort of his mother's arms.

"Yew're too soft with that boy!" he hissed between his teeth. "He's turnin' into a right little namby pamby."

"Well, yew shouldn't force him then should yew?"

"Aw, I'm goin' to watch the jazz band competition!" he shot back as he stomped across to the marching bands at the far side of the field where anxious parents and band managers were willing their particular troupe to win.

From the middle of the field a clamour of noise caught my attention. A crowd of spectators were shouting encouragement to a couple of burly, young miners in the 'dads only' egg and spoon race. Half running, half walking they gingerly made their way to the winning line.

"I'm goin' to beat yew," puffed Jack Blainey his lungs already clogged with coal dust.

"Not if I can help it," retaliated Joe Gittins.

They were neck and neck as they reached the finish, chalked out on the grass with a length of string suspended between two posts. Jack caught his toe in a clodge and fell headfirst over the line.

"Yew've won dad, yew've won!" screamed his delighted daughter rushing to hug her father.

"That's not fair," complained Joe. "Yewer feet didn't go over the finish line."

"'Course they did."

"Well, let's see what 'e's got to say," Joe suggested looking expectantly at Herbert the Judge.

"This is a difficult one boys. Yew did go over the line Jack so I suppose yew *could* say yew've won, but…."

"No bloody 'buts' about it mun; 'is feet didn't go over the line and that's that!" argued Joe.

"Are yew sayin' I'm tryin' to cheat, yew cheeky buggar!" Jack hissed in a loud whisper looking round to see if he could be heard.

"Well, if the cap fits," seethed Joe.

"That's enough of that boys and watch yewer language right. There's women and children over by there."

"Sorry missus, didn't see yew b'there mun," murmured Jack shamefacedly as they went into a ruck with Herbert muttering and gesticulating. Finally, the judge emerged grabbed the men's arms and raised them high declaring,

"It's a draw!"

Red-faced Jack and Joe glared at each other over a tight-lipped grimace posing as a smile.

Satisfied that a winner had been declared I headed for the 'Flying Fox', otherwise known as 'The Death Slide', where I bumped into Anwen and Mati.

"I dwn't fancy *that*," Anwen remarked eyeing the wire that the army had constructed between two towers.

"Well, I'm having a go!" I exclaimed relishing the thought of whizzing down the wire like Tarzan.

"Not if yewer mother sees yew, yew won't," laughed Mati, but I wasn't listening.

I headed for the queue and waited impatiently until I could climb up the tower.

My heart gave a little lurch when I realised how far I would fall if I lost my grip. A soldier grabbed my arm to steady me ordering,

"Dwn't look down, look straight ahead. That way yew won't get giddy."

"Right," I said feeling very nervous but too proud to back out.

"Hands even on both handles and dwn't wriggle around. Are yew ready?"

"Yes, I'm ready," I said faintly.

With his hand on my back the soldier instructed,

"Hold tight." then gave me a gentle push to set me in motion.

I careered down the line fervently regretting my foolishness. The crowd below milled about their voices muffled by distance and the sound of rushing air round my head.

"Oh God, oh God," I prayed, "dwn't let me fall off. I'll never do anything stupid again."

Hanging at arm's length I hurtled downwards towards the opposite tower unable to control the speed. At the bottom a soldier stood waiting to halt the 'Foxy Flyer'. Suddenly, a man's voice shouted,

"Keep yewer head back or yew'll break yewer neck!"

Confused, I tried to look down at him and saw the ground hurtling towards me.

"Keep it back I said!" shouted the soldier as he caught me with a lurching thud.

"That was great!" I laughed nonchalantly as I wobbled towards Anwen, my courage renewed by the feel of firm ground under my feet.

We watched as the next intrepid 'flyer' started her journey down the wire. About ten feet from the tower she started to slow down then gradually ground to a halt.

"I'm stuck!" she screamed. "Quick, someone help me!"

A hush fell over the happy crowd below as they sought the source of the scream. Suddenly, somebody yelled,

"Look, up there on the wire."

A sea of upturned faces gazed at a girl dangling by her arms twenty feet above the ground.

"Dwn't move!" ordered one of the soldiers as she wriggled trying to move herself forward. "We'll have yew down in no time."

One of the soldiers gave the line a gentle shake to loosen the mechanism which brought petrified screams from the suspended body swinging to and fro and gasps of horror from spectators.

From behind the tower a group of men appeared with a tarpaulin, held it under her and shouted,

"Jump and we'll catch yew."

"No, I can't, I'm afraid!"

"Yew'll be okay, just let go and yew'll fall into the tarpaulin like the fireman do it."

"No!" screamed the terrified girl desperately grasping tighter on the handles.

She shifted her hands to get a better hold almost losing her grip. A corporate gasp swelled from the crowd below. Women covered their eyes waiting for the sound of a thud, but nothing happened. Suspended in mid air she swung precariously over the upturned faces below.

"Keep the tarpaulin underneath. I'm going to try something!" yelled a squaddie.

He clambered up the tower, grabbed a set of handles and launched himself down the wire. Spectators gasped as he hurtled towards the girl who was craning her neck at the sound of the wheel behind her.

"He'll knock her off the wire like that, the *silly* fool! They'll both be killed!" cried an elderly woman peering through the gaps in her fingers as she covered her face.

Suddenly, the squaddie made contact and managed to wrap one arm round her just as the wheel dislodged sending them hurtling, at some speed, towards the tower. They 'flew' to earth like a pair of trapeze artistes to the resounding cheers of those below whose anxious expressions soon turned to smiles. Relieved, the crowd dispersed to mingle amongst the stalls and gossip with friends and neighbours about the near catastrophe.

Later, as the mellow sun melted towards the west the thwacking sound of racquets connecting with balls could be heard from the tennis courts. Some moved into the small putting green for a family game. Others watched the white-garbed, elderly bowlers on the green wearing intense looks of concentration before aiming their ball.

"Lovely day wannit, except for that poor old girl?" Anwen giggled as we walked down Park Road.

"It's nothing to laugh at," I chided, "she could have been killed yew know."

"Yeah, I know but she did look funny danglin' up there 'specially when she was trying to keep her dress from blowin' up," she retorted heading for the stream that ran along one side of Park Road.

Some of the older men popped in to water their flowers and vegetables in the allotments that sat behind the high, privet hedge bordering the other side of the narrow road. My mother ambled in front chatting to neighbours who were heading home with sleepy, fractious children. Families meandered slowly while youngsters searched in the stream for newts; cupped their hands to catch a butterfly or wriggled their fingers amongst the tiny, gleaming, silver fish that darted in and out of the stones in the shallow water.

"Look," I breathed, " a dragon fly."

Fascinated, I tip-toed forward and gazed at the delicate, scintillating body, its diaphanous silvery wings streaked with blue and green. It hovered over the water, almost motionless, then zoomed over the surface of the stream its wings glinting in the sunlight.

I looked up as my mother's voice called breaking the spell,

"Come on yew two if yew want a strawberry and ice in the Bracchi's."

The dragon fly darted past my face then disappeared amongst the 'lily pond' leaves floating on the water, searching for sustenance.

"We're goin' up the mountain tomorrow for a picnic. I just 'eard them arrangin' it," Anwen said indicating my mother and Mrs Cadwaladr chattering animatedly as they walked on ahead of us. I felt a tug of excitement at the prospect of climbing the mountain high above the village: to lie on Table Rock in the 'long grass' before it died under a thick blanket of golden-red leaves.

As autumn approached a gloom settled over us until the joy of Christmas spun its magic then faded to be stored with other memories. Wrapped up against a frosty winter we trudged to school under leaden skies until the first green buds appeared on the trees. Spirits lifted by the birth of new life and warming sun we breathed deeply on the sweet air; excitement filled our hearts like the gentle fluttering of butterfly wings. Another summer to come, another 'season of the long grass', another wedding to anticipate.

REVENGE OF THE WELLIES' GIRL

"Another wedding, great!" I exclaimed when Rita's forthcoming marriage was announced after Christmas.

I danced round the room with excitement chanting,

"Rita's getting a-married. Rita's getting a-married!"

"Well, yew'll have to have a new outfit for the wedding," my mother declared that evening. "We both will. We'll go to Ponty Saturday morning. If we can't find anything there we'll go down to Cardiff."

"I want yew to have something *really* pretty and lacy."

"But I dwn't *want* anything lacy. I'll feel like a fool," I wailed.

"Well you're having something pretty and that's that! It's no use wheedling, my mind's made up."

Nine o' clock Saturday morning we stood at the top of Doctor's Hill waiting as the Red & White 'bus screeched to a halt. Clambering up the steps of the bull-nosed vehicle we made our way down the aisle, swaying from side to side, as it lurched towards the bend.

"Sit down here quickly!" my mother ordered falling into a seat as the 'bus careered round the corner and down the steep hill to the next stop at the foot of Ynysmeirig Road.

"Good mornin'; lovely day innit?" shouted Mrs Burton who was still settling herself in for the ride after getting on near Albert House on Abercynon Road.

"Yes, beautiful day," my mother responded.

"Goin' to Ponty then?"

"Yes."

"Shoppin' is it?"

"Er, yes."

"Anything special like?"

"Oh, this and that."

"Oh aye, this and that; sounds interestin'?" probed Mrs Burton realising she wasn't getting anywhere with her questioning.

Thoroughly disheartened with the way the conversation was going she sniffed loudly, gathered up her ample bosom and looked intently through the window for the rest of the journey.

We got off the 'bus behind the town hall, crossed Gelliwasted Road and ambled towards Taff Street.

"We'll just have a look in the windows first to see what's around."

Knowing my mother's energy and capacity for shopping I urged,

"Let's go straight to the clothes shops, shall we?"

"No, I'd rather have a look around first. I dwn't want to buy the first thing I see."

I groaned, this was going to be a long, arduous day.

We traipsed the length of Taff Street and back again before deciding to go into Theophilus' ladies' wear.

She tried on various garments all of which suited her slim, petite figure. Shaking her head she made a moue at her reflection and sighed,

"I dwn't like this, the skirt's too full; it makes me look fat."

"It looks lovely," I assured her hoping to make a quick exit.

"Hm! I dwn't know; I think I'll try on the one I tried on first of all."

Fifteen minutes later we emerged from the shop empty-handed.

"There's nothing I *really* liked," she complained. "Come on, we'll go to Paige's. If I dwn't see anything suitable we'll go and get your outfit."

In Paige's she tried on a beautiful muted, eggshell-blue two-piece suit with a fitted bodice that accentuated her small waist.

"If madam will allow me," cooed the assistant, "I'll fetch a lovely hat that I think will suit beautifully."

In seconds she reappeared with a dainty hat, that fitted close to the head, tastefully covered with a little tulle on one side.

"Perfect madam, even if I do say so myself."

"Ye-e-s, it does look nice," my mother said rather hesitantly.

She twisted and turned before the mirror to get a better view.

Delicately she manoeuvred the hat into the most fetching position murmuring,

"Yes, yes, I think I'll take it."

"At last!" I thought breathing a sigh of relief. "Now we can go in the café for a drink."

As I made for the door she called,

"Well, I've got nothing to go with this. I'll need matching shoes and a handbag."

After trying on numerous pairs of shoes, in as many shops, we went off in search of my wedding outfit.

Hours later we wearily lugged our purchases towards Princes café and restaurant.

"I'm worn out, still we've got everything now so we won't need to come down again. Those white sandals I bought for yew last week are in nana's ready," my mother said as she gratefully collapsed into a chair.

"Roast pork sandwiches twice please and tea for two," she said knowing I didn't like fizzy drinks. "Do yew want a cake as well?"

"A custard slice please."

I'd seen them in the window; perfect oblongs of thick custard on a thin layer of pastry topped with white icing.

"I'm *glad* I bought yew this frock now," she commented as she riffled through one of the bags. "Yew always look so nice in blue."

"Yuk!" I thought visualising the creation she had picked. "At least it didn't have any lace."

"Oh no, it's started to drizzle and I dwn't want yew to get those socks dirty!" my mother exclaimed as she peered through the window. "What a shame, still it looks as though it's going to clear up."

Dressed ready for the wedding I looked down at my socks trimmed with white lace.

"Oh, yew look really pretty in that dress," she clucked fussing at the tiny, tight ringlets caught either side of my head in matching blue bows of satin ribbon.

The blue and white dress was quite simple with puff sleeves and a Peter Pan collar.

"We'll pick the new shoes up from Nana Howells' before we go to the church. Yew'd better wear those tan sandals for now"

"But what if it rains again? I could wear my Wellingtons? That'll keep my socks dry."

"Yew can't wear Wellingtons in summer. It doesn't look right, does it?"

Abruptly, the fine drizzle turned into a heavy downpour hammering on the roof and slashing against the windows.

"Oh no, look at it now; we'll get soaking wet!" she wailed as silver stair-rods of rain descended from ponderous clouds plunging into the thirsting summer earth.

"I think yew'd better wear Wellingtons after all!"

Murky, grey clouds hung over Abercynon turning an August day into temporary winter. Through the canopy of cloud a barely perceptible glimmer of silver light battled to take hold of the sky. We huddled inside our 'Macs' desperately trying to keep the umbrella positioned in just the right place.

"Tilt it over this way a bit and stay underneath or the ringlets will fall out," she instructed patting them back into place.

"Where on earth is that 'bus? I wish Dad Smith could have taken us up in the car. Why did he have to work today of all days?" my mother tutted tapping her elegantly shod foot impatiently. "We're going to be late at this rate."

Just at that moment we heard the grinding of gears being shifted to haul the 'bus up the steep slope of Doctor's Hill.

"Here it comes," I said as it nosed round the bend onto the flat.

"Thank goodness! Make sure the seat is clean before yew sit down," she whispered, "just in case."

But, as usual, the seats were spotlessly clean. Miners coming up from Abercynon Colliery never used the service 'buses, except on very rare occasions. Consideration for other passengers ensured they never sat on the seats. Regardless of how tired they were they stood for the whole journey or sat on a newspaper on the step of the 'bus.

We rattled up through Tynte and Penrhiwceiber lurching to a halt at every 'stop'. As another Red & White 'bus came into view its driver flagged down our vehicle, stuck his head through the window and whispered furtively. Both drivers let out a raucous laugh followed by more whispering and guffawing.

"Well, *they* may have all the time in the world, but *we* haven't," remarked a stout matron to the conductor.

"Call that work. No consideration at all. They should go down the pit for a bit mun. They'd know what 'ard work is like then instead of wastin' our time jokin' about and laughin' like hyenas," remarked a grizzled ex-miner as the 'bus staggered forward up Oxford Street towards Mount bridge.

We hung onto the metal pole by the front seat and waited for the 'bus to shudder to a halt. Hastily, we walked over the bridge dismayed to see the wedding cars drawing up at the church. Faint strains of organ music reached us throwing my mother into a panic.

"We'll just make it in time if we hurry up. Only the bridesmaids have arrived so far," she observed.

Unknown to us the bridal car had already left in the opposite direction taking the longer route along Granville Terrace. Finding the house deserted my mother shouted over the neighbouring wall.

"P'raps they've been left with Mrs Francis," she panted breathless after the exertion of climbing the hill.

"Hello, Mrs Francis, is anyone at home?" but there was no response.

In all the bustle and excitement they had forgotten that I was going to pick up my shoes.

"Well, there's nothing else for it. Yew'll have to go as yew are, Wellingtons or no Wellingtons," she moaned, "and look at your hair, the ribbons are soaking wet."

"P'raps they'll dry out," I muttered trying to avoid her grooming.

Sighing, she scraped at my hair with a comb moulding it into various positions as she walked behind me down Austin Street looking more disconsolate with every step. She was even more miserable when Nana Howells pushed me into the front row for the wedding photographs. A vision in blue; flattened hair, water-logged ribbons and feet clad in Wellington boots. A fitting revenge for Eira the 'wellies' girl.

"I can't believe this weather for August can yew?" complained a guest. "It was bucketing down earlier, now look at it."

Miraculously, the clouds had parted to reveal a patchy sky. The wedding party smiled at the camera while guests thronged round the church. Within minutes an invisible hand moved across the sky and swept away the remaining clouds leaving a hot, yellow sun blazing in a canopy of blue.

The sun maintained its feeble hold on the sky until autumn blazed into colour. Frost hardened the ground for Christmas followed by howling winds and heavy rain that lashed window panes and ran deep in gutters. Women, huddled in heavy coats, struggled to hold on to children and umbrellas as they trudged up Doctor's Hill; sodden, paper carrier bags threatening to split and spill over the pavement.

Undaunted, they stored jars of pickle onions, tins of custard powder, jellies, hundreds and thousands, vermicelli and trifle cases in the back of the pantry. Women gathered in front parlours to discuss strategy, vie for positions on the organising committee, munching Marie biscuits and sipping endless cups of tea. Their thoughts were on more important matters: street parties, bunting and the coronation.

LITTLE DAI STRIKES AGAIN

Grey clouds in a white sky hung ominously overhead threatening promised rain. Outside Albert House 'Old Mother Riley' moved up and down the line of children checking on positions ready for the fancy dress parade. 'She' pushed 'Dilly Daydream' into line next to the dentist who was brandishing a pair of pliers at Laurel and Hardy. 'Old Father Time' flicked his long, white beard at special agent 'Dick Barton' as he ogled the pretty blonde nurse in front. Hoisting her umbrella into the air 'she' called in a vaguely familiar, manly voice,

"Pa-r-a-de, quick march!"

A buzz of excitement filled the air: drums began to beat a steady rhythm as the motley ensemble moved off skipping steps as they tried to keep in time with the beat. A Jack Russell bounded out of the tight group of spectators and raced up and down the line yapping and playfully nipping at the feet of the marchers.

"Gerroff, yew stupid 'apporth!" muttered 'Dilly Daydream' peering vacantly through black-rimmed glasses.

A boy emerged from the crowd grabbed the dog by the collar and pulled him, yelping loudly, back to the curb.

The pavements were crowded with people waving little Union Jack flags, blowing kazoos or shaking wooden rattles above their heads in celebration of young Queen Elizabeth's coronation.

"Yoo hoo, Mary!" called Mrs Beynon from the crowd as her daughter, resplendent in 'Cinderella' costume, marched past on the arm of her brother, 'Prince Charming'.

"Doesn't she look gorgeous!" she exclaimed. "It took me weeks to make that dress yew know. I wouldn't like to say how many sequins are on it."

"I hope the rain keeps off," remarked her companion eyeing the delicate net overskirt. "Yew wouldn't want that to get wet now would yew?"

"I tried all ways to get *her* to dress up but she wouldn't budge. She sulked that much I just gave up in the end," my mother complained shooting me a black look.

A vision of my devastated 'daffodil dress' drifted across my memory making me squirm with remembered embarrassment.

She waved furiously as Roger passed in his '*Dick Whittington*' costume with 'Brummie', our tabby cat, sitting on his shoulder. Michael scampered alongside in long, white nightshirt and tasselled nightcap carrying an old-fashioned round, metal candlestick.

"What's 'e supposed to be then?" asked Mrs Winter.

"Well, it's obvious innit mun?" chortled Mrs Tolley her ample bosom shaking with laughter. "'E's '*Wee Willie Winkie!*'"

The parade marched on round the bend into Mountain Ash Road. As it drew level with Bethania Chapel '*Old Mother Riley*' ordered in a deep, manly voice,

"Pa–r–a–de, halt!" bringing the children shuffling to a stop. "Pa–r–a–de, fall out! Have a good time!"

The words were lost in the sound of scuffling feet as children surged through the wrought iron gates of Bethania's grounds and disappeared down the steps into the hall underneath the main chapel.

Inside white-clothed trestle tables were laden with party food: sandwiches, finger rolls, pickled onions, beetroot, cheese, ham and little iced sponge cakes. Welsh cakes, Bara Brith, various shades of jellies and oblong cases of home-made trifles covered with hundreds and thousands; jugs of lemonade and orangeade placed at strategic points along the tables. Red and blue paper, table napkins, alternately placed at the side of each plate, had been fashioned into small half-pyramids. On a corner table an enormous tea urn gurgled and spat steam as it came to the boil. Dozens of cups and saucers lined the table from end to end.

"Aw, look at all this!" exclaimed Anwen. "There's enough to feed an army in 'ere."

She reached out to take one of the flags that formed the centre-pieces on each table.

"Dwn't touch those, I think they're just for decoration," I said eyeing the flags on the wall whilst noticing the sharp glance of one of the lady helpers.

"Well, come along now sit down everybody so we can get started," said a solidly-built woman wearing a frilled pinafore crowned by a fancy, straw hat, its brim covered with a peculiar concoction of flowers and shiny, red artificial cherries.

"For what we are about to receive may the Lord make us *truly* thankful," intoned the black-clad minister of Bethania.

He had barely uttered the final word before dozens of hands were reaching for sandwiches to join the ham and tomatoes on their plates.

"Where's the trifle?" Little Dai asked looking around.

"No trifle for yew 'till yew've eaten yewer savouries, my lad," ordered Fancy Hat firmly as she passed our table.

Little Dai scowled as he picked up the bits of crusts he had left, sighed loudly, and shoved them into his mouth. Fancy Hat raised her eyes to the ceiling with a pained expression on her face.

"Tsk! Tsk! That's not very nice now is it?"

Little Dai gulped the last piece and washed it down with a mouthful of orangeade.

"I've finished mun, 'aven't I so I'm ready for my trifle now," he said smothering a burp.

Looking daggers at Little Dai she picked up a trifle and put it down in front of him with a look that said,

"I hope it chokes yew."

Tight-lipped, she smoothed imaginary wrinkles from her pinafore, stuck her nose in the air, and retreated to the comfort of the tea urn to wait for the Loyal Toast.

Excitement increased when 'Old Mother Riley' announced the start of the Fancy Dress competition. Children walked around the hall in circular fashion while the judges leaned towards each other, whispered, smiled and made copious notes. Tension mounted as the bulk of the parade was eliminated leaving five children on the floor. 'Wee Willie Winkie' was ousted but 'Dick Whittington' continued his march around the room. Finally, the judges were ready to make an announcement.

"The standard was so high it was very difficult to pick the winners. Congratulations to all of yew for making such a wonderful effort. And the runners up are....."

His words were drowned by onlookers shouting their congratulations. My mother's face fell as she saw the look of imminent disappointment on Roger's face suddenly changing to a wide smile of excitement as the judge continued.

"And first place goes to, '*Dick Whittington!*'"

Loud clapping filled the room as Roger went to collect his prize. Startled by Little Dai cheering at his elbow 'Brummie' jumped from his shoulder and darted across the room. As a dozen hands reached out to catch him he leapt onto the nearest table knocking over plates of food. A lurid, orange stain spread outwards from an overturned jug of pop as the frantic feline raced from one end of the table to the other hitting little flags like a skier in a slalom race.

"Close the door!" a voice shouted.

Too late, 'Brummie' was out of the door and over the wall into Thurston Street. We chased him into the lane and watched as he scrambled up our back wall into the garden and safety.

Still laughing at 'Brummie's' antics we walked up to Sid Jones' field, above the stream, ready for the races. We ran in the sack race, laughed at fathers hobbling in the three-legged event and mothers mincing along balancing an egg on a teaspoon. Flushed and triumphant I flopped onto the grass besides Anwen and Mati.

"I've come first in nearly all the races. I've won 1s and 9d altogether," I bragged. "Two shillings if I hadn't had thruppence for coming second last time."

"Last race now," Sid Jones called. "This time the prize will be 9d."

"On yewer marks, get set, go!" he shouted.

I ran as though pursued by the devil; down the dips, over the tumps, through thistles, catching my feet in clodges of earth and grass until I fell through the finish line flat onto my face. Sid Jones picked me up and raised my arm in the air.

"The winner!" he declared handing over my nine pennies.

Still puffing from my exertions I showed Dad Smith my handful of winnings.

"I've got 2s and 6d now."

"Give me all that small change and I'll give yew something smaller," he said squeezing half a crown into my palm.

Half a crown! I was already on my way to making a fortune!

As dusk descended we made our way down Margaret Street to join another street party. Herbert Street had been cleared of tables and chairs leaving it clear for dancing. Red, white and blue bunting stretched across the road between the houses; flags hung from windows. Music blared from a radiogram that had been carried into the street. In the middle of the road couples danced to the sound of Nat 'King' Cole's '*Unforgettable*' mouthing the words to their partners.

Children ran in and out of moving legs eating ice-cream or emulating the adults with their own improvised steps. A little girl jealously tugged at her father's trouser leg as he danced closely with her mother. Lifting her up he whirled her round and round as she threw back her head and laughed with delight. Holding her close the threesome danced together under the fading canopy of light.

Golden shafts of light spilled from open front doors, candles flickered, the breeze breathed gently on bunting. Old ladies sat on kitchen chairs, eyes moist, remembering the dead king who had lived with them through the horrors of war. Others toasted the young queen and the beginnings of a new era. This night a shared spirit and sense of community still lived in the valley. The 'season of the long grass' beckoned once again and entered my heart as I dreamed of the mountains asleep in darkness above the village.

MAGGIE, MARG AND THE MOUNTIES

That September I jumped a class and went straight into Standard Five, the scholarship class. Some of my friends moved into Standard Four which meant that they would move into the secondary modern at the end of the year. Margaret MacLucas, a pretty woman with a voluptuous figure, was class teacher of Standard Four. Her sleek, dark hair smoothed away from her face and caught in a chignon gave her an earthy, Latin look. She sometimes wore flattering, figure-hugging sweaters that made the older boys ogle inanely and nudge each other theatrically. Miss MacLucas was also a member of the local drama group that often performed plays on the small stage in St. Donat's Church Hall.

"I want yew to ask your parents to buy tickets for the play next week. I'm sure they'll enjoy it," beamed Maggie.

"Can we come as well Miss?" we chorused.

"Yes, of course yew can. It's half price for children."

We squealed with delight when she informed us that she was to act in the forthcoming summer production the following week: we could hardly wait to see her on stage.

Enjoying the remnants of a warm, early summer day we strolled along past the Workmen's Hall and Ynysmeirig Hotel, nicknamed 'The Spy'; so-called because it had been frequented by a German spy who lived on Ynysmeirig Road during the First World War.

As we climbed the steep incline of Well Street a welcome, faint breeze touched our faces gently ruffling our hair. Old men stopped half way up and rested on their sticks wheezing painfully; breathing hampered by the coal dust clogging their lungs. The drab black and grey of the miners' Sunday best suits contrasted sharply with the summer dresses of the young mothers and bright hues of their children's cotton shorts as they filed into Church House.

Metal folding chairs squeaked and scraped on wooden floors as the audience shuffled into comfort. Mothers mouthed shushing warnings as children craned their necks for a glimpse of Miss MacLucas.

"Oh look, there she is; there's Miss MacLucas!" exclaimed Gareth

"Be quiet, for goodness sake. Can't yew behave for two minutes!" said his mother in an exasperated tone.

"Never happy until everybody's looking at yew, are yew? Stop attracting attention to yourself," she said in the affected superior voice she saved for occasions like these.

After a final shuffling and positioning of chairs the audience settled down to enjoy the play.

"It's gonna start now," whispered Gareth.

"Any more noise and home yew go to your father, my boy!"

On cue a bodiless hand, either side of the stage, pulled back the curtains and the hall fell silent.

Maggie was co-starring with a tall, thin, eagle-faced, bespectacled academic. The closing scene required them to kiss until the curtains closed to signal the end of the play. They kissed and kissed, occasionally coming up for air, but frantic attempts to close the curtains failed. We loved it. Fancy, one of the teachers kissing in public in front of the children. Finally, two of the cast pulled the curtains together and held them as the red-faced couple fled off stage to howls of appreciation from parents and children alike. Maggie had acquired a new respect from her charges. After all she was a star!

Her colleague, Marjorie Thomas, played the piano in assembly. She played with gusto; hands leaving the keys theatrically and upper body swaying to the melody. A handsome woman, quite tall, well-built with dark hair pulled back in a severe chignon. She squinted short-sightedly whenever she took off her glasses, vigorously cleaning them with a spotless, white handkerchief. Carefully placing them back on her nose she fidgeted, moving them this way and that with the tips of her fingers, until they were in just the right place.

Miss Thomas lived on Plantation Road. Every Christmas we sang carols outside her door. After a few renderings of, 'In the Bleak Mid Winter' and 'Once in Royal David's City', she peered round the door and said,

"That was very nice but you're too early. Come back nearer Christmas and sing again."

Dutifully we obeyed and next time round she presented us with two pennies between four of us. Never more, never less.

She ran the Girls' Guild Club in the evenings in the 'Clock', the local secondary school at the foot of Doctor's Hill. Most evenings she concentrated on teaching us how to sing in the hope of entering us in local and area competitions. Looking over her shoulder as she played the piano she mouthed the lyrics of the melody in an exaggerated manner encouraging us to emulate her pronunciation. Reluctantly we sang a melancholy Welsh hymn rising to an ear-splitting crescendo as we hit the last line.

"Girls, girls, this is supposed to be a serious piece of music."

"Aw, but miss, I dwn't like this kind of mewsic," complained a rosy-cheeked soprano.

"How *many* times do I have to tell you. Not mewsic girls, meousic, meousic! You must enunciate! Now then all together!"

This would be followed by, 'Nymphs and Shepherds' and 'On Wings of Song', although Marjorie pronounced it 'neemphs' and 'weeings'. Finally, she came to us triumphantly and told us that we had been entered in the South Wales Girls' choir heats in Barry. A month later we found ourselves singing on stage watching Miss Thomas carefully as she played and looked at us to ensure we were singing what she was mouthing at us. We made her proud as we carefully copied her grimacing and sang with much feeling about "neemphs and weeings and meeousic."

We sang for what seemed hours until, released, we rushed headlong to the lavatory. Impatiently queuing outside we could see Miss Thomas dimly silhouetted behind the half-glass door, the upper part covered with a patterned paper pasted to the glass; a very popular device at the time. Unaware that she could be heard Marjorie completed the necessities to the hilarity of the girls she had lined up outside. Every sound and trickle appeared to be amplified as each girl took their turn. Always painfully shy I held back until Miss Thomas pushed me inside with some frustration and said,

"Oh, for goodness sake *do* come along girl! We haven't got all day, the 'bus is waiting!"

Closing the door I waited a respectable length of time then came out and shut the door quietly behind me, still bursting. I had been too embarrassed to pass water in case they heard me outside.

Dougie Davies, a ruddy, stocky man with dark, curly hair, brilliant blue eyes and a ready smile taught the scholarship class. He had a wealth of stories to tell us about his time overseas when he was in the forces. On winter mornings we crowded around the roaring, coal fire surrounded by an ornate, black fireguard and waited for our little bottles of milk to thaw. Taking off our shoes we warmed our wriggling toes and listened to his stories about Canada, especially Alberta, where he hoped to emigrate one day.

"It's so cold in Alberta in the winter that if a mug of hot tea is thrown outside it'll freeze before it hits the ground," he told us.

I tried visualising the liquid freezing as it hurtled through the air, the endless whiteness of the snow-covered fields and rugged mountains.

Fascinated, I imagined myself in the glamorous, red uniform of the Mounties sitting astride a sinewy, chestnut horse as it ploughed through the thick snow. Precipitous crevices gaped below as I carried my wounded friend to safety across a bridge of snow with gun-slinging criminals in close pursuit.

"Steady now: get down on your stomach and slither across bit by bit. Easy does it Joe."

"Look out!" I cried as the edge of the bridge gave way almost plummeting us to the bottom of the chasm.

Safely on the other side I wrapped my now unconscious friend in warm, animal skins promising to get him back to the nearest trading post.

"Mush! Mush!" I shouted. "We must find shelter before the blizzard gets worse!"

The sharp crack of the whip sounded loud and clear in the freezing air as the powerful huskies dragged the sleigh through the snow-laden trees of a Canadian forest. Dougie's voice broke into my thoughts,

"Open your books at page nineteen please."

With a sigh I floated back to earth for the morning maths session.

One morning Dougie sat at his high desk, clasped his hands tightly and leaned forward with his elbows resting on his desk for support. As he started to tell us about our forthcoming scholarship examination his hands and legs started to tremble until his knees were banging against the underneath of the desk. Beads of glistening perspiration stood out on his forehead as he struggled to control his movements.

"What's wrong with Dougie?" whispered a boy in front of me. "E's sweatin' like a pig!"

Dougie tried to make light of his trembling by blaming the cold weather.

"It's freezing in here; almost as cold as Canada," he said attempting a weak laugh. He could see by our stricken faces that we were very frightened.

Hands tightly clenched on the desk he instructed,

"Go and fetch the headmaster for me, will yew ?" he nodded to the boy nearest the door.

"There's no need to be alarmed," Mr Bevan assured us when he came in and saw our anxious faces.

Attempting a wobbly smile in our direction Dougie staggered from the room supported by Mr. Bevan. Emlyn Jones, a tall, sandy-haired man, came to take us for the rest of the morning. He told us gently that Dougie was suffering an attack of malaria that he had picked up serving overseas. We felt miserable, convinced that he would die, but the following week he was standing over us as we recited John Masefield's 'Sea Fever' and struggled with fractions, areas and volumes in readiness for the scholarship examination.

Scholarship day dawned after a sleepless, fitful night tossing and turning. Fiddling with pens, clutching lucky charms, some futilely tugging at socks, rubbing at imaginary smudges on desks we waited anxiously for the papers to be distributed knowing that the outcome of this day would influence our lives in the years to come.

The day passed in a blur of composition writing and calculating. Like every other candidate I was convinced that I had failed. In the ensuing months we talked of nothing else except the impending results, some with worried looks, others with feigned nonchalance.

All too soon results' day arrived. We watched with baited breath as Mr. Bevan walked in: all eyes riveted on the sheet of paper he was holding. Looking at us gravely he gently reminded us that not everyone was suited to an academic education.

"Some of yew are better suited to more practical work. Yew will all eventually find your own niche in the community."

"That's it, I've failed!" groaned the girl next to me hanging her head.

Seconds later her face was wreathed in smiles as she heard her name called from the list of successful candidates.

Face flushed I waited in fevered anticipation, covering my face with hot, sweaty hands; not daring to hope. When my name was called out I didn't move a muscle. I just stared ahead.

"I've passed," I said quietly, not quite believing what I had heard.

Hardly a sound could be heard until the last name was called out. Unable to control our relief the hushed mutterings turned into a babble of joyful excitement. Congratulations for some, commiserations for others. Elated, I skipped school dinners and ran all the way home from Carnetown to tell my mother and grandparents.

She was throwing a bucket of disinfected water over the path which splattered all over my shoes. Jumping aside I gathered my composure not wanting to look too excited. Nonchalantly I said,

"Well, I've passed the scholarship. I'll be off to grammar school in September."

Delighted she threw down her brush, dragged me to my grandparents house to tell them then rushed down to tell her friend, Aurona May. Nana Smith proudly snipped out the list of successful candidates published in the newspaper and filed it with her treasured cuttings.

That weekend we went to Pontypridd to buy a congratulatory present. Still hoping for a bike I pleaded, but I knew it was no use asking. Instead, I had a gold-plated watch with matching bracelet to wear on my first day at grammar school.

Towards the end of term Dougie Davies announced he was emigrating to Canada. His adventure was brief, his dreams shattered, because the climate was too cold for him. He probably hadn't even managed to have a cup of tea before it froze. Our last day was tinged with sadness because we were leaving Dougie, but simultaneously filled with anticipation of the time that stretched ahead of us: time we would spend in the 'long grass'.

JEZEBEL AT ELEPHANT ROCK

On the horizon a galleon in full sail slowly drifted into view like a sleeping swan with folded wings.

"Ship ahoy!" I shouted scanning the gentle swell of the sea through my imaginary telescope.

"It's gaining on us. I can just make out its flag. It's the Jolly Roger me hearties! Let's give 'em a run for their money shipmates!"

Puffing and blowing sailors hauled on ropes, others swung in the rigging or fired the cannon with a loud,

"Boom! Boom!"

"They've lost their main mast!" shouted Little Dai. "We've got 'em now!"

"Argh! We've been hit!" screamed Denny. "There's water pourin' in!"

"Abandon ship! Abandon ship!" I screamed.

"Land ahoy! Swim for the shore!" yelled Anwen.

A snapped branch followed by a muffled thud and loud squeals signalled a painful landing on the lush grass below. Lying across a huge branch I 'swam' frantically, flailing my arms and legs until I reached 'land' and collapsed in gales of laughter on the 'beach'.

Tired out I leaned against the gnarled branches of the ancient oak and gazed over the rooftops of Abercynon, the mining village where I was born. Terraced houses snaked up the valley or clung tenaciously to the side of mountains tracing the line of the narrow, main road. North of Abercynon mountains, once green and lush, stood stark and blackened with coal tips. Across the valley the steep, green slopes of Cefn Glas dotted here and there with craggy rocks. Behind me the mountain stretched across to Pen-y-Foel covered in oak, silver birch, pine and other species.

It was still summer, 'season of the long grass', when we played all day on the hills. Sometimes the gang picked bunches of harebells and celandines avoiding the poisonous foxgloves, or filled capacious pockets with unripened hazelnuts to eat as we sprawled in our make-shift den hidden away in the long, honey-coloured, dried grass surrounding Table Rock.

Heaving a loud sigh I climbed down not wanting to return to reality, but the game was over. It was time to go home to report to the 'admiral of the fleet' who had promised fresh supplies of food and water for our afternoon expedition to Elephant Rock.

Leading off from Mountain Ash Road, hidden between the houses, was a steep, pot-holed, narrow road that led directly to the mountains. Mainly used by farm traffic it also led to the main gates of Abercynon Cemetery set on the mountain behind Pontcynon. Panting with exertion we climbed doggedly onwards past Brown's slaughter house slowing down to look fearfully at the rundown shack.

"There's a ghost of a murderer in there," whispered Gareth. "No, dwn't stop to look yew ninny! It'll come out and grab yew and chop yewer 'ead and legs off!"

"Aw, dwn't be so daft mun," grinned Denny nervously as he quickened his pace and struggled up the hill.

The slaughter house had long since ceased to exist, but was reputedly haunted by this legendary character because of his grizzly trade. Villagers spoke in hushed tones about the spectre of 'Brown the Slaughterer' who appeared at midnight. Apprehension, accompanied by a thrill of terror, coursed through me each time the image of this man, holding the blood-soaked head of a sheep in his hands, encroached on my mind. In reality the place was just a wooden shack surrounded by dirt and stones while the faint odour of horses' dung seeping into the nostrils brought our hands up to our noses in protest.

At the top of a steep incline the road forked. To the right it undulated gently and rose up directly in front of the enormous cast-iron gates of the cemetery, simultaneously imposing and intimidating. The road was like a dark river pulling us into its depths; waiting to sweep us along towards the mouth of the ghoul that lurked beyond deep inside the gates to envelop us in oblivion.

Instead we turned left, onwards and upwards, towards our destination moving over a still rougher incline covered with rugged boulders and flat, smooth stones as big as manhole covers. The road wound round in an 'S' shape and took us past Horse Rock where we sat astride it, legs dangling, hair flying in the wind as we whooped delightedly across our make-believe prairie.

"Giddy up! Giddy up!" yelled Little Dai face flushed with excitement.

"Dig your heels in and hold tight to the reins boys!" I yelled.

"Look out for arrows and Apaches coming down the hill! Hundreds of 'em!"

"Arrrrgh! They've got me!" groaned Gareth falling off his make-believe steed whilst firing his invisible six-shooter at the approaching Indians.

Adventure and suspense, experienced in a moment of almost painful pleasure, was transfixed in our minds for eternity as we escaped through the undergrowth.

Red Indians lurked surreptitiously behind every bush and tree as we slid along on our stomachs to avoid capture.

"Phew! We lost 'em." Little Dai whispered.

Carefully parting the ferns I peered into a small clearing in front of a huge rock formation. Momentarily, I hesitated before signalling to the gang to run towards Elephant Rock and safety where a new adventure would begin.

Chins held high, hands shading our eyes looking for signs of head-shrinking cannibals, breath held in suspense at the sudden snapping of a twig.

"Get down, quick!" I urged.

Voices and movement in the ferns behind Elephant Rock interspersed with girlish giggling. We crept slowly forward, inch by inch, hardly daring to breathe.

"Damn!"

It was just another sloppy, courting couple locked together in passionate embrace.

Wide-eyed we stood watching with rapt attention while they kissed and fondled each other and wondered why.

"What's 'e doing then? I think she's bein' murdered," said Gareth in a hushed tone as the woman struggled and pushed the man's hands away.

"We'll 'ave to save 'er before she gets killed!"

"Dope! She wouldn't be giggling now would she?" said Denny scornfully. "They're just wrestlin' tha's all."

Suddenly the man looked over his shoulder and caught sight of us staring at them.

"Oi yew lot, shove off!" shouted the man with the greasy hair and pock-marked chin. "Why don't yew bloody kids play somewhere else?"

"We always play up 'ere. This is our rock, innit?" exclaimed Gareth indignantly looking at the rest of us for support.

"Yeah, it's our rock," we chorused.

We held our ground: this was our territory and we were not going to capitulate without a fight. The man shuffled uncomfortably under the direct gaze of six wide-eyed and angrily whooping warriors. Finally, in desperation, he groaned,

"Aw, come on Joan. Doesn' marra where yew go round yuh mun. there's no peace. Look at them kids. They're all bloody mental mun!"

With that they slunk into the undergrowth never to be heard of again until the scandal broke some weeks later. They had been discovered lying in the shade of Elephant Rock by the man's young son who had rushed home to tell Mam the good news. His father, apparently, pledged never to be influenced by a Jezebel again. Who could blame him with two blackened eyes and a split lip caused, so rumour tells, by slipping on a bar of soap in the tin bath whilst bathing after a shift down the pit.

PIGMASH AND HAY

At the crest of the hill leading to Cook's field the dirt road forked to the left and then arched upwards towards the 'long grass' and Van Poucke's farm. On the curve of the bend was a large, metal farm gate with a stone stile at the side. Beyond the stile a number of fenced off fields full of Michaelmas daisies, pignuts, burdocks, feverfew and buttercups stretching away towards the houses on one side and the mountain on the other.

Descending crookedly through these fields ran a narrow path littered with small, loose stones and deeply embedded rocks fenced off with barbed wire. At the end was another stone stile that led into Bateman's field and downwards into Plantation Road.

"Oh come on, for goodness sake will yew. Yew're always day-dreamin' yew are!" yelled Anwen who was striding in front. "Look at 'er, she's always the same, dawdlin' as usual!"

"I'm coming!" I said impatiently.

Unlike my friends I was curious about my surroundings. Kicking over the loose stones I watched the wriggling worms and scurrying insects. I prodded them gently with a discarded lollipop stick watching them disperse and hide under other stones. Fascinated, I observed the movements of a group of ants gathered round a small piece of bread, marvelling at their strategy before they dragged it off to their nest.

Languidly trailing behind I listened to the sounds of this pocket of countryside filling the air. The day was hot and sultry. The familiar chirrup of crickets and the flap of birds' wings followed by other more mysterious noises escaping from the undergrowth nudged at my senses; noises that simultaneously filled me with apprehension and a magnetic curiosity. A smattering of fluffy, white clouds slowly sailed across an azure sky steered by a gentle breeze. Momentarily, my attention was caught by a barely perceptible rustle from the grass that brought me to a dead stop.

"It's nothing, just my imagination," I thought.

Still, I listened, not daring to breathe or move a muscle.

Suddenly, I caught sight of a snake wriggling along from the bank into the path. Heart pounding painfully, brain seething with anxiety and fear, I stood transfixed with horror.

"Please God, please don't let it come near me," I begged silently.

The snake, long and greenish grey, recoiled as it sensed my presence its tongue flicking in and out menacingly.

"Go away, please go away!" I screamed inside my head willing the reptile to disappear from sight, but no sound came from my lips.

Too frightened to move I stood, frozen in dreadful fascination, listening to the blood pounding through my temples and the thudding, suffocating motion of my heart until the snake raised itself up like an Egyptian carving on a tomb then dropped back and slithered underneath the fence. My legs felt leaden but after a while I tentatively moved one of them forward, very slowly.

"Help! There's a snake after me!" I screamed, ignoring the fact that it had disappeared from sight.

Like a maniac I sprang forward not wanting to touch the ground where the snake had lain in case I was infected by some deadly poison.

Leaping over the stone stile I remembered, too late, that the other side was much lower and landed with a crashing blow onto the sharp stones at the foot of the stile.

"Ow, my knees!" I groaned as I struggled to my feet and limped as fast as I could towards the rest of the gang who, safely on the other side of the fence, were laughing hysterically.

"It's not *funny*, is it?" I complained humiliated by their laughter, grazed knees smarting with every step.

"I could've been poisoned. Died in agony with no antidote like that man in the '*Tarzan*' film."

"Aw, dwn't worry mun. We wouldn't let yew die. We'd 'ave sucked the poison out wouldn't we boys?"

"Humph, not likely! I'd rather die in agony!" I retorted as I hobbled painfully after Anwen who was laughing raucously as she ran down to the bottom of the field.

Reaching the safety of Bateman's field I rushed towards Ship Rock and flung myself onto its flat surface letting out great gasps of air as I tried to regain my composure.

"What are yew all laughing at? I nearly died then!" I exclaimed dramatically as the others clambered onto the boulder.

This was a rock of what seemed to be gigantic proportions, wide at the stern and gradually tapering to a sharp prow. Shallow hollows in the stone were portholes and an eight inch high ridge, stretching the width of the rock, was the 'bridge' from where fierce battles were won and pirates were forced to '*walk the plank*' duly bound and blind-folded.

This ceremony was accorded all the aplomb of a band of unruly matelots as a child was prodded towards the edge of the rock while the others shouted,

"Into the sea! Into the sea! Look out for sharks!"

Landing in the 'sea' brought howls of laughter, especially wallowing in a cowpat or a cluster of sheep droppings that were liberally scattered over the whole area of the field, along with abundant thistles and 'stinging' nettles. We searched arduously for the creatures that had deposited their signatures, but rarely did we see a cow or sheep to blame.

Until now it had been eerily quiet: a calm, even silence delicately encroached upon my senses as I lay on Ship Rock penetrated only by the sounds of the bees busying themselves around the wild flowers and the occasional chirp of a bird. The sun blazed down; a shimmering ball in an unbroken, blue sky. Now the field began to fill up with other youngsters of my own age and a few older boys and girls from the surrounding streets. It was harvesting time and every year we helped to rake in the hay. The memory spun its magic with the feel of the rake in my hands as we worked joyfully in the sweltering heat; raking until blisters formed on our hands and our eyes hurt from the glare of the now mellow, golden sun.

As evening approached and the sun turned blood orange on the horizon we sat on Ship Rock and ravenously gorged on thick slices of Swansea bread smothered with Welsh Shir Gar butter and generous lashings of strawberry jam washed down with luke-warm Tizer. We were pioneers, adventurers harvesting our future in the spirit of youth; filled with camaraderie and the fulfilment of being alive and close to the warm, earthy smell of the land.

When approaching dusk threatened to spread its blanket over the sky another task, not for the faint-hearted, awaited us in the potato store. Standing ankle deep in rotten potatoes we took childish pleasure in throwing them into huge vats being boiled up into mash for the pigs, our fingers sinking into the stinking mass as we scrabbled for more.

"Aw, what a pong!" I exclaimed gingerly picking up a slimy potato and throwing it into the nearest vat.

Screwing up my nose in disgust I edged towards the shed door and gasped for air, but I couldn't show the others I felt squeamish. Reluctantly, I went back inside, closed my eyes in silent acceptance and plunged my hands into the malodorous mess.

With the sun still lingering on the horizon, bone weary and satisfied, hair matted to our heads with perspiration, faces glowing with health, burnt pink by the sun, filthy all over and smelling of pig's swill we walked slowly home, dragging our feet, not wanting the day to end. Dragging our feet because we knew we were in for a scolding for helping with the pig mash.

"Great day wannit?" Anwen beamed.

"Fantastic!" agreed Little Dai looking at his blistered hands with pure contentment as Tom the big, black carthorse lumbered towards us and nuzzled up against his shoulder.

Stan the Milk put Tom out to graze in Bateman's field after his milk round had been completed. Early every morning the great, muscular beast pulled the milk cart around the streets of Abercynon, holding up cars and 'buses. Stan's band of young, eager helpers leapt agilely on and off the cart dragging crates onto the pavement ready to put the milk on each doorstep in time for the morning tea.

The Co-op also plied its milk and bread rounds with big, red wagons pulled by enormous horses who puffed and snorted and shook their long manes. Switching their tails to keep off the summer flies they impatiently waited for the driver to flick the reins and move on to the next set of terraced houses clinging to the side of a hill. The horses pawed at the tarmac, neighed and curled back their lips in anticipation of a treat. Relics of a gentler age they snuffled contentedly in the palms of some of the children who brought sugar lumps or apples. Hysterical shouts from some of the rougher boys,

"Look out, the 'orse is 'avin a pee pee!"

Children suddenly jumped to one side amid hoots of laughter as the horse urinated like a fast-flowing waterfall over the road setting the gutters awash and immediately followed by the animal relieving itself still further in the middle of the road.

Vacant steps and doorways suddenly came alive as men rushed into the street with their shovels to scoop up the hot, pungent, steaming mess to be dutifully deposited under their rose bushes or rhubarb.

"Aw, tha's disgustin' mun!" exclaimed Little Dai as he watched Jack Dung fill his bucket.

"Duw mun, nothing like a bit of 'orse manure to make them rhubarbs grow. I bet I'll 'ave the biggest rhubarb this side of Ponty too at this rate. Dur, they were big last year wan' they?" he said looking at his wife who was turning up her nose with distaste. "But this year they'll be flamin' gigantic, just yew wait and see now!" he exclaimed as we raced up the street, holding our noses, desperately trying not to breathe until we were a safe distance away.

After the drama of the rounds Tom, glistening with sweat, ambled lethargically into Bateman's field to enjoy a well-earned rest away from the monstrous fume-filled motor cars that had slowly, but surely, overtaken these faithful animals. Some afternoons his idyllic paradise was disrupted. While he snuffled, nostrils deep in the fragrant grass, the boys waited for him to nibble alongside a rock where they stood in wait ready to throw themselves onto his broad back two at a time.

"Hold 'im by the mane for me to get on," Denny urged as he attempted to climb up on Tom's back.

"Aw, yew stupid 'apporth!" complained Denny as Tom moved sideways leaving him with one leg planted on Ship Rock and the heel of the other leg resting precariously on Tom's back at an angle reminiscent of a Bluebell girl's high kick. One final push and Denny was sitting triumphantly astride the carthorse while the other boys scrambled clumsily up behind him.

Startled, Tom neighed loudly and snorted indignantly at this encroachment of his rest and liberty, but to no avail.

"Giddy up, giddy up! Come on Tom, move will yew?"

The unruly lads, hanging onto his mane, urged him into a canter across the field until they either fell off or Tom stopped and stubbornly refused to move an inch further. We loved this gentle creature. Oceans of tears were shed when Stan turned up one day to do his rounds with a new van. It could never replace old Tom. His demise was the end of a period of history as he was the last horse to pull a trade cart through the streets of Abercynon.

FOOD FOR THE DEAD

The days of my childhood were quiet and free; free from the boom of jet planes, the rumble of heavy lorries and the deafening pounding of car radios. Free to play without fear in the 'long grass' on the green hillsides behind the houses. Our lives unfettered, protected from harm by a strong sense of community. From the mountainside children looked towards their back gardens where mothers waved their tea towels signalling the onset of mealtimes accompanied by;

"Yoo hoo! Yoo hoo! It's time for tea."

Five minutes later another call; this time urgent and edged with irritation.

"Yew'd better get down 'ere now or yewer father will be up there after yew."

Silence then,

"Do yew 'ear me? If I 'ave to come up there my boy yew'll be in serious trouble! Now get yewerself down' ere now!"

Those were the days when very little traffic interrupted our lives unlike the present day. Now there is a constant stream of cars, motorcycles, school and factory buses. Harassed motorists ramming their fists down on the horns of their cars confident in the belief that roads were created for motorists and should not be crossed on foot. Any pedestrians daring enough to take their lives in their hands and cross the street are greeted by a polyphonic blast of noise; noise that encroaches into every aspect of our lives. The harsh abrasive 'honking' of the car horn startles old men and causes them to brandish their walking sticks at red-faced motorists exasperatedly devil-drumming on their steering wheels, while old ladies lethargically cross the highway as if it were still a tranquil summer in the halycon days of their youth.

As a child I played multifarious games on Mountain Ash Road safe from the harm of the mechanical beasts that had been spawned by increasing technology. Memories of ethereal figures lunging for the ball to avoid being '*Piggy in the Middle*', ghostly voices calling,

"Queenie, Queenie, who's got the ball?"

The thump of the ball as it struck my shoulder in a frenzied game of '*Cabbage*' leaving me bruised and sore though totally unaware of the immediate pain as I was enveloped in the spirit of the play. The fortunate winner of the toss was 'keeper of the ball' while the rest of us weaved and dodged until he shouted,

"Cabbage! Yew moved then Little Dai! Dwn't anybody move now or yew're out!"

Standing stock still, bodies quivering with the effort of controlling our energy; breathless with the anticipation of being the target of a hit or the sudden exultation of becoming 'keeper'.

School summer holidays were idyllic and crammed with excitement. The sun shone hard and bright; the days long and happy in those post-war years of the 1950s when we climbed puffing and gasping like steam engines, picking our way over the rocks grazing our knees and hands, oblivious to the pain. The only thing that mattered was reaching Table Rock and 'the long grass' where we dreamed and talked and dreamed again.

At the top of the hill the road was quite level and dirt-smooth with just a few tufts of grass growing between isolated stones embedded into the earth by horses' hooves and farm vehicles. A few more laborious steps and we were upon it – Table Rock in the midst of the whispy 'long grass'. Just above Bateman's Field, it was a safe place to play without the unwanted presence of watchful parents. Agricultural vehicles, on their way to Van Poucke's farm, bumped slowly over the rough-hewn, dirt road that skirted Table Rock and the 'long grass' now parched golden after long days of summer sun.

On the rock's weather-beaten surface we spread our picnic and ate sighing contentedly with every mouthful. Appetites satisfied we stretched out with our faces to the sky.

"I'm going to join the WRENS and travel round the world on an aircraft carrier," I announced, remembering the stories I had read about life on the high seas and the glamorous uniforms tailored to fit the stars of the black and white films, "then, I'm going to write about all my adventures in different countries."

"Well, I'm gonna get married and have six children: three boys and three girls," said Pauline a pretty, chubby-faced, blue-eyed blonde, "after I've joined the WRAF and learned to fly planes."

Such dreams; dreams nurtured by imagination and the magic of our secret place. Dreams impossible for young girls in the 1950s.

All around us the whispy 'long grass' golden now in the light from the sun in its zenith, while the faint breeze carried our whispered thoughts and hopes forward into the distant, unknown years that dropped away into infinity. In later years I wondered about those companions and how fate had catapulted us through time and space to place us into our allotted compartments in life.

Looking down from Table Rock I could see the unified streets of Pontcynon. On one side of the main road terraced houses with grey, slate roofs and sun-blistered front doors that opened on to the pavement. Opposite, terraced, bay-windowed houses with tiny gardens. Lower, and to the left, the creamy, yellow 'prefabs' of Nant-y-Fedw and the factories of Ynysboeth industrial estate their white, sanitised walls glistening and shimmering in the midday sun. To the right the dark, circular, reservoir tank separated from the 'long grass' by a weathered, dry-stone wall with another looming over the cemetery.

"I wonder 'ow deep they are?" mused Gareth. "P'raps we could 'ave a swim."

"No fear, I'm not going in; it's too deep. Besides, I'll have a good row if I go in there," I said, thankful I had an excuse to stay away from its murky depths.

"Mam told me it's about one 'undred and fifty feet deep," said Little Dai in an awed voice.

"Aw, that's stupid. Trust yew to say something like that."

"Crikey, yew think yewer bath water's fifty feet deep!" laughed Denny slapping him on the back.

"Well, I dwn't like water tha's all, do I?"

"I've 'eard that dead people from the cemetery come out of their graves in the night and swim in 'em," said Gareth. "The water glows a greeny colour and an 'orrible green mist comes down the mountain. Tha's 'ow people know they're in there."

"Aw, nuts!" said Little Dai fearfully looking from one to the other. "You're 'aving me on in yew boys?"

Everyone screeched with laughter and rolled around in the grass exaggeratedly clutching their stomachs with delight. Nevertheless, the reservoir was a magnet for older children in the area who were warned about swimming in its depths. One had reputedly been found drowned after a long night of searching and weeping. On our many walks we skirted around them in fear and trepidation owing to the macabre tales of drowning and the ghosts of suicidal lovers.

Below the reservoir the walls of the cemetery loomed ominously even at this distance; damp and sinister, ivy choking the stones and reaching out to draw us into its tentacles. Sometimes on our way home we crept towards the entrance, squeezed guiltily through a gap in the railings at the side of the gate, and filled our bottles with water from the taps which were supposed to accommodate visitors with water for their flower vases.

"All the little babies are buried by the wall over by there," whispered Anwen.

Creeping forward on tiptoe, as if our presence would somehow waken them, we looked at a small, wooden cross but no name was visible. Silently, we stood gazing down at the spot until Little Dai giggled nervously,

"My friend's dog is buried up against the wall outside. There's loads of cats' and dogs' graves there."

"Aw, shurrup up Little Dai. It's not funny mun," murmured Denny digging him in the ribs. "These are real babies mun, not dogs."

The sight of the tiny graves filled me with sadness and gave me a curious sense of loneliness. Even in those far-off days I was a covert loner; in the crowd yet slightly detached as if my body and spirit were constantly separated; justifiably accused by my friends of being distant and aloof. I was not really with them, just an onlooker who occasionally made a conscious contribution to their games, but I played thinking games of my own of which they had no part and did not understand.

The melancholy atmosphere was relieved when Little Dai, who had wandered off towards the graves after his rebuke, suddenly shouted,

"Look boys, there's some really big wind berries over by 'ere!"

Enormous, succulent wind berries grew in uncontrolled profusion on some of the graves. Sitting on the edge of a tombstone Little Dai grabbed handfuls of the juicy fruit and stuffed it into his mouth until his face was purple like a boxer's after a particularly gruelling fight.

Horrified at the crowd's disrespect no amount of taunting could persuade me to participate in such a nauseating past time.

"I bet they're big and juicy 'cause they feed on the dead bodies underneath," I said.

Denny, eyes wide, stopped short, a handful of wind berries halfway to his mouth,

"Dwn't be daft!" he said turning quite pale as he threw the berries back onto the grave.

"Who cares? It won't 'urt yew mun, will it?" said Little Dai, looking at me for support.

"Oh, do what yew like Little Dai but I'm not eating them. There could be bits of corpses in them. They could feed on your insides until there's nothing left and then eat their way out!" I exclaimed dramatically eyeing him in mock horror.

"Dwn't believe a word of that, I dwn't," he said throwing a frightened glance at the graves.

Feigning bravado he made his way to the gates urging us to follow. As we walked past my eyes were involuntarily drawn to the inscriptions on the gravestones. I ruminated on the lives of the occupants wondering what they had been like in life. I did not understand the feelings of poignancy only that it filled me with a restlessness of spirit and a sense of urgency to fulfil the web of dreams we had spun on Table Rock in the 'long grass'.

BUCKETS AND BOMBS

During the school summer holidays our mothers packed a picnic and took us higher up the mountain. We skirted the cemetery walls and trekked up to Gilfach-y-Rhyd, a beautiful sequestered spot, only reached after a long, arduous climb through a pine forest that stretched endlessly up the mountain until it met the sky. Through this forest ran a narrow, tortuous path. Even on the hottest, brightest day the path was sheltered from the sun because of the expanse of trees on either side. An aura of gloom and foreboding permeated the woods causing one to look over one's shoulder; feelings that an unknown presence stalked our footsteps.

Trees huddled close together their branches almost touching. High ferns grew in profusion and covered their lower trunks as did the lichen. It was dark and eerie, the silence broken only by the constant buzzing of swarming gnats.

"I dwn't like in it in 'ere; it's creepy," Anwen whispered waving her arms to ward off the gnats. "Try and walk a bit faster will yew?"

"There's loads of snakes in the ferns," I whispered back warily. "I'm sure I heard one slithering around in there."

Creeping slowly forward we listened for any sign of movement.

Suddenly, a sound of rustling came from the ferns. Screaming loudly we ran and ran up the incline until we could see an opening a short way ahead. Gulping in huge gasps of air we collapsed onto the stone encrusted path.

"We're all nutters runnin' away like that mun. There's nothing in there," giggled Mati trying hard to convince herself and us.

"C'mon, let's go before we all start acting as if we're stark, raving bonkers!" I laughed struggling to my feet. I ploughed up the path with the gang at the rear, but we were all very watchful of our surroundings barely reassured by the sound of our mothers' voices behind us.

Gradually, the pathway became much narrower and steeper until we reached the entrance to the field. We climbed laboriously hands pressing down on knees at every step to support the weight of our weary bodies. One concerted effort and we were over the stone stile and in another world.

Towering in front of us a high, bright-green hill; long grass that shone as glossy and glowing as a young girl's hair cascading down the mountain like an emerald waterfall. To the far right a tall forest of pines, with an isolated orphan from another species more indigenous of the Welsh valleys, intermingled with waving fronds of ferns around their trunks. To the left open ground covered with shrubs, wind berry bushes and sweet-leaves beyond which the bottle-green forest curved around skirting the hill in a great arc.

It had an almost Tyrolean splendour; a panorama of pine trees with green hills fading gradually from purple to blue as they receded into the distance. Wire fences enclosed the trees to keep out farm animals that frequently strayed near the perimeter. Little tufts of sheep's wool clung to the wire where animals had tried to force their way through the fence.

"I love it up 'ere. It's peaceful like, innit?" Anwen sighed contentedly as we flung ourselves onto the soft grass.

"Yeah, you can 'ear the birds flyin' out of the trees and the stream comin' down the mountain. It's great innit? I could stay up 'ere forever," murmured Denny shielding his eyes against the midday sun.

"Look, there's our favourite tree! Come on, let's play 'Tarzan'," I enthused running over to swing on a low-lying branch that overhung the water.

On the banks of the stream a tree of massive proportions, its branches covered with verdant foliage, gave us protection from the sun. Cut into the hillside nature had carved a huge cleft down which fresh spring water tumbled and cascaded. The sun's rays caught the droplets in crystal bursts that danced and gleamed as they fell into natural, miniature waterfalls over which the water rushed and plunged into deep, translucent pools. Our pool was naturally calf deep, but almost chest high after our strenuous efforts to build a dam across the stream where we could swim just a few strokes in either direction.

Underneath our shorts and tee-shirts we wore swimming costumes. Halter-necked monstrosities with fine elastic woven through the material to form bulbous squares that swelled on contact with the water and made us look like giant pineapples with arms and legs. Feet slipping and sliding on wet stones we found a partially submerged rock. Very gingerly sitting down on the cold stones covered with green, slimy, gypsy soap we dipped our toes into the stream with sharp, staccato movements that sometimes sent our feet prematurely plunging into its depths.

"Dur, it's cold innit!" screamed Mati pulling her toes out of the water.

"You're right, it's freezing, but it's a bit warmer over here," I ventured tentatively jabbing a foot into the shallow end.

Gasping involuntarily, breath momentarily frozen by the shock of the cold water, we feigned mock terror as the spring water poured icily over the waterfall to cool the summer-warm stones.

Days were long and lazy; in our imagination, our games became reality. No longer Gilfach-y-Rhyd, but the cascading waterfalls of Switzerland that I had seen in Nana Smith's encyclopaedia: African jungles where head-hunting cannibals lurked camouflaged by exotic undergrowth.

"Look out boys, there's one behind yew! Run for it!" screamed Denny.

Frantic, breathless, running to climb into a tree for refuge or paddling through the stream to put them off the scent.

"They've got me this time," I moaned clutching my leg dramatically whilst rolling my eyeballs to reveal the whites. "A spear got me in the ankle. I'm goin' to bleed to death."

"Dwn't worry, we'll get the missionary to bury yew if yew die won't we girls?" Anwen promised her eyes cast down in sorrow.

"And we'll cut some branches from our favourite tree to make a cross then we'll carve yewer name on it," Denny offered sympathetically.

"That'd be great, but not yet!" I screamed hysterically as I jumped up and careered down the mountainside.

Voices accentuated with feigned fear and mounting excitement of the play interspersed with cries from the adults of,

"Dwn't run down hill like that. Yew'll lose your balance!"

Children paid scant heed as they ecstatically rolled over and over again flattening the lush grass. Others took sheets of brown, cardboard to use as makeshift sleds. Knees pulled up under their chins, hands gripping the sides, they hurtled down the mountainside shrieking with pure joy until the cardboard developed a hole and put paid to their enjoyment.

Too soon it was time to go home as our mothers gathered up the remnants of the day. We hung behind and dragged our feet limply; snivelling, complaining, begging,

"Please, just a few more minutes."

Not wanting the day to end we sulked while the adults chattered away nonchalantly, unconcerned with our grievances. Down through the pine woods hazy with the melting sun of evening slanting through the foliage. Occasionally, a rustling amongst the dry leaves underfoot, or an unfamiliar sound, found us creeping closer to our mothers. Everyone fell silent until we had passed the cemetery and emerged onto the road leading from the main gates of the graveyard to the Thorn Hotel near the bottom end of Abercynon Road where the spell was broken until another day.

Sometimes our walk extended through the pine forest along a wide, deeply-furrowed, dirt road that had been cleared of trees by the foresters. Strewn on either side, somewhat haphazardly over the road, were enormous logs. Some freshly felled, leaves gently moving in the breeze, looked like fallen warriors majestic even in death. Other logs lay ravaged and sawn into manageable blocks littering the ditches, spilling into the gaps between the trees.

"Cor, there's a lot of Christmas trees up 'ere mind," Mati remarked. "P'raps we could cut one down and take it 'ome with us."

"Yew'd 'ave the forestry man after yew and yew'd end up in jail for twenty years, at least!" retorted Anwen looking rather frightened at the prospect.

"Oh, come on let's balance on the logs." I yelled yearning for some action. "Look, they stretch right across to 'Bottom Peak!"

Jumping onto the tiered logs I climbed up onto the highest one and walked precariously, one foot in front of the other, steadying myself with my arms like a tight-rope walker, whilst looking warily over my shoulder at our parents ambling behind us deep in conversation.

The forest seemed to reach endlessly into the distance then suddenly banked gently into a treeless, grassy clearing on the ridge of Darren-y-Foel above Carnetown Junior School. This dell, known as 'Bottom Peak' by the local children, fell away precipitously to present a magnificent view of the southern end of Cynon Valley. Sometimes we climbed to the summit of Pen-y-Foel or 'Top Peak'. On a clear day the Bristol Channel could be seen glinting in the far distant west with a view of the Brecon Beacons to the north.

Below 'Bottom Peak' sat Abercynon railway station with its two platforms: one serving the line from Merthyr Tydfil and Penydarren from where Richard Trevithick ran the first railway engine on rails to the Basin in Abercynon in 1804. The other line snaked down through Cynon Valley from Aberdare, stopping at Abercynon, before following the banks of the River Taff to Cardiff.

Sitting on the ridge I saw steam belching from the black locomotives as they screeched metallically to a halt followed by the muted slamming of carriage doors.

"Listen," I said, "yew can hear the stationmaster blowing his whistle from up here."

"Naw, yew can't," said the pretty, petite, raven-haired Mati.

"Yes yew can then if you keep quiet for a minute!"

"Ooh, 'ark at bossy boots!"

Suddenly, the faint shrill of a whistle floated up the mountain followed by the clank of train wheels as it departed from the station.

"See, knew I was right, so there!" I exclaimed triumphantly. "Yew can see the river too."

At Abercynon, the natural junction of the valleys, the rivers Taff and Cynon, separated after their birth in the Brecon Beacons, flow into each other like lovers with an all-consuming passion. They meet in clandestine unison at 'Watersmeet' near White Bridge, below St. Thomas' Catholic Church, from where the Taff flows sedately to Cardiff to join the sea.

Nestling below Travellers' Rest, one time coaching inn and garage, lay Abercynon Colliery grey and drab amidst the surrounding hills. Dirty, coal-blackened lorries trundled to and fro with their loads of coal like black, hump-backed beetles homing in on their nests. The huge, black frame supporting the winding gear that brought the miners up in their rickety cage from the bowels of the valley loomed stark and ugly against the blue of the sky. Little oblong-shaped buckets, attached to an aerial line, moved out of the pit yard and soared over the main Cardiff road to deposit their contents onto the slag heap on the ridge of Craig Evan Leyshon that runs above the common from Fiddler's Elbow to Cilfynydd.

"I'd love a ride on one of those bucket things. They look like the ones in Barry Island except they're all different colours," remarked Mati wistfully.

"Oh yeah! What happens when they tip yew out on the slag heap the other end? What if yew sank up to your neck in that small coal on the top? They'd just keep tipping all the other buckets of small coal over yew and yew wouldn't be able to get out. Your mother wouldn't recognise yew, would she?"

"Aw, trust yew to think of that! Well, I think it would be great myself, so there!"

"No, I'm joking. I think it would be fabulous; like flying. We could pretend to be pilots and drop bags of small coal down like bombs then they'd set off the sirens like they used to in the war. I could be the pilot and yew could drop the bombs," I said gaining enthusiasm for the idea as I carefully crafted the details.

"Let's go down by the pit one day to 'ave a look!" Little Dai urged.

Below us the pithead stretched away, drab and grey, beyond Martin's Terrace. Until 1954, when little gusts of steam spurting from the red, brick buildings heralded the opening of the new pithead baths, miners released from their shift trudged home faces blackened with dust, nails encrusted with coal, hands covered in blue scars. Army style metal boxes, rounded off at one end to carry their sandwiches, dangled from their sides along with their water jacks. Trousers secured by solid leather belts, old ties or strong lengths of cord; hob-nailed boots clattering, carrying round bundles of chopped sticks tied with wire to light the morning fire. Old men's chests wheezing, ragged clothes clinging damply to their bodies, helmets still perched on their heads; young men's jauntily, blissfully ignorant of when they too would gasp and pluck at the air; living, dying men. Others weary and pathetic over the blood-shot eyes of the wearer looking forward to a hot bath and a backwash with a soothing, hot, soapy flannel before sitting down to the evening meal.

In winter sunlight rarely touched their faces. They trudged to work in early morning darkness and home again in the gathering twilight of late afternoon. As they marched down the street an apparition manifested itself flitting in and out of gateways and lanes. Mrs Jenkins the Milk hastened round the doorsteps delivering the daily 'pinta'. Grey hair sticking out from under her woolly hat, feet shod in black, zip-up bootees topped with thick socks: an old overcoat tied at the back by the sleeves served as an apron. Too early for the street lights to appear she scurried round, camouflaged by darkness, suddenly appearing from a gully to startle a passing miner.

"Dear God, Mrs Jenkins, yew frightened me 'alf to death!" he exclaimed clutching his chest. "I thought yew were a witch mun all dressed in black like that."

"Mornin', just finishing off the deliveries," she replied as she disappeared down Thurston Street and into the side entrance of the dairy.

On Saturdays local lads helped to deliver the milk or worked in the dairy fitting caps on bottles. As the machine sent them round and round a boy clamped on a foil top with a metal device while another took them off the conveyer and placed them in crates. Mrs Jenkins, still in her black, ragged clothes, hauled the crates and stacked them ready for her husband, Bob, to collect for his rounds.

Miraculously, once a week, Mrs Jenkins emerged like a butterfly from a chrysalis. Gone were her ragged clothes; on Thursdays she emerged as a vision in lavender. A well-cut, expensive costume, smart shoes with a fox fur over her shoulders. His shooting brake safely garaged Bob held open the door of the huge Armstrong Siddeley for Mrs Jenkins and they swept off to Cardiff for lunch. When their granddaughter came down from boarding school in Surrey they took both of us with them to Penarth, indulged us with Knickerbocker Glories in a seafront restaurant, then walked us sedately up and down the pier.

In summer the miners breathed deeply on the sweet, warm air savouring the daytime smells of roasting meat; the faint odour of beer as they passed the Thorn. In the searing heat the acrid smell of melting tar at the side of the road caught in their throats making them cough painfully. Sometimes a great steam roller painted red and green, brass funnel polished to blazing gold, moved laboriously over the road. Workmen threw spades full of gravel into the liquid tar to be embedded by the huge rollers.

"Wet tar boys; walk on the sides!" shouted the driver to the men who minced their way along the gutters laughing or complaining.

"Stupid buggars doin' the road at this time mun, especially when we've got 'ob-nailed boots on," declared an irate miner.

"Never mind butt, we can 'ave a breather up the mountain on Sunday," consoled his pal.

"Oi, when's the rag and bone man round next? If I dwn't get rid of that old fender in the back garden the missus'll be creatin' again."

"I wouldn't mind bettin' e'll be round next week 'cause 'e was in Ponty yesterday," his neighbour called back as he mounted his front steps.

SUNDAY PICNICS

Dad Smith ambled across a silent, Sunday road shading his eyes against an afternoon sun that shone fiercely from a shimmering, azure sky. The air hung still and heavy threatening an expected thunder storm. Coming into the cool of the living room he hesitated adjusting his eyes to the gloom of the curtained room. Looking round censoriously he exclaimed,

"Why on earth are yew sitting here with the curtains drawn? It's a beautiful day. Yew should be out and about in the fresh air not lounging about."

"I've pulled the curtains to keep the room cool. I can't stand the heat; it's so hot and sticky," my mother replied. "Yew never know where yew are with this weather. The week before last it was pouring every day now it's so hot yew can hardly breathe."

"Well, pull yourself together 'cause we're going up the mountain teatime for a picnic."

"I dwn't feel like dragging up there dad," she said but he was already on his way out.

"It's too hot to eat much," I complained as she started rummaging in the cupboard.

"What about salmon and cucumber?" she offered. "I think I've got a couple of tins in the cupboard."

Without waiting for a response she set about washing lettuce, tomatoes and 'jibbons' packing them into a big shopping bag along with a loaf of bread, tinned fruit, Nestlé's tinned cream, a loaf of cake, apples and lemonade.

Early afternoon we climbed up Cemetery Road, at the side of R.Ts., shop, to picnic on the mountainside above the lower end of Abercynon Road. Cool fingers from a faint breeze fanned the still air caressing our flushed cheeks. Chattering children's voices carried over the crest of the hill as we emerged onto the undulating road that led to the great, iron gates of the cemetery.

"Oh, there's Anwen and Mati." I cried running over to the Cadwaladr's.

"We're goin' to pick wind berries after tea," Anwen said wielding her father's 'Tommy box'. "I've got a big toffee tin as well."

"Yeah, I've got this," I replied flourishing a large, square biscuit tin as I flopped onto the grass.

Wrapped in my special Sunday feeling I gazed over to Cefn Glas watching the afternoon shadow paint the hillside a muted green-blue as it moved over the ridge. Muffled voices deep in conversation, children running amongst the wind berry bushes, stopping to examine an ant hill or pick sweet leaves. No sounds of traffic, no intrusive mobile phones, ghetto blasters or computer 'pings': no boisterous revellers emptying the pubs, no television to trap and isolate people from their neighbours. Birds soared overhead, bees hummed in the undergrowth; miners released from the dark bowels of the earth breathed deeply on pure, sweet air. Peace and quiet wandered the mountain touching the hearts and souls of a community at rest.

Families, mostly neighbours with children of the same age, dotted the mountainside below Edwards' Field. Miners, businessmen, councillors, professionals and war widows claimed their own piece of hillside on summer Sundays. The Vickery's, the Bowcott's, the James', the Davies', the Owens', the Williams', the Jones', the White's and others gathered round to talk about the week's events. Snobbishness prevailed as groups of like-minded individuals drifted away from the 'hoi polloi' to commandeer a particular rock or patch of grass with whispered warnings from the self-elected elite to their children,

"Yew mind what I said now. No playing with that grubby lot over by there."

"But mam, mun!"

"Dwn't mam me; just yew mind. Yew dwn't know what yew'll catch!"

After spreading out a blanket they settled back relishing a few minutes of peace and quiet. Children rushed off with their metal sandwich boxes to explore the surrounding area for wind berries that were always plentiful on the mountain. Competitive youngsters raced to be first to fill their tins. Really ambitious pickers had large toffee or biscuit tins donated by the local grocer or saved from Christmas. After a relatively peaceful lull a shrill voice pierced the air.

"This is my bush so gerroff! I was 'ere first mun," insisted Ronnie, a ruddy-faced boy in grubby shorts, as he vigorously pushed a blond-haired lad to one side.

"No yew weren't then!" said Blondie shoving the boy off his feet.

"Oi, what do yew think yew're doin'? Gerroff!"

"Now then, now then, tha's enough of that boys. There's plenty for everybody mun," ruled an older lad picking nearby.

"Oi, yew get yewer 'ands off 'im; 'e can pick where 'e likes," growled Ronnie's burly brother shooting him a menacing glance.

"Idwal, dwn't get involved!" cautioned his mother as Blondie started to shape up to Ronnie. "Get over here now!"

Idwal slunk over and dropped onto the grass.

"Do yew 'ave to show me up like that. I can fend for myself mun."

"Well, I'm not having yew brawling with the likes of *that* lot," glared Mrs Fancy Probert carefully enunciating her words.

She cocked her nose in the air looking around at her neighbours.

"Well, we dwn't behave like that do we?" she said smoothing down the blushing Idwal's cowlick.

After about two hours with scratched arms and legs, mouths purple from stuffing themselves with wind berries, children returned to their parents proudly displaying how much they had gathered. Exhausted, I lay sprawled on my stomach, waving my legs in the air, shading my eyes from the late afternoon sun.

"I've filled my tin," I said, proudly exhibiting my spoils. "We should get loads of tarts out of these."

"Lovely, yew can help us top and tail them later," said Nana Smith.

I pushed the image of the tedious job to the back of my mind replacing it with the sweet smell of cooking tarts wafting out of the kitchen.

Thirsty, appetite whetted by my frantic picking under a hot sun, I waited impatiently for my mother to prepare tea. She preferred to prepare fresh food at the picnic site claiming that it was fresher and safer to eat. The task of preparing food had been perfected into an art form over the years. The three of us held plates whilst she distributed salmon with thin slices of cucumber; tomatoes, mountains of lettuce, 'jibbons' and sticks of celery. Lastly, a Swansea loaf spread thickly with Shir Gar Welsh butter.

A sudden breeze blew up the corners of the tablecloth.

"Get the tablecloth quickly!" cried my mother.

The fluttering cloth covered the butter dish then blew away to dip its corners into a bowl of beetroot painting its edges a lurid maroon. The kettle on the ancient Primus stove hissed spitting little bursts of steam. Finally, after much huffing and puffing, the adults settled down with a cup of steaming tea.

"This is lovely," sighed Nana Smith leaning affectionately against my grandfather's shoulder.

"Look at their faces Harry, wind berry juice everywhere. Still, as long as they're enjoying themselves."

"Great stuff this," mumbled Dad Smith munching contentedly on the heavy, fruit cake my mother always insisted on taking to our picnics. Later, hunger sated, they sat back and leisurely read the Sunday papers occasionally commenting on some interesting titbit of news.

While the children played cricket with makeshift stumps some of the men gathered in small groups to talk about their work. Standing hands in pockets, bald heads covered with knotted handkerchiefs; the flat caps of the miners or panamas of the 'crachach' drawn low over their eyes. Nodding their heads conspiratorially they engaged in serious discussion. Snatches of their conversation filtered across the grass.

"So, what do yew think about the roads we've been making up?" said a local councillor referring to some of the unmade streets still left in Abercynon.

"It's long overdue if yew ask me?" retorted one of the men fiercely. "It should 'ave been done years ago."

"Georgie Fag End was caught tryin' to smuggle a cigarette down the pit last Thursday," remarked a sinewy youth standing with a group of miners.

"Eisht now, do yew want everybody to 'ear yew?" an older man remonstrated looking around to see if he had been overheard. He thrust his hands deep into his pockets, "Mind yew serves 'im right. He'll cop it now wun 'e, daft 'apporth? I wouldn't mind bettin' e'll be sacked. Good enough for 'im though putting us all at risk like that."

Nearby their wives gaggled and chattered over the latest gossip.

"Yew wouldn't catch *me* going down to Margaret Street in a turban. I think it's common, dwn't yew?" chipped in Mrs Bedford. "Not like that one over by there."

She inclined her head towards a scrawny, bleary-eyed woman in shabby clothes who was half-heartedly trying to control her squabbling children.

"Well, what do yew expect, poor old so and so. She 'asn't got much now 'as she?" tutted Mrs Vaughan sympathetically.

"Aye, well, it doesn't stop 'er keepin' those kids clean now, does it? Poor little mites are runnin' round in wellies all through the summer. I ask yew now, what does it cost for soap and water?"

"Are yew going on Moriah's Sunday School trip this year? P'raps it won't rain this time. Fat chance though!" Mrs Bedford said changing the subject.

"Yewer boy leavin' school this year?" Mrs Vaughan queried looking at Mrs Fancy Probert. "Down the pit is it?"

"*My* boy's not going down the pit. Not while *I'm* breathing. I've seen enough with my Big Idwal. He can hardly breathe poor beggar. He's got a good head on him. Little Idwal's passed the scholarship yew know. He's off to grammar school in September; wants to be a doctor."

Chest puffed out with pride, Mrs Fancy Probert spoke as precisely as possible being the mother of a prospective professional.

Mrs 'Frizzy' Bowen, nick-named because of her over-zealous

home perms, folded her arms across her ample bosom, a look of indignation and disgust on her rosy face.

"Well, I never! I didn't think *she* was the type who'd stand for that now did yew? Mind yew he's always been a pig of a man that one. Giving her all those babies and fathering another one with that *hussy*," she aspirated emphasising her aitches in order to impress. "Yew know who I mean," she indicated with a knowing glance, "but to invite his fancy woman to his son's engagement party and pass her off as one of his son's intended's friends. Well, I think that's more than going too far now, isn't it?" she reproved speaking very correctly. She had standards to keep up. After all she was the wife of a man who wore a suit and tie to work every day.

"Well, we all know better than that now, dwn't we, knowing *his* behaviour," interjected Mrs Fancy Probert. "Yew wouldn't think he'd have the energy after being down the pit all day now would yew, but there yew are. I'd be ashamed if he was *my* husband. Y cha fi! Disgusting!"

"He winked at me the other day," said a stout woman with podgy, thread-veined, red cheeks, her black eyes bright with mischievous merriment. She always looked pregnant because she walked with her ample stomach sticking out while her bottom waddled from side to side like a sailor on a heaving ship.

"He was still covered in coal from 'is shift down the pit. Disgustin' it was."

"Oh, I dwn't believe *that*," said Mrs Frizzy Bowen behind her hand to her neighbour. "I can't imagine any man winkin' at Beatie Bloomers can yew?" so called because one could always see her voluminous knickers, gartered demurely just above the knee, showing below her dress as she waddled along. The lads in the area followed her around and spied on her as she slated the front steps to a gleaming silver-white. Giggling surreptitiously as she bent over unaware that her knickers were caught up in her dress and visible for the world and his wife to see.

And so it went on until the sun melted and shadows stretched their fingers over the streets below at the foot of the mountain. Families packed up the remnants of their picnics and meandered down the steep hill grateful for the cool breeze that fanned approaching evening. Weary children dragged behind mothers; infants, legs dangling limply, asleep in their fathers' arms. For a few moments they lingered outside to finish a story or wind up a conversation before thankfully closing their front doors against the world and the night.

Later, when the boys were undressed ready for bed, we settled down to listen to the wireless. You could hear a pin drop in the stillness of the living room as we waited for the intriguing voice which invited us to travel with him on his "*Journey into Space*" then we were lost in the excitement of Jet Morgan's adventures.

In the 1950s television had not yet encroached on family life in the valleys. Sunday evenings, especially in winter, was a time for card games; New Market, Trumps, Fish or Old Maid. Sometimes I brought out the compendium of games I had been given for Christmas and played Snakes and Ladders, Ludo or Tiddlywinks with the boys. When my grandparents came over we played Monopoly. The thrill of buying Park Lane, Oxford Street, little red and green houses and hotels delighted me

"P'raps I'll be a millionaire when I'm older," I beamed when I looked at the pile of make-believe money and property I had accrued.

"P'raps yew will," said Dad Smith, "but remember money can be lost. Best stick to your education and your family my girl: yew won't go far wrong. Now time for bed."

RAG AND BONE MAN

A carthorse, pulling a flat cart, ambled down the main thoroughfare of Abercynon urged on by the rag and bone man while an impatient motorist trailed behind startling the horse with an occasional, feeble toot of his horn.

"Whoa, steady boy! Easy now Sultan!" soothed the lean, sinewy ragman his shrewd, black eyes darting from side to side of the street watching for open doors. He glared at the motorist with undisguised contempt on his leathery-skinned face. Thick-soled, hob-nailed boots, collarless shirt, sleeves rolled up to his elbows: course, brown corduroy trousers, open waistcoat topped by a flat cap, perched jauntily on the side of his head, the rag and bone man moved purposefully down Abercynon Road plying his trade.

The 'season of the long grass' also brought Jimmy Adlam, the local tramp.

"Mam! Mam! Jimmy Adlam's round again," shouted children as they rushed indoors.

"Mornin' missus," smiled Jimmy raising his battered hat, "anything to throw out?"

Mrs Evans disappeared inside re-emerging with a pair of men's shoes and a pop bottle filled with water. Next door he acquired half a loaf of bread and a wedge of cheese before the door was firmly closed in his face. He moved along, from house to house, doffing his hat at every door. By the time he had reached the end of the road he had acquired an old shirt, jacket and trousers to go with the shoes. Jimmy visited Abercynon, year after year, until one day a rumour circulated that he had frozen to death on the road in the depths of winter.

Summer also brought the knife-sharpener, in his little pushcart, who honed kitchen knives and repaired umbrellas ready for the winter months. Unlike the rag and bone man he politely knocked on doors to promote his services working on spokes and blades with quiet efficiency. Now it was the rag and bone man who excited our interest.

"Rag a' bone, rag a' bone. Any old rags missus?" he shouted across to a woman standing on a wooden, kitchen chair energetically polishing her front room window.

"Money for old rags! Take the kids to the seaside with pennies from your old junk!"

At intervals along the road heads popped out through doors followed by the upper halves of their bodies as they strained to see who was outside. Just as quickly they disappeared only to emerge a few moments later to trail the rag and bone man down Abercynon Road before he disappeared round the bend. The ragman continued to walk lethargically holding the horse's bridle as people threw their unwanted items onto the back of the cart. Rusty buckets, old clothes, heavy flat irons, cast-iron fenders, a three-legged chair, a pram chassis and a cracked chamber-pot.

"Tuppence for the flat iron missus," offered the ragman to a buxom matron in a wrap over apron who was purposefully approaching his cart.

"It's worth more than that mun," Mrs Ellis snorted holding fast to the iron.

"Thrupence then, but not a penny more missus. I've got to earn a livin'."

"Well, arright but it's a bit stingy I think!" she exclaimed barely concealing her resentment.

A handful of coppers changed hands and were immediately tucked into her pinafore pocket to be ceremoniously dropped into a redundant jam jar hidden away in the farthest recesses of the pantry.

An occasional clink of the reins accompanied his raucous shouts as the ragman disappeared round the corner past the Thorn Hotel into Mountain Ash Road where I lived.

"Whoa!"

The big grey jerked up his head with a loud whinny as the rag and bone man tugged at his bridle and reined him to a halt.

"Time for food and wa'er my buooty," he said in an unfamiliar English dialect.

Children gathered shouting,

"Look, it's the rag and bone man! 'E's feeding is 'orse! Come on, p'raps we'll be able to 'ave a ride on the cart!" they chorused watching with delight as the horse nuzzled deep in his nosebag.

Sultan's tail switched lethargically at the summer flies as he slaked his thirst with a bucket of cool, clear water provided by one of the women.

We fussed and petted the old, grey horse offering him sugar lumps and apples. Tentatively, a plump, fair-haired girl with long plaits, tied at the ends with tartan ribbons, stepped forward to feed Sultan.

"He licked me!" she cried jumping back yelping with fear and delight her hand still outstretched. Sultan snuffled in the palm of her hand to eat the sugar cube whilst stretching his head looking for more treats then snorted loudly curling back his lips to whinny his approval.

"He won't hurt yew," I said holding on to his reins as Dad Smith had taught me.

I stroked his huge head as he turned to nuzzle against my shoulder and ran my hands gently along his back screwing up my nostrils against his hot, primitive smell.

When the rag and bone man moved off towards Doctor's Hill a few of the older boys jumped onto the back of the cart laughing and swinging their legs over the side as the horse clattered off over the tarmac road ignoring the first anxious calls from their mothers.

"Bobby Ellis yew come back 'ere at once, do yew 'ear me?"

"Aw Mam mun, only a little ride please!"

What 'ave I told yew about 'anging about with that rag and bone man? In! Now! Do yew 'ear or do I 'ave to get yewer father to yew!" said Mrs Ellis glaring menacingly down the road.

Bobby jumped down off the cart, red-faced, head hanging in shame. The other boys jeered loudly as he snivelled his way towards his mother who ushered him, none to gently, indoors.

Exciting though it was the rag and bone man's annual visit was always tinged with sadness, for it heralded a new school year and the close of the 'season of the long grass'.

"Come on," I called to Anwen and Mati who were still staring after the over laden cart, "let's go down the bank opposite the park."

"Yeah, we can sit on the grass and count the different trucks as they pass, "Anwen suggested as we headed for the lane.

RIDING A BOGEY

Until the footbridge was built opposite the park the foolhardy still crossed the railway line to avoid the long walk round Quarter Mile while someone watched for approaching trains. We caught snatches of conversation as we tailed a group of boys.

"We'll cross down by 'ere is it?" said Alan.

"If my mother finds out I've crossed the line I'm tellin' yew now I've 'ad it," replied Mervyn.

"Aw, dwn't be such a drip. She's not goin' to find out is she?"

"Yew can bet somebody'll be lookin' through their windows up by there," Mervyn pointed nervously towards the back of the houses on Abercynon Road.

"Well, quick then before anybody sees us," Alan urged.

They looked furtively behind them before disappearing round the bend into the gully on their way to the park.

By the time we arrived at the bank overlooking the railway track they had vanished.

"Somebody's bound to see 'em from 'the tump'," I declared indicating a flat area of open ground opposite Albert House.

"Well, as long as *we* dwn't get in trouble there's no problem is there?" Anwen remarked sanctimoniously.

Lethargically, Mati picked up a stick and dragged it through the 'stingy nettles' while Anwen and I trailed behind shading our eyes against the glare of a yellow, shimmering sun surrounded by loose clusters of fluffy white clouds like a Michaelmas Daisy.

"I know, let's go down by the Roman Road," Mati suggested.

"I dwn't feel like traipsing down there now. It's too hot," I moaned throwing myself onto the grass. "Listen, there's a train coming."

The clank of a lumbering, steam engine grew louder as it chugged its way down the line. Almost like a living being it snorted and belched hot, white steam throwing out little particles of soot into the air. Sitting on the lush grass above the track we waved at the passengers en route to Pontypridd and Cardiff. The stoker, face soot-smudged and shiny with sweat, was closing the door on leaping orange flames after feeding the hungry boiler. Leaning on his shovel his face broke into a wide grin when he saw us waving.

"Hello there!" he shouted signalling acknowledgement with a grimy arm.

"It's Mr. Harris, Eddie's father, from down the road," I chuckled standing up to wave.

"Hello-o, yoo hoo!" we chorused arms flailing wildly over our heads as we flung ourselves back on the bank.

Later another engine passed by its wagons loaded with coal destined for the docks. Then another came up the track from Cardiff dragging closed containers of Fyffe's bananas on their way up the valley to their distribution points. The black beast thundered past with a wave from the driver and a 'toot toot' as he pulled the cord to sound the hooter.

For a while peace and tranquillity descended lulling us into a delicious torpor. Just the sounds of wild life; the gentle flutter of a bird's wings and the soughing sound of the breeze in the trees. Suddenly, there was the sound of movement lower down the track. Squinting our eyes against the sun we stared in disbelief as a maintenance cart came into view. Alan and Mervyn were operating the bogey's handles, pushing up and down furiously to gain as much speed as possible while Tudor sat on the platform with his legs dangling out over the rails. As they spied us, gawping in amazement, they slowed down to a gradual stop.

"Come and have a ride!" Alan yelled. "It's smashin' fun innit Merv?".

"No, I dwn't think so," I said warily. "I'm not allowed on the line."

"Aw, blow yew then!"

Disdainfully, they moved off pumping their way up the track then back again to show how easy it was.

"See, it's easy innit?" said Mervyn completely forgetting his mother's wrath.

A stirring of interest and excitement, coupled with fear, welled in my chest. Still, I was cautious visualising the consequences of being found out.

"Nobody can see us from here," I thought, "so perhaps I could get away with a very short run up the line without being caught."

"Aw, come on! We'll stand guard won't we Alan."

We hesitated every few feet while sliding down the grass bank until we were level with the cart.

"I dwn't know," I bleated, "if my mother or my grandparents find out I'll really cop it." But temptation was already winning the battle of wills. As the boys egged me on I stepped gingerly up onto the platform of the bogey and slowly started to pump up and down to get it moving.

As it gathered speed so the exhilaration mounted until we were whooping and laughing with delight.

"Great innit," Mervyn beamed with pure enjoyment.

"It's fantastic!" I yelled over the metallic whine of the wheels and the rush of wind through my hair.

"We'll go up as far as Pontcynon and back."

Elated, the boys fired imaginary six-shooters from the cart ducking and weaving to avoid returning 'fire' from the gunslingers hidden in the bushes along the bank. Then we heard it; a distant, low, rumbling sound. My heart seemed to be filling my chest and I couldn't speak for the thumping of blood in my ears.

"It's a train! It's a train!" I screamed.

Time stopped as we froze in tableau for what seemed an eternity then I shrieked at the others,

"Jump! Jump!"

We lunged forward onto the park side of the track, landed with a jolting thud amongst the gravel, then rolled into the nettles. With bated breath we watched as the train lumbered along the track, waiting for the collision, but nothing happened. Moving excruciatingly slowly the enormous engine trundled past towing a long line of coal carriers.

Still wide-eyed with horror we gasped with relief and disbelief as the last container passed on the northern line while the' bogey' still sat on the southern track. In our intense fear we had forgotten that there were two tracks and just jumped for our lives.

"Aw, I feel awful sick," moaned Mervyn clutching his stomach.

"Me too," I said still lying in the nettles. "Do yew think anybody saw us?"

"I dwn't think so," Tudor replied looking about furtively. "Let's make a pact. Put yewer 'ands over mine and swear never to tell a soul."

We swore each other to secrecy vowing never to go near the railway line again. Shaken and ghastly pale I staggered to my feet suddenly aware of the burning nettle stings. I picked a 'dock' leaf and pressed it against my leg hoping to alleviate the pain. Legs trembling, nausea threatening to engulf me, I limped down the bank on the park side. Too terrified to cross the line again we dragged slowly home round Quarter Mile bridge full of trepidation at the thought of being found out.

My mother was making our favourite custard slices when she saw me hovering in the doorway of the kitchen. She stopped halfway to the oven and stared at the grazes on my knees and elbows.

"What on earth have yew been up to?" she demanded.

"Nothing much," I whined.

"Nothing much! Look at the state of yew!"

"We were just playing and I fell in the 'stingies' that's all."

"That's all?" she queried suspiciously.

"I haven't hurt myself," I said lamely.

"Well then, yew have a lot of explaining to do my girl!"

Miserably, I scratched at the inflamed, white lumps that covered my legs, arms and face.

"I told yew to stay by the 'green' didn't I? Well, yew can stay in the back garden now with the boys."

"Just wait 'till I get hold of that Alan," I whimpered to myself as my mother rushed off to get the calamine lotion.

THE ENTREPRENEUR

Blistering heat, the road a shimmering mirage broken only by the occasional car or an increasingly rare, flat cart ambling sedately along while the horse twitched its tail in indignation at the driver's,

"Giddy-up boy! Giddy up!"

Neighbours sitting chatting idly in their front gardens.

"Lovely day Mrs Smith," Jack Parry called over the wall. "Can't keep 'em still for long," he remarked eyeing his four sons engaged in rolling around on the grass.

"Oh, they're not doing any harm, just high spirits," countered Nana Smith watching their wrestling antics.

"That's boys for yew," laughed Mrs Vickery on her way to John Evans' shop. "Well, well, look at those girls, and in all this heat too."

A group of girls were playing 'bumps', a strenuous skipping game, while Anwen and I bounced two tennis balls against the pine end of my house chanting as we juggled,

"Betty Grable is a star S.T.A.R. Two, four, six, eight, Mary's at the garden gate."

Grades of difficulty were obtained by throwing the ball under one leg or turning full circle to catch the ball before it hit the ground. Eventually, tiring of the game and the heat, we walked through the house to the cool of the back garden where the boys were playing, and out onto the 'green'.

In one of the neighbouring gardens a young mother had filled a large, tin bath with cool water for the toddlers and their friends to splash around in. Cooing mothers and watchful grannies sat in deckchairs round the bath gossiping.

"Look at 'im tryin' to swim. 'E's got all the right actions mind.

I'll take 'im down the park when 'e's a bit older where 'e can learn proper," said one of the grannies proudly.

"Well, I've told Councillor Owens up the road it's about time we had a footbridge over the line by the park. Yew mark my words there'll be an accident one of these days," declared her companion indignantly. "We pay enough rates after all. Now, now, yew mustn't put 'is head under the water," she chastised as she hauled her errant daughter out of the bath kicking and screaming.

Howls of laughter and muted conversations drifted over the wall from the older children.

"They're a bit quiet all of a sudden. I wonder what they're up to now?" she continued peering over the wall.

Behind the gardens older children played 'dick stones' in Bassett Street or swapped glass beads from broken necklaces protectively stored in old tobacco or sweet tins. Turning the cut-glass in their fingers the sunlight reflected the colours of the rainbow. Girls bartered their wares to obtain a complete collection of their favourite 'precious' stones.

"I'll give yew these rubies for that diamond," offered one of the girls flourishing two garish red beads.

"But this is a *real* diamond. It's worth more than rubies!" argued Mati.

"Well, all right, two rubies and an emerald."

"*Two* rubies and *two* emeralds!"

"Aw arright then, but tha's daylight robbery innit?" declared the girl grudgingly handing over her treasures.

Traffic was almost non-existent behind the houses so it was safe for children to play outdoors. Boys congregated to play cricket or football or haggled with marbles: transparent marbles with blue, red or green encapsulated in the smooth, round glass. Outsize 'pop allies' and giant, silver-coloured ball-bearings passed from hand to hand. Tempers flared exploding into hot-tempered indignation and exclamations of,

"Yew're cheating! Yew said I could 'ave a 'pop alley' for two marbles not three!"

Scuffles ensued until a mother came out and broke up the fracas.

With lumps of rough chalk others drew numbered circles, spirals or 'T' shaped boxes to play 'scotch'. Some sat on the grass colouring their little, wooden tops with intricate chalk patterns ready to play 'whip and top'.

"Look out!" yelled a young lad running down the road guiding a metal hoop with a stick. In hot pursuit a group of laughing youths on a 'gambo' made from orange boxes and pram wheels.

"Young hooligans!" muttered Mrs Davies Snobby as she scampered across the road. "Why dwn't yew play in yewer own street and give us some peace!" she hurled back at them as she slammed her back door.

"Spoilsport!" bawled the 'gambo' boys boldly as she disappeared from sight and earshot.

Suddenly, the back door re-opened to reveal Mrs Davies equipped with a brush to sweep the back path.

"What was that yew said then?"

"Nothin' Mrs Davies, honest. We wouldn't say anythin' would we boys?" spluttered a freckle-faced lad hanging his head contritely.

"Well, just mind yewer cheek or yewer mother will be hearing from me, dwn't yew worry now."

"Yes Mrs Davies, sorry Mrs Davies," they choMrs Davies, safely indoors again, the boys collapsed into a heap laughing and threshing arms and legs until they were breathless.

"Well then just yew mind, do yew hear me?"

Mrs Davies, safely indoors again, the boys collapsed into a heap laughing and threshing arms and legs until they were breathless.

Roger and Michael were playing happily in the garden while my mother kept a watchful eye through the large, picture window in the kitchen. Armed with beach buckets and spades they were happily making castles from a box of wet sand using cone-shaped sweet bags, stuck on sticks, as pennants.

"They're playing quietly now," she said with relief, " but once Roger starts making up some game or other…." Her voice trailed off uncertainly.

"Oh, they'll be all right. What can they get up to in the garden?" queried her friend Aurona May as she sipped her coffee.

"That's what worries me!" my mother retorted.

Blessed with a very vivid imagination Roger incorporated this asset to develop his entrepreneurial skills.

Close in age the boys were eons apart in terms of temperament and personality. Roger always emerged from play dirty, covered with cuts, bruises, bloodied knees and the inevitable tears. Michael stayed as immaculate and shiny as a new penny. She knew Michael never wandered but Roger was more adventurous. The natural leader of the two he was always the boss while Michael was expected to follow his instructions.

"I'll be Robin Hood and yew can be Little John," Roger instructed.

"That's not fair, yew were Roy Rogers *last* time and I was only a cowboy. It's my turn to be the boss this time!"

"Yeah, but yew'll be the hero 'cause yew'll be saving me from drownin'. Get down and I'll jump on your back."

Michael hauled Roger out over an imaginary river and promptly shrugged him off to land heavily on the grass.

"Yew did that on purpose. I've hurt my leg now *and* I nearly drowned."

"I didn't do it on purpose Rog, honest I didn't," Michael laughed, a look of triumph in his dark eyes.

Silence, then the sounds of make-believe six-shooters and slapping of thighs heralded a new game. Peering through the kitchen window my mother observed,

"They're playing cowboys and Indians now. That'll keep them occupied for a bit."

Satisfied they were playing happily my mother continued her baking. Suddenly, she stopped, hands covered in flour, head cocked to one side.

"It's gone very quiet down there. Go and see if they're all right."

"They must be on the 'green' outside," I called from the garden. "I'll go and look."

"But I locked the back door. If those Thomas' boys have been over the wall again opening the back door they'll be in trouble this time," she declared anxiously. "And yew were supposed to be keeping an eye out for them."

We searched the lane behind the houses, but there was no sign of them anywhere. It had only been a few minutes but, as usual, my mother panicked. Dashing back into the house we heard a loud knocking at the front door. Mrs Lewis from the end of the road, a plump, blonde, matronly woman stood giggling at something beyond our view.

"Yew must come and see this," she chortled her ample breasts wobbling precariously as she laughed. "I've already made a purchase just for his pure cheek."

Looking past her we saw Roger and Michael moving from house to house, arms full of the cone-shaped bags they had been playing with in the garden.

"What on earth have yew got there?" Mr. Moses laughed.

"Bags of small coal Mr. Moses. Only 'tuppence each or three for fourpence."

"Small coal, but why are yew selling coal boy?"

"Me and Mikey are saving up to buy my mother a Christmas present, but it's a secret," Roger said proudly.

"Well, in that case I'd better buy a bag, but I've only got a 'thrupenny bit'," he rejoined fishing in his pocket.

"I've got plenty of change in here," Roger smiled fishing in the toffee tin he was using to hold his spoils.

"Yew can keep the penny. Yew've thought of everything, haven't yew?" Mr. Moses observed desperately trying to conceal a smirk.

Like the others he parted with a 'thrupenny bit' even though they had a shed full of small coal at the end of their gardens.

"Right yew two, inside now!" my mother fumed.

Looking contrite they scurried in and scampered upstairs without a word.

"What have I told yew about shaming me with your antics?" She glared at Roger knowing he was the instigator.

"Sorry," they chorused in unison. "We won't do it again."

Tears coursing down their cheeks they sobbed at the injustice of being punished for using their initiative. After all they had only sold the coal to get money for her present, but they kept silent about their plans.

"That's what yew said last time when yew sold those bunches of bluebells," she spluttered, "and those tins of blackberries I'd picked. Well, this is the very *last* time yew show me up like this. Yew can stay up here; there'll be no supper for yew tonight."

Behind the bedroom door I stifled a laugh knowing it was an idle threat. An hour later they were sitting at the table devouring enormous slices of bread pudding to keep them going until dinner.

THE RUM BARREL

The Pontings' had emigrated to America in their youth. In late middle-age, comfortably off, they had returned to their roots and taken over the grocery and sweet shop on top of the steep hill at the corner of West Street and Mountain Ash Road.

"Nice mornin'. How are ya today folks?" Mr Ponting said reaching for Nana Smith's ration book on his first day behind the counter.

"A quarter of liquorice allsorts please."

"All righty, ma'am. Anything else?" he queried as he started to cut out the tiny coupon from the ration book.

"On second thoughts you'd better make that two ounces, and two ounces of jelly babies," Nana Smith answered quickly. "I'll keep my husband's coupons 'til later in the week."

"Let's have some chocolates as well nana?"

"No, we must save some coupons or we won't be able to have any for the weekend."

"Can't yew just give money?"

"No, sweets are still on ration and we're only allowed so much. We'll all be glad when it's over."

"We sure will ma'am," Mr. Ponting agreed.

When sweet rationing had ended in 1953 a queue of children stretched from the shop down past Bethania Chapel.

"We can buy as much as we like!" exclaimed a delighted lad. "I'm goin' to spend all this on sweets!" displaying a handful of coins.

Clutching fists full of copper pennies, 'thrupenny bits, 'tanners' and shilling pieces, begged from parents and grandparents, children waited impatiently for their turn.

Excitement mounted as each child left the shop brandishing an assortment of sweets and chocolate. Fry's chocolate mint bars, toffee apples, sherbet lemons, Mars bars, acid drops, wine gums, nougat, fruit pastilles, everlasting strips and coconut mushrooms: gob stoppers, peanut brittle, parma violets, elegant little boxes of variety creams and squares of sherbet that rapidly melted in the mouth.

"Smashing innit boys? Can't believe it mun," mumbled Little Dai as he walked the length of the queue taking huge bites from a chunky chocolate bar.

"Yeah, great innit!" marvelled the animated queue.

Beaming with happiness children gathered in groups, chocolate-smeared cheeks bulging.

Soon they were dipping into each other's bags sharing their various sweets and chocolates.

"I feel a bit sick like all of a sudden," groaned Denny.

"Serves yew right then for being so greedy," his father admonished as he dragged him up his front steps.

"I'll never eat chocolate again as long as I live," promised his waxen-faced son.

"Oh, yew'll live to eat another couple of bars," his father grinned.

By nightfall smiles had turned to groans as children gratefully went to bed clutching their stomachs and fighting off the sickness caused by over-indulgence. Who could blame them after years of Spam, powdered egg, 'pom' and sweet coupons?"

Determined to spend the proceeds of their venture into the coal industry on a Christmas present for my mother Roger and Michael had struck a deal with the Pontings'.

"What can I get ya boys?" Mr. Ponting asked in a broad American accent typical of the 'yanks' we saw in the 'pictures. Broad-shouldered, brilliant blue eyes and well-groomed, snow-white hair fashioned into a 'college boy' cut he was the epitome of glamour.

"How much is that please?" Roger pointed at a miniature, china, rum barrel fashioned into the figure of a clown with matching cups hanging from hooks on either side.

"Too much for ya, I guess."

"There's lots of other things like that vase in the window," I pointed out.

"But we dwn't like anything else, do we Rog? We want that," interjected Michael who was already looking disappointed.

"We've got lots of money," they chorused emptying their pockets onto the counter, "*and* we can save more by Christmas."

Beautifully made-up and be-jewelled, Mrs Ponting, a well-built woman with coiffured, blue-grey hair whispered something to her husband.

"O.K guys, here's what we'll do. We'll count up ya money and give ya a lil' card. Every week ya can put some more on it 'till ya pay the full amount. It'll be our lil' secret," he winked at me. "What'd ya say? Is it a deal?"

"Yes, Yes, it's a deal!" they piped with excitement. "It's a deal!"

"Dwn't worry, I'll look after the card for yew," I assured them.

"And yew've got to promise not to tell mammy," they babbled as they bounced out of the shop.

For months they took their saved pennies to Mrs Ponting who dutifully marked the amount. On Christmas Eve morning they rushed to the shop, picked up the rum barrel that Mrs Ponting had packed in a cardboard box surrounded by scrunched up strips of old newspaper, and carried it with exaggerated caution back to the house.

"What are yew three up to?" my mother called as we sneaked upstairs to hide the treasure.

"Nothing much," I called back, "just packing some presents."

Christmas morning they raced downstairs squabbling as they both tried to hold her present.

"Do yew like it Mam?" they queried as she unwrapped it.

Anxiously, they waited for a response from my mother, but she was too overcome with emotion to speak. Finally, she whispered in a querulous voice,

"It's beautiful, beautiful. I never expected........," she gulped, her voice trailed off as tears filled her eyes.

"We bought it from Ponting's shop," Roger enthused, "and we saved all our pennies until we had enough, didn't we?"

"Mrs Ponting gave us a card to save on," Michael interjected breathlessly.

"Did yew know about this?" she eyed me suspiciously.

"Yes, but they wanted to keep it a secret. They used all the money they had from selling those bags of small coal in the summer."

"Well, I'd better have a word with Mrs Ponting when they open up after the holidays, just in case," she blathered.

"Mrs Ponting didn't mind at all. She told us we can do it again for your birthday!" they piped.

Too emotional to be angry with them she just 'cwtched' them to her. Days later Mrs Ponting told her,

"Ya couldn't help but laff. They looked so serious I didn't have the heart to say no. We don't mind if they want t'save up again."

"Let's, let's!" the boys cried.

"Well, all right," she laughed, "but no more antics like trying to sell small coal."

Christmas, like a bright jewel glowing in the dark depths of winter, soon faded. Dismal days and dark nights kept us indoors wistfully longing for the 'season of the long grass'. Summer days spent on the hillside, picnics in the long grass, languorous hours beside the River Wye and the banks of the Usk; the train chugging its way to the coast giving us out first glimpse of the sparkling sea after a dreary, indolent winter.

WHAT'S THAT THEN? SCOTCH MIST?

Peering out through my bedroom window I was confronted by ponderous, grey clouds scudding along the sky. Across the road trees above the stonecutter's shop swayed gently as a few spots of rain started to splatter against the window pane. Feeling warm and clammy the slightest exertion made perspiration stand out on my upper lip. I groaned out loud,

"Oh no, not another wet Sunday School trip to Barry Island!"

Once again the weather forecast had failed us. Promised sunshine had turned to grey skies and the threat of rain. Most summers saw people dashing for shelter into the arcade on Barry Island beach for cups of hot tea and a steaming plate of fish and chips. Every few minutes I went to the front door and held out my hand to feel for more spots of rain, but they never came.

The kitchen was a flurry of activity. Loaves of bread, cakes, lemonade, tinned fruit, cream and salmon were all waiting to be packed into a big, canvas shopping bag.

"Come on or we'll miss the train," urged my mother making for the door.

"We'll carry everything and yew bring the boys. Make sure they stay on the pavement."

Grabbing the boys' hands I set off at a trot to keep up with her as she half ran, half walked towards Doctor's Hill.

"The train's due to leave Abercynon at nine o'clock so we'd better hurry!" she panted.

Brightly-coloured beach towels under our arms, buckets and spades rattling, we trooped to the railway station along with the rest of the people living in our road.

The Cadwaladr's and the Bolyes' walked down with us

exchanging pleasantries and anecdotes relating to the last trip.

"I dwn't know about yew but if it rains like last year I'm comin' back early," declared Mrs Cadwaladr to her husband. "I couldn't stand wandering round in the wet all day again."

She prattled on occasionally tossing a question at him, but she didn't really expect a response. Hands in pockets both fathers, who had longed for just one boy each amongst their brood of girls, lagged behind in a perfunctory manner.

"Buggar Barry Island. Wish I could go for a pint instead," whispered Mr. Cadwaladr.

"Oi yew, I 'eard that. Not in front of the children, if yew dwn't mind!" hissed Mrs Cadwaladr indignantly.

The Cadwaladr girls were like their mother; dark with liquid eyes and long, black lashes; all endowed with a Silurian beauty but Anwen was the odd one out. Tall, thin and bespectacled, but blessed with a chirpy, sunny disposition that made it impossible for her to be melancholy for long.

" We're goin' to Barry Island! We're goin' to Barry Island!" she sang in high-pitched, nasal tones, completely unfazed by the possibility of a miserable, wet day.

The Boyles' were a mixture of both parents. Only one had the dark good looks of her father, a strong-willed man who over-shadowed his fragile, delicate wife. The others were a hotch-potch of lips, eyes and bone structures from various parts of both families. One thin and delicate-looking like her mother; another tall with well-defined features, another short and round. As an only girl, raised with an extended family of boys, I felt slightly envious of their sisterly closeness and the secrets they shared.

The boys clanked along carrying brightly-coloured, metal pails covered with cartoon characters and long, wooden-handled spades; one red and one blue.

"We can build a sandcastle and get water from the sea for a moat," chattered Roger excitedly.

"And put flags on top, too!" Michael added.

Dressed alike, in a combination of the same colours; Roger in red cotton shorts, Michael in blue. Both with striped red, white and blue tee-shirts, tan T bar sandals and white socks with a band of the predominant colour of their clothes around the ankle. Formal, grey, short-trousered suits were worn with different coloured shirts and ties. With only thirteen months between them they looked like fraternal twins.

Wiry, slightly built, blond hair, brown eyes and a quick, mischievous grin Roger resembled my mother's brother, Emrys. Grazed knees and cut hands brought on piteous crying especially when he was scolded for getting too dirty. Tears coursed down his face making white channels on his smudged, tear-stained cheeks arousing the strongest maternal instincts in my mother who petted and fussed him interminably. After suffering a fractured skull in an accident she kept him very close to her, spoiling and coddling him at the slightest sign of discomfort.

After a few weeks in hospital he was indulged even more by the nurses. Once he was on the mend the ward sister carried him around the hospital where older patients cajoled and cosseted him even more. His hold over my mother's love and attention was firm and absolute.

Michael was sturdier with the same brown eyes but platinum-blond hair that fell softly around his face. My mother wound his hair into fat rolls round her finger adamantly refusing to have them cut off until he went to school. Rivers of tears flowed when Fluff, the Barber, cut off his precious ringlets and swept them into a bright, blond pile on the floor.

Fluff was a small, wizened man with tight, wavy hair reminiscent of a 1920s matinee idol. Donned in his khaki work coat he listened to endless accounts of the various problems of his clientele. Mostly, boys were taken by their fathers because women were not allowed in the shop, except for special days when small boys could be taken for haircuts by their mothers.

"It's time yew let the boy have a haircut," declared Dad Smith, "*before* he goes to school."

"Do yew think I dwn't know that!" my mother had retorted in a hurt voice tinged with acrimony.

"I'll take him when I'm ready."

"I'll take him. I know yew my girl. Yew'll be sitting there with tragedy written all over your face."

Finally, she gave in but she couldn't bear to send him for his first grown-up haircut without her to grieve over the demise of the shining, white baby ringlets that never grew back.

"Look at all his baby curls," she choked staring at the gleaming mass of hair on the floor. "He looks so different, so grown-up."

"Well," soothed Fluff, "all the little boys have their hair cut before they start school. Yew'll soon get used to it."

Stiffening in silent misery tears sprang to her eyes as Fluff picked up his flaming taper and proceeded to burn off the ends of the hair at the back of Michael's neck. The acrid smell of burning hair filled my nostrils with an odour that wafts into my memory every time I think of Fluff's barber shop in the front room of his house on Abercynon Road; the red and white pole, declaring his trade, suspended diagonally beside his front-room window.

The motley band moved like a multi-coloured sea along Abercynon platform; a kaleidoscope of children in green, bright-yellow, red and blue intermingled with grey, brown and black of elderly men and women who dressed for a trip to the seaside as though they were going to chapel for the morning service at Moriah English Baptist Chapel. The seething mass moved forward and poured into the open carriages of the specially chartered, steam train amid squeals of delight from children.

"Oh, great, it's a corridor train!" exclaimed Mati dashing for the nearest compartment.

"If yew go next door to us we can go in and out all the way to Barry."

After a great deal of scuffling and bobbing in and out of compartments the throng of bodies finally settled in. Whole families commandeered compartments for themselves. Bags, beach towels and jumpers were casually placed on seats to make it look as though the seats were taken.

"Any room in 'ere then?" asked Gwladys Fawsty.

"No." said my mother who was never able to lie without giving herself away.

Nobody wanted to sit by Gwladys Fawsty, because she smelled so badly of stale urine and wet dog caused by sheer lack of personal hygiene. Short and squat, with a protruding stomach, unkempt hair matted to her head combed into a style that kept its shape due to the stiffness of dirt and grease. Sharp, intelligent eyes shot a look at my mother from Gwladys' florid face ingrained from years of inadequate washing.

"What's that then, scotch mist?" said Gwladys looking at the space we had saved for Nana and Dad Smith.

"Mam and Dad are sitting there, sorry," said my mother defensively, eyelids fluttering rapidly and looking decidedly uncomfortable from the effort of trying to lie convincingly.

"Oh, there they are now!" she exclaimed with relief. "Where've yew been? Yew nearly lost your seats then!"

Fussing with the surplus space left after my grandparents had seated themselves my mother arranged and re-arranged cardigans and towels moving the boys around desperately trying to ensure that Gladys Fawsty did not sit down.

"Can't yew shift up a bit to make room then?" queried Gwladys.

"We would if we could, wouldn't we?" muttered Dad Smith.

He looked beseechingly at my grandmother for some support, but she was gazing through the window with a haughty look on her face determined not to get involved in the argument. From her demeanour it was obvious that she was equally determined that she would move to another compartment if Gwladys Fawsty dared to sit down.

"Look, yew can see there's no room, can't yew, so yew'll have to try further up the train and that's all there is to it! All right?"

"Humph! All right then, if *yew* say so!"

Gwladys stomped off glaring back over her shoulder muttering to other passengers about,

"That lot down there! I dwn't know who they think they are! It's a free country innit, after all?"

All along the corridors children were standing looking through the windows, some sticking their heads out to feel the rush of warm air as the train sped towards the tunnel. One of the boys, who had been leaning out of the window as the train chugged out of the station, quickly pulled his head inside as he caught a speck of soot in his eye. A tall, insipid looking boy with pale, vacant, blue eyes, a round cherubic face and dough-coloured skin.

"I've got s-s-something in m-m-my eye mam!" he stuttered.

"Serves yew right yew soft article for putting yewer 'ead through the window in the first place. For goodness sake 'ave some sense mun will yew?" his father rejoined.

'Dough Face' stared through the glass with a sulky expression on his face and a cuff around the ears. Five minutes later his head was out of the window again and we were treated to a repeat performance of his previous activity.

Two small children were careering up and down the corridor, screaming and pushing past people, completely out of control.

"Look at them," said Aurona May, the petite, raven-haired mother of my friend Nia. "They're like heathens and their mother big in the chapel. Yew'd think they'd have more decorum wouldn't yew? Goes to show yew doesn't it; all chest and no sense. Dear, dear; no control whatsoever!" she complained. "Well, they'd better not come in here with their cheek or she'll know about it, dwn't yew worry now!"

Scornfully, she looked out into the corridor 'tut tutting' at their unruly behaviour.

"Thank God ours dwn't behave like that. It wouldn't pay them to anyway, would it? They know what they'd get," she said self-righteously. "Mind yew, I've *never* had to smack mine."

"Neither have I," said my mother with a smug look on her face. "They're not *angels*, of course, but they do know how to behave in a civilised fashion when they're out. That's one thing I can say about mine. I can take them anywhere and I know I'll never be shown up."

With a self-satisfied smirk on her face she turned and glared at the boys as they began to look restless from behaving themselves.

Disdainfully, both women folded their arms under their bosoms as people, now tired of the children running about, started to complain loudly.

"Come and control yewer kids Mrs Jones before there's an accident mun. Duw! Duw! Duw! No control at all. The woman's as 'alf-soaked as a piece of soggy, bread pudding mun," observed Bill Sticks; a burly collier with a heart of gold who was always bringing neatly, chopped sticks home for the old people in the neighbourhood.

Mrs Jones finally came to retrieve her children and hauled them, kicking and screaming, to her compartment. Aurona May and my mother looked at each other knowingly and clucked their tongues indicating their disapproval at this unseemly behaviour. I thought how comical they looked; a caricature of two disdainful mothers with perfect offspring, but it was true, neither of them had ever smacked their children.

"Severn Tunnel coming up!" shouted one of the boys as the carriage lights came on.

"Dwn't be daft! It can't be Severn Tunnel. It's the wrong way yew fool!" retorted one of the older girls.

"Close the window or we'll 'ave fumes in."

There was a rush to the windows and the sound of slamming as they were tightly closed with the thick leather straps secured to the brass button on the door.

"I hate going through the tunnel," squeaked a skinny girl from the corridor. "What if there was a crack in the tunnel wall and all the water poured in. We'd all drown if the train couldn't get out on time."

"Aw, dwn't be daft," muttered the dough-faced lad uncertainly.

The compartment seemed to get smaller and smaller as people popped in and out for a chat from the carriages lower down the train. Noise levels increased as time passed and children became increasingly restless to reach the seaside. Most of the adults were enjoying themselves talking animatedly to friends and acquaintances.

"The sea! The sea!" squealed a little girl held tightly in her father's arms.

Children surged into the corridor for their first glimpse of the sea that year. A thin strip of bluish-brown water sparkled on the horizon, gently rolling waves glinting in the watery sun forcing its way through the clouds.

"Ooh, it's smashin' innit boys!" said Billy Candles jumping up and down with excitement while he furiously explored his nose with his index finger. Billy had acquired his nick-name because his nose was constantly running; a physical trait that lost him many friends during the school lunch break.

The acrid smell of steam hissing from the engine accompanied our approach to Barry Island station. Slowly, the train shuddered to a halt to wait as an oncoming goods wagon shunted past. Billy howled in agony as his finger went too far up his nose. As he started to bawl a hand came out of the compartment next door and yanked him back inside. Instead of sympathy he received a hefty smack on his backside as punishment for his dirty habits.

"How many times do I have to tell yew about playing with yewer nose? One of these days yew'll damage yewer brain if yewer finger goes too far up. Yew stupid boy! Yew keep on and yew'll pull yewer brains through yewer nose, yew nincompoop!" said his father with exasperation trying to speak in hushed tones, but not quite succeeding.

"Try to speak properly for goodness sake!" said Mrs Candles.

After all Billy Candles senior had been elevated to foreman and shared a cramped, dingy, little room he grandly described as his office. He held no truck with these common working class habits his son had picked up from school.

"Never mind angel," said Mrs Candles who had attended secretarial college and could type and write in shorthand, "it won't be long now then yew can bury daddy in the sand. Won't that be a treat now?" she said sweetly.

As we approached the station the train ran parallel with the main road linking the island with the rest of Barry; Cold Knap, and the sea to the right with the road in between. Directly in front of us was the fairground with the scenic railway towering above it. A ride was in progress, the occupants of garishly, decorated cars screaming wildly, their hair blowing in the rush of wind, eyes screwed up tightly, hands gripping the rails of the car. They hurtled round the bend, plunged down the steep incline and careered out of sight inside the massive structure, fear mixed with ecstasy written on their faces.

"I'm havin' a go on that," said Nia.

"Me too!" yelled Roger.

"Oh no yew are not then," said my mother dismissively emphasising every word. "It's not safe and anyway you're too young. They won't let yew on there so think again!"

Dragging him back inside she gathered up towels and bags in readiness for our arrival. Imploring glances from Roger were studiously ignored even when he climbed on to her lap with easy tears in his eyes.

SAND IN OUR SANDWICHES

The train finally sidled into the platform and ground to a halt. Carriage doors flew open as people spilled out onto the platform like ants and scurried towards the exit anxious to get to the beach and bag a good spot. Favourite places were near the entrances which led from the colonnaded promenade because they were close to the teashops, fish and chips and gift shops. We often went into the fish restaurant owned by Jimmy Wilde, a boxer Dad Smith had admired in his youth. Outside, at the back of the restaurant, long, trestle tables and benches were laid out in the open during the summer months. Children were allowed to eat their own sandwiches as long as their parents had bought the minimum pot of tea and a bag of chips.

Off we trooped through the fragrant fairground, past the rifle stalls and the carousel, breathing in the multifarious smells and relishing the fairground sounds that all children love. The briny odour of cockles, the sweet smell of candy floss and the enticing aroma of fish and chips mingled with the salty tang of the sea filled our senses. A kaleidoscope of brightly-coloured rock in all shapes and sizes: giant sugar dummies, candied bananas and flat, striped lollipops tempted us to drag our feet and gaze longingly at the stalls crammed full of delights. As we crossed the road to go to the beach one of the children shouted,

"The bird 's movin! Let's stay and watch!"

They had spotted the Guinness mechanical clock. A crowd of small children gathered to watch entranced as it commenced its display. By the time the bird finished its performance the sky had started to clear.

The sun had miraculously taken a hold on the heavens while

thunderous clouds had blown over to reveal a clear, azure sky. I could feel the warmth of the sun on my back as we trundled down the concrete ramp onto the beach. Everything looked brilliant and dazzling: sun glinting on seahorses while white foam lapped around the ankles of bathers. Little heads bobbing in the water, rising and falling, as the sea rose with the swell of a wave. Sometimes heads disappearing from sight until a wave broke towards the shore.

Small children were jumping over the waves holding tightly to their mothers' hands; other children were lying in the shallow water pretending to swim; elderly men paddling with their trousers rolled up to their knees, collarless shirts and thumbs sticking in their braces. Some had knotted handkerchiefs on their heads to protect their bald heads from the sun. Their wives, often plump little women, minced into the water holding their skirts demurely to avoid them getting wet; bare arms and full, large bosoms that met their waists, straw hats perched jauntily on their heads. Grey-haired matrons, now girlish and giggly, danced lightly over the waves that rippled towards the shore. Their male protectors occasionally picking up a brightly-coloured beach ball to throw back to the children whose laughing faces shone with excitement and the rapture of being by the sea.

On the beach young boys played cricket with a tennis ball and make-shift stumps. Children, furiously building sand castles, were carrying pails of water from the sea to fill hastily-dug moats. Some had placed little paper flags on the turrets and stood proudly to attention whilst admiring their handiwork. Two girls and a boy nearby were busily burying their sleeping father in the sand. All that could be seen of him was his bright-red, bald pate burnt badly from a combination of salty air and sun which was now beating down unmercifully. It had turned into a glorious day.

"There's a good spot; look just over there!" cried my mother pointing to a large area of clear beach. We all trooped over to the vacant space.

"Oh! I dwn't know though, it's a bit exposed here and I want to make sandwiches. We dwn't want sand in them do we? Let's go over there between that young couple with the pushchair and the family

135

with the windbreaker. Right, put everything down and let's get sorted out. Hold the blanket and put it down carefully. We dwn't want sand all over the place."

"Plenty of sand here all right," I laughed. "You can't miss it!"

"Never mind about that Leonard," she said to my stepfather who had been rummaging in the contents of the beach bag.

"Can yew fetch three deckchairs? Dad, will yew go with him and get two for yew and mam. The boys would rather lie out on the blanket."

Muttering thankfully, both men disappeared up the ramp towards the pile of stacked deckchairs. They hadn't been gone more than two minutes when my mother, who had been scanning the beach said,

"On second thoughts I think we'll go back to that spot by the wall where we were first of all."

"Oh, make up your mind!" said Nana Smith with frustration. "I'm fed-up of trudging from one place to another and back again."

We reached the wall after an arduous trek over soft, fine, deep sand that was difficult to walk on and gratefully sank down by the wall. I took off my shoes and socks wincing as my bare feet touched the burning, hot sand. Wet sand didn't bother me, but the feeling of dry sand between my toes sent shivers up my spine. Michael was tugging at my mother's skirt laughing and pointing across the beach.

"Look mam, dad and grampy don't know where we are!"

We looked across the beach from where we had moved. It was a seething, kaleidoscope of colours; a sea of moving bodies, brightly-striped deckchairs and windbreakers. Both men were standing holding the deckchairs, eyes screwed up desperately searching the crowds. My mother stood up and waved her arms about excitedly trying to catch their attention.

"Go and fetch the silly devils. They must be blind as bats. Dad, over here!"

Suddenly, my grandfather caught sight of us and began to thread his way through the mass of sprawling bodies. They dragged laboriously up the beach towards the wall and, exhausted from their efforts, dropped the deckchairs onto the sand.

"Thank God for that! Why did yew move before we came back?" grumbled Dad Smith. "That's it, I'm not moving again and that's that!"

"Put up my deckchair Harry," said nana. "Yew know I can never get the contraption to stand up properly."

It was she who had started calling him Harry when they were courting. To his family and friends of his youth he was always known as Henry.

The men fiddled and muttered and got into more of a pickle putting up the deckchairs, increasingly harassed by the heckling of the children and 'tut tutting' of the women.

"Oh, for goodness sake!" my mother exclaimed raising her eyes to the sky. "Yew can't do anything properly can yew? Let go, and I'll do it!"

In seconds the deckchair was erected and she was sitting in it looking with contempt at Leonard who had thrown himself on to the sand scowling darkly.

Nana Smith lay back, her head covered by a wide-brimmed, straw hat and a towel over her shoulders to protect her arms from the sun. Although predominantly dark-haired, with dark eyes, she had a very fair, milky complexion. In strong sunlight you could detect a hint of auburn lights threading her hair. Dad Smith sat next to her with a newspaper over his face, feigning sleep, while my mother started the usual ritual of making sandwiches.

Out came the bread and butter and the proverbial tin of salmon. Next came the lettuce, cucumber and tomatoes with a generous wedge of cheddar cheese. Further mutterings and rummaging in the bag revealed a tin of pineapple chunks, Nestlé tinned cream and an enormous loaf of home-made fruit cake.

She hated pre-packed sandwiches and always insisted on making them just before we were ready to eat. For ten minutes she fussed, slapping butter generously on to bread with great relish. She loved these days out with all the family and did not look on preparing food as a hardship, but as an enjoyable part of the trip.

"There!" she said triumphantly. "Not a bit of sand in them and as fresh as a new-laid egg."

"Yes mam," I said as I bit into a sandwich and started to chew on the sand that had miraculously eased between the layers of bread.

"I dwn't understand it!" she wailed. "I was so careful. Yew must have been flicking sand when I turned my back!"

I started to protest but changed my mind. There was no point.

"Right Leonard, will yew go over to the café and bring a tray of tea for us and some lemonade for the boys while I finish the picnic?"

"Mam! Mam! Can I have an ice-cream please, please?" clamoured Roger.

"No, not yet. Yew can have an ice-cream later on. Have an apple."

"I dwn't want an apple. I want an ice-cream!" he cried.

"I want an ice-cream too!" said Michael echoing his older brother, as usual.

"Oh, all right. Mam, dad, do you want ice-cream? Right then, seven ice-creams, five teas and two lemonades."

Leonard trudged off in the direction of the tea stall muttering to himself,

"Yew watch now, she'll change her mind before I get there, yew can bet on it!"

Thirty minutes passed and there was no sign of Leonard. My mother scanned the crowds for a sign of him, but he was nowhere to be seen. An hour later he returned without the tea or the lemonade.

"Where have yew been?" she hissed through her teeth looking furtively around to ensure that she was not being over-heard.

She was livid with anger and demanded a full explanation of his absence as he was wont to disappearing acts when he was sent on a shopping expedition.

"Yew'll never believe this," he said. "I was standing in the queue and this chap kept staring at me. Suddenly he said,

'It's Len, isn't it? Eighth Army. Desert Rats!' Well, we were so excited we got talkin' and before we knew it we'd lost our place in the queue; then he insisted I went for a glass of beer for old times' sake. Well, what could I do? Yew could have knocked me down with a feather."

"I'll knock yew down in a minute," whispered my mother, "and it won't be with a feather! Drinking in the middle of the day and us sitting here nearly dying of thirst. I've never heard the like of it. Dwn't yew dare come near me, yew, yew, drunkard!"

"But I've only had half a pint!"

She dodged him as he tried to put his arm around her in a cajoling way.

"Dwn't yew come near me until yew stop smelling like a brewery!"

She smiled sweetly, gave a nervous laugh and glanced at the surrounding families just to make sure they hadn't eavesdropped on the proceedings, grabbed the boys and signalled for me to follow.

"Come on!" she said cocking her nose in the air. "We'll go for a ride on the 'duck'.

The 'duck' was the big, amphibious, ex-wartime craft which came right up the beach to pick up passengers for a ride in the bay. I was fascinated and spent a great deal of time trying to work out the mechanics of the vehicle as it surged through the blue-brown waters of the Bristol Channel rising and falling with the swell.

"Great," I enthused, "then we can go up the fair."

THE MONEY WHEEL

Out of the many attractions in Barry Island fairground the most lucrative, by far, was a device which looked like the top of a children's roundabout. Just a flat, round circle of wooden boards skewered to the ground secured by a screw and nut through the centre and surrounded by sandbags. The whole contraption appeared to be pointless and innocuous until I saw it in action. Children paid sixpence each to sit on the wooden wheel. It spun very quickly until, in turn, every child was thrown off with a thud onto the sandbags. Those who managed to stay on for a whole minute won sixpence and also kept the sixpence paid for the ride. One after another boys and girls came flying off the wheel. Again and again they tried their luck, to no avail. It was impossible to stay on.

I paid my sixpence and was duly thrown off once the wheel gathered momentum. After three attempts I realised that the closer I got to the middle the longer I stayed on. It was difficult to move towards the centre because of the mass of wobbling bodies being thrown about, but I was determined to try out my idea.

"I'm having a go at that," I said as I rushed to the wheel, "and I bet I can stay on it."

"Bet yew can't then!" Anwen snorted with amusement.

Once on I had to be content with sitting on the outside because older boys were spread out over the surface. Twice I was almost thrown off, but I managed to cling to the surface by lying flat and holding on to one of the other children. As each child was hurtled into the sandbags I crawled nearer to the middle of the wheel. Triumphantly, I reached the nut and bolt in the centre of the contraption and sat on top of it. It was very uncomfortable, but I was sitting firmly on top just as I had thought. I wasn't being thrown off, but I *was* beginning to feel very nauseous.

The fairground worker spun the wheel faster and faster. Feeling very sick I was about to ask him to stop it when one of the men watching the antics shouted at the operator,

"Oi, come on now, she's been on there for nearly two minutes! Chwarae teg mun! She's earned her sixpence!"

The man stopped the wheel, looking very shame-faced, and duly paid me my sixpence plus my own sixpence. I tried four more times before I was banned.

"Clear off you young buggar," whispered the man in my ear, "and dwn't come back!"

Feeling very dizzy I didn't argue about honesty or integrity, a word I had recently learned from my forays into the huge Oxford Dictionary housed in Nana Howells' bookcase.

My friends, who had been watching with mounting admiration and excitement, were even more impressed when they realised I now had five shillings to spend instead of half-a-crown.

"Dur! 'ow did yew do that then?"

"It's easy, but I'm not telling yew yet. Yew'll have to wait."

They all wanted to know the secret, but I wasn't ready to reveal it until I had exploited it to its full potential. Knowing that the man would go off for a break, sooner or later, I waited and watched.

We circled the fairground going on the dodgems and the gallopers. After the second circuit my time had come. There was a different man attending the wheel. Two more shiny sixpences were won before the new man realised that I knew what I was doing.

"Right yew. I've 'eard about yew. You're the clever little sod my pal warned me about. Clear off!"

"Humph!" I said indignantly. "I won this money fair and square. Yew'd better not swear at me again or I'll tell my grandfather about yew, then yew'll be sorry. He won't let *anybody* swear at me!"

Normally, I was a shrinking violet when it came to confrontations with adults and would never answer back, but I was stung by his remarks because it offended my sense of justice. After all I wasn't cheating, just using my initiative after working out how to stay on the wheel. Now, I decided, the time had come to give my friends the benefit of my experience. Out of sight we huddled together and I told them what to do. The first two won their sixpences, then the next two, before the wheel was prematurely closed for the day. The older girls, who were supposed to be in charge of us, were chatting and giggling with some boys outside the ghost train. We were sworn to secrecy about the boys and they were sworn to secrecy about the wheel.

The fairground was beginning to fill up with day trippers having a final fling on the rides before catching their trains and coaches back home to the valleys. People were bumping into neighbours, enquiring about platforms and how they had enjoyed the day. Grannies shaking sand out of shoes; chattering, recalcitrant children shaking off mothers trying to cover naked shoulders, pink from the sun, with sea-dampened towels. Vague smells of ale, orangeade, chips and hot engines mingled with the sweeter odours of candy floss, toffee, marshmallow and talcum-powdered ladies. Children clamouring for just one more ride while grannies dipped into their purses to buy sticks of bright, pink rock with Barry Island imprinted through the centre: sugar mice with black eyes and little cord tails, slabs of fudge and giant bars of nut-filled, nougat. Mothers urging toddlers,

"Yew must have a 'wee wee' before yew go on the train."

Dads trailed slowly behind, hands thrust into their pockets, looking longingly at the nearby pub. Young parents standing by the kiddie roundabouts waving while their offspring drove the latest racing car, or motor-bike, with intense concentration on their furrowed brows.

"Look at 'im. He's a born driver in 'e Bill? One day yew'll own yewer own car lovely and yew can drive mam and dad to Barry in it, can't 'e Bill?" cooed one of the mothers proudly.

As the golden sun of early evening glinted on the sea the motley crowd surged towards the exit by the scenic railway and moved, in a colourful mass, over the road towards the railway station to mingle in loose groups on the platform relating the events of the day.

"Did yew 'ear about Mr. Brewin?" said a plump stalwart of Moriah English Baptist Chapel. "He lost his false teeth in the sea. Dived in smilin' and came up without a tooth in his head. What a laugh. He had to keep on divin' until he found them. Still, all's well that ends well."

And so the conversation went on until the great train, gasping and throwing out sulphurous fumes, steamed into the platform. The crowds pushed towards the doors as eager to get on as they had been when they left the valleys. Children, bags, buckets and spades were pushed onto the great beast. Doors clunked shut and windows lowered by their straps to shout last minute goodbyes to friends in other parts of the train. Mothers sank thankfully into their seats cradling weary toddlers, now fast asleep, hanging limply in their protective arms. The guard's whistle screeched shrilly, the train groaned out of the station towards home and the end of another 'season of the long grass.'

LADIES IN CRINOLINES

I stood outside the big, wrought iron gates of Duffryn House, emblazoned with the coat of arms of Lord Aberdare, whose home it had once been. September, still warm and bathed in early golden sunlight, saw children walking past the lodge and up the drive towards the school. Some marching confidently others chattering and laughing with their friends.

"Cor, it's big innit!" whispered a lanky, dark-haired lad with a hint of awe in his voice. A bit posh like!"

"No need to whisper mun. It's only a school innit?" said his chum in a hushed voice betraying his bravado.

Other children tagged along with older boys and girls, apprehension and awe alive on their faces as the impressive house came into view.

In my imagination the buzz of voices fell away. Genteel ladies in long gowns twirled their parasols on a Sunday morning stroll while others lunched delicately from a picnic laid out on snowy, white tablecloths. Liveried servants carried silver trays laden with crystal glasses of cooling drinks for the children. Young men doffed their top hats or slapped riding crops against their shiny, black boots as they sauntered past on their elegant, well-groomed horses. The bell rang and the spell was broken.

Hurriedly, I walked up the drive and down the narrow road that fell away into a hollow. Sweeping lawns, scattered with flowering cherry trees, woodland and an orchard made the school grounds the most beautiful in South Wales. At each of the entrances stood a lodge with stables nestled against the outer, stone perimeter wall surrounded by woods on three sides. Lush, green lawn and mature rhododendron lined the main drive leading from the main gates to a small, ornamental stone bridge spanning a stream.

Once on the bridge the land fell away to meet the stately, old house sheltered from the elements by a backdrop of tall trees. Narrow paths leading from different parts of the house dissected the manicured lawns.

"Oh, it looks just like the houses in Jane Austin's books!" I exclaimed admiring the heavy, double doors that fronted the imposing foyer as we were ushered towards the covered way that led to the assembly hall.

A sea of green, red and white uniforms met me as I walked into the hall; the colours of the Welsh flag. Our blazer badge proudly displayed a red dragon rampant inscribed with the school motto, 'Deuparth Bonedd Y Dysg'; 'Three parts of a Gentleman is Learning'.

Quietly fidgeting I sat wondering what was going to happen next. Suddenly, a hush spread through the room as Idris Jones, the headmaster, swished down the aisle in his black gown, ascended the stage and turned to gaze benevolently over his charges.

My chest swelled with pride when he said in his reedy, nasal voice,

"Welcome to Mountain Ash Grammar School. You are the few who are fortunate enough to attend this school," he announced his eyes sweeping the room.

"Why are you here? I'll tell you why. You are here because you have proved you are the brightest. You are here to be educated to the highest standards: to fulfil your potential. Slacking, bad behaviour, impudence, will not be tolerated!" he emphasised.

"Now we will sing,' *Holy, Holy, Holy*.'"

"'Ooh, ark at 'im!" giggled Jane, a gangly cheeky-looking brunette, nudging my elbow.

Her giggling quickly subsided as Idris Jones homed in on the sound and fixed his eagle gaze in her direction. It was to be the first of many near misses for Jane, especially in her attempts to mimic Beaky while he imparted his scholarly wisdom.

Academic gown held in classic scholar pose Beaky sauntered haughtily up and down the rows of desks announcing the attributes of the more illustrious, past pupils while we sat riveted to our seats. Sparse, white, receding hair atop a meagre frame, piercing eyes and a razor-sharp brain whirling towards us announcing,

"If you work hard you too could be one of our distinguished

alumni; or even an Einstein or Marconi contributing great things to mankind. You might become an inspirational teacher, a skilled surgeon or historian. I could go on!" he exclaimed raising his arms in a sweeping gesture.

Boys and girls listened with rapt attention, glowing from the flattery; their hopes and desires melting into a kaleidoscope of mental images of their successes. Brushing chalk dust from his gown he enunciated in clipped, precise tones, peering at us intently with his eagle eyes,

"These are the learning fields for greatness yet to come. Remember this magnificent setting where you are so privileged to be educated. Remember these words well!"

I remembered his words on my second day when all thoughts of "greatness to come" eluded me. Filled with shame I found myself lost at the foot of the stone stairs that was originally the servants' entrance. Wandering up and down the steep, winding stairs I emerged to find 'top' corridor completely deserted and eerily quiet.

Bewildered, and a little scared, I listened at one of the heavy, tightly-closed doors and heard muffled voices. Footsteps, accompanied by the sound of the door-knob turning, took me by surprise. Alarmed, I bolted along the corridor and started down the grand staircase stopping in my tracks as a man's voice barked,

"What are you doing here miss! These stairs are out of bounds! Boys only!"

Turning round I froze, feeling my chest constricting with apprehension, as I looked up into the steely eyes of Idris Jones, M.A. I muttered something unintelligible as he directed me back up the stairs and along the corridor to the French room. Looking every inch the proverbial headmaster, to be found in story books on public schools, he gazed after me with an icy glance that could have frozen the waters of the North Atlantic. He was not an unkind man, but his naturally, haughty demeanour, snow white hair, aquiline nose and academic demeanour silenced every pupil as he swept purposefully down the corridor his gown flowing behind him. Beneath the dignified presence and insistence on firm discipline he had a true humanitarian desire to nurture and develop the best in his pupils.

Endless stories circulated about the grand staircase and the ghosts that haunted Duffryn House particularly the spirit of, 'The White Lady'. Her boudoir had been commandeered as the ladies' staff room that looked onto the back of the house and the little stone, ornamental bridge. Eerie sightings had been reported of her standing on the bridge. Others had sworn they had glimpsed her sitting forlornly on the window seat behind the huge, leaded light windows that ran along the back wall, or gliding down the carved staircase. Cleaners and staff had reported intense, cold spots on the stairs and an overpowering smell of perfume. The heavy, ornate, mahogany door, reputedly imported from a 14th century Italian monastery, was heard creaking open after the cleaners had struggled with its weight to close it.

In a hushed voice one of the caretakers told how he had locked up after patrolling the school, closing open windows and ensuring nobody was in the building.

"I was crossin' over the bridge after lockin' up when I 'ad this feelin' that someone was lookin' at me.

Frozen to the spot he had felt an overpowering sense of foreboding. Covered in goose bumps, the hairs on the back of his neck standing up, he forced himself to look back towards the house.

"I could see a young woman sittin' in the window seat in the ladies' staff room lookin' straight at me through the leaded windows. She was all white, but I swear she looked real as though she lived and breathed!"

Cleaners often hurriedly terminated their employment after reporting weeping sounds or being touched by an icy, cold hand on the stairs accompanied by a strong whiff of 'The White Lady's' perfume.

Duffryn House was the only mixed grammar school in the valley, but segregation of the sexes was assiduously enforced. Separate entrances and separate cloakrooms were manned diligently during breaks to ensure that fraternisation was kept to a minimum. Only boys were allowed to use the magnificent, grand staircase. Girls were relegated to the narrow, stone, servants' steps, a practice that was vehemently resented by those who dreamed of a Bette Davies descent as the boys watched in awe at the foot of the stairs.

Boys managed to watch in awe and frustration from the art

room. Set away from the main buildings, it was the venue for much hilarity especially when older girls ran past to the hockey pitch. Pressing their faces to the window, while pretending to look for equipment, captive boys mouthed suggestive remarks; eyes rolling in their heads as the girls' breasts bobbed up and down and their bottoms wobbled like jelly in their bottle-green, gym knickers.

"Cor look at them," sniggered Danny Boy flinching as he received a hefty swipe across the back of his head.

Every few yards a girl extracted her handkerchief from a little pocket on the front of her drawers covering her face with embarrassment while an invisible hand yanked the boys back into their seats. At the sound of the whistle, that heralded the end of the match, they developed an urgent desire to be helpful; cleaning the tables by the windows while gazing earnestly towards the girls innocently bouncing back to the changing rooms.

Trying to cover my backside with my hands I looked the other way as I passed the art room and saw the pale images of boys bent over their work. Face scarlet, stomach churning with captive, multi-winged butterflies, I slunk over to the gym where a shapely Ma Dav, who floated around the school in a short, navy, gym skirt, waited impatiently for the stragglers.

"Into the showers!" she ordered.

Having been raised in a very male environment I always had my privacy and was not used to the feminine camaraderie of most girls who wandered around the changing rooms completely naked. The thought of communal showers was torture but, still clad in my bottle-green knickers, clutching a towel to conceal my bosom, I dutifully obeyed. As I passed she gave me a scathing glance, whipped away the towel and bellowed,

"Do take off your knickers you silly gel!"

Fortunately, my ringlets fell over my face hiding my blush. My humiliation was complete when one of the more sophisticated girls said with a sneer,

"A bit old for ringlets aren't yew?"

TWINKIES AND CURLERS

During my time in the scholarship class Dougie Davies had found all of us pen-pals. The black and white photograph I received was of a well-built girl with a pleasant, oval face, hair parted in the middle and long pig-tails that fell below her shoulders. Lively letters had passed between us describing our lives, hopes and dreams for the future. A year after I moved into grammar school our mothers agreed to meet in Bristol Zoo where we could spend the day getting to know each other better.

Helen had written that her pig-tails had recently been cut off and she had a more modern, short hair style. Armed with this information I complained to my mother that I was too old for ringlets and big bows of ribbon. Remembering the way the stylist brandished her smoking, curling tongs to create fat ringlets whenever my mother was taking me somewhere special made me shudder. Something modern appealed to me more in keeping with my approaching teens. Besides, if I had my hair cut I would no longer have to suffer the indignity and discomfort of going to bed in 'rags', a ritual that produced tantrums and tears. Finally, about a week before the visit, my mother gave in and took me off to the hairdresser's.

"Bubble cuts are all the rage," the stylist told me.

Whatever it was I wanted it!

She cut and snipped at my long hair until I felt quite naked. Looking at the pile accumulating on the floor I felt the back of my neck alarmed to find it so bare. After vigorously washing my hair Mrs Parfitt combed it away from my face. Looking at my cropped image in the mirror I wanted to cry. It was horribly flat.

"Oh, dwn't worry, it'll be fine!" she laughed as she wound my hair around prickly rollers before squeezing me under the dryer.

Feeling flushed and anxious I was relieved when Mrs Parfitt finally popped up the lid of the dryer. Red-faced from the heat, ugly rollers sticking up all over my head, covered with a pink hairnet, I wailed in dismay. Closing my eyes I resigned myself to spending my time in the zoo looking like a freak. Finally, Mrs Parfitt exclaimed,

"There now, finished! That wasn't so bad was it?"

Afraid to look in the mirror I eventually plucked up the courage to squint between my fingers and was amazed at the reflection gazing back at me. I looked entirely different and there was definitely nowhere to put ribbons.

"Yew look *lovely*," Mrs Parfitt said. "The soft curls frame yewer face. It really suits yew."

Even my mother grudgingly agreed that she liked the new style.

My hair had a natural kink but it only fell into waves when it was long. Cut short the curls didn't take long to fall out. A few days later my mother complained,

"I knew I shouldn't have let yew have your hair cut. Yew can't even put ringlets in that. It's too short!"

Despondently, I moped about the house feeling increasingly sorry for myself. My plans to meet my pen friend looking 'cool' and modern were in tatters. Suddenly, it came to me. The solution to my problem was simple. One of my school friends had told me, with grown-up pride, that her mother had given her a perm. She had twirled around the playground, tight little curls completely under control.

"Dwn't be ridiculous! Yew are not, definitely not, having a perm! No arguments, that's final! I don't agree with girls your age having perms!" my mother asserted.

There was only one thing for it. I had to make my hair look as awful as possible; so awful that my mother would be forced to let me have a perm.

Every time it rained I went out and got my hair wet combing it into spikes so that when it dried they stuck up all over my head. This went on until a week before the planned trip.

"I dwn't understand it!" my mother exclaimed. "Your hair looks worse now than it did last week. We'll have to do something about it. Yew can't go to Bristol like that!"

"I could have a perm?" I said hopefully.

In desperation my mother went into the hairdresser's to make an appointment, but they were fully booked because of a number of weddings. There were only a few days to go before the trip.

"Oh well, I'll have to do it myself. Home perms are supposed to be quite easy to do."

I was elated! I was going to have a perm; a real grown-up perm! After a swift consultation with Mrs Parfitt, who was very apologetic, she trooped off to the chemist with me in tow and asked for a '*Twinkie*' and some perm curlers.

"Sorry, perm curlers are out of stock," said the assistant, "but lots of people use pipe cleaners. They're just as good."

The picture of the young woman on the box smiled out at me with confidence. Soon I'd have a '*Twinkie*' and I'd *never* have to have 'rags' again.

Hair freshly washed, towel wrapped around my neck to catch the drips, I sat looking in the mirror as my mother wound my hair around pipe-cleaners using little pieces of white, tissue paper. Fumes from the solution made my eyes water, but the worst thing was the neutraliser. It was cold and very messy; icy rivulets coursing down my forehead into my eyes and down the back of my neck soaking the towel. I dabbed frantically dragging the towel up as close to my face as possible. Gazing in the mirror I reflected on how ridiculous I looked, but any indignity was worth restoring my 'bubble cut'.

Peering short-sightedly at the instructions my mother undid one of the curlers to see if the perm had 'taken'.

"It *looks* all right," she said in a cautious tone. "We'll give it another couple of minutes, just to be sure, and it should be ready."

Willing the time to pass I breathed a sigh of relief when she finally took out the curlers and shampooed my hair.

"That's *lovely*!" she exclaimed.

It looked very pretty after my mother had styled it into big, soft curls although it still stank of perm lotion. Moving my head from side to side I thought how grown-up I looked and how modern I would seem to my pen friend.

The following Saturday we caught the train to Bristol Temple Meads to meet Helen and her mother; dressed in my best yellow dress with puffed sleeves and a little Peter Pan collar embroidered with silk flowers. Thinking how sophisticated and ladylike I looked in my tweed coat with its tan, velvet collar we walked briskly to the station hugging our coats closer as a chill breeze clutched at us penetrating the warmth of our clothing. Catching sight of my reflection in the Co-operative shop window I gloated,

"Yes, the hairdo is a definite improvement!"

"It's a bit nippy out here: we'll sit in the waiting room until the train arrives." my mother said turning the brass knob of the heavy, wooden door.

In winter the little stone-built station with its shiny, dark-polished bench seats looked warm and cosy. Travellers sat and basked in the red glow of a huge, coal fire besides which sat a coal scuttle and tongs that the station master used to bank up the fire. Travellers luxuriated in the heat oblivious to rain, hail, snow or wind that lashed against the window panes. Now, without a fire, the waiting room looked cold, its drab, beige walls adding to its starkness.

Remnants of dull, grey ashes, that had died overnight, sat forlornly in the grate heralding the death of a winter that still hung on the air. Shafts of pale sunlight revealed swirling motes of dust that danced their way to darkness in the corners of the room. Outside tiny specks of soot, disgorged from the funnels of passing trains, clung to the window panes.

We waited impatiently in the gloomy room until we heard the laborious puffing and clanking of the Great Western Railways' train pulling in to the station.

"It's a corridor train, thank goodness!" my mother exclaimed as we boarded. "We'll have a bit of privacy now."

She hauled the sliding door closed and settled back in the empty compartment. A few people passed up the corridor, stopping momentarily to gaze inside, then moved further up the carriage to try their luck elsewhere. My heart fell as two young men, discussing the merits of their favourite football teams, pulled open the door.

"There's room in 'ere," said a lanky lad with washed-out blond hair falling over his eyes like an Old English Sheep Dog.

"No, not in there mun, let's find one to ourselves," replied his companion giving us a doubtful glance.

"Good, if we're lucky we'll have the compartment all to ourselves if no-one gets on in Pontypridd," my mother sighed with relief.

A cold, white, watery sun struggled to maintain a hold over a blue sky spattered with just a few pale, grey clouds as we left the station. Steaming and blowing, as though it had a life of its own, the engine chugged along leaving behind the terraced streets clinging resolutely to the slopes of the valley. Watching the houses disappear I settled into my seat lulled by the rhythm of clattering wheels.

Through the soot-smudged, carriage window I gazed at emerald fields that stretched away from the once-green mountains scarred with discarded coal: the legacy of pits that provided work for the men of the valleys. Steam coal that had powered the engines of great liners sailing across the Atlantic; their passengers enjoying the voyages made possible by the sweat and clogged lungs of miners: ominous warships that had ploughed rough waters engaging in fierce sea battles guns blazing in the pursuit of peace.

As we approached Severn Tunnel the guard walked along the corridor and slammed closed an open window jolting me back to reality. I held my breath as the train moved into the yawning blackness and the dim carriage lights came on. Everything looked rather surreal in the half light. Sepia-coloured, framed pictures of countryside scenes adorned the wall above the seat opposite. Eyeing the communication cord I wondered what it would be like to pull it and bring the clanking beast to a sharp, shuddering halt.

Gradually, I drifted off into the folds of my imagination. Emergency scenarios broke into my thoughts flickering like rapidly turning pages of a book until the train shot out of the tunnel into the bright, white light of an early spring day.

As we alighted from the train at Temple Meads station a light drizzle started to fall, but it wasn't enough to get really wet.

Protected by an umbrella we scurried out to catch the 'bus to the zoo struggling against a grasping wind that threatened to snatch the umbrella from our hands. Gratefully, we climbed on board, glad to be out of the wet, and sat down heavily in our seats. My mother turned to me to say something but nothing came out of her mouth. She just sat staring at me speechlessly with a look of utter dismay.

"What's the matter?" I said nervously.

"Your hair!" she half choked on her words. "Your hair! The perm's gone frizzy!"

She continued to stare until I thought she was going to cry. Patting my hair all over it felt capacious, coarsely thick and springy to the touch. She glared at me,

"If yew had had 'rags' like I wanted this wouldn't have happened! Yew look so pretty with ringlets!"

By the time we stepped off the bus the sun was shining again and my spirits lifted. I recognised Helen straight away as she and her mother came to greet us.

"Oh," she said, "you don't look anything like your photograph."

"No, I've had my hair cut and permed," I replied feeling rather smug and superior as my mother edged me towards the ladies' cloakroom.

Muttering apologies she ushered me into the ladies and stood me in front of the mirror. Staring back at me was the startled image of an auburn-haired, wild child. The gorgeous, 'bubble cut' I had been so proud of had vanished. In its place was a mop of hair that had exploded into a voluminous blob that looked like a cross between a badly-cut Afro style and a giant lavatory brush. Looking as if she wanted the earth to swallow her up my mother tetchily nudged me outside towards a grinning Helen.

We wandered round the zoo my mother constantly lamenting the state of my hair to Helen's mother; commenting on how lovely my ringlets had been only a few weeks before. She was finally consoled when my pen friend's mother admitted sympathetically to a similar catastrophe when her wilful daughter had hacked off her own hair with a pair of dressmaker's scissors.

Every window and mirrored surface mocked me with the

vision of a pale face surrounded by an explosion of tight, wiry, auburn hair. Salvation came when my mother spotted some straw hats among the gifts on sale. Ramming it on my head she hissed between her teeth.

"Dwn't ever ask for a perm again! It's ringlets for yew in future my girl!"

As far as I was concerned the dreaded 'rags' had gone forever. When the perm finally fell out I had discovered a new style; a D.A. like Doris Day. Some months later I learned the meaning of the abbreviation when one of my nastier acquaintances shouted across the road,

"Dur! Look at 'er, the grammar school snob! She's got a duck's arse!"

COOKING SKIMMERS

Subjects in Mountain Ash Grammar were strictly compartmentalised: woodwork for boys, needlework and cookery for girls. How I longed to be able to design a bridge, saw up pieces of wood, wield a hammer, make a coffee table instead of a Victoria sponge or squashed, baked apples stuffed with sultanas. Flossie, the vague, fussy, little cookery teacher, fluttered endearingly through lessons, face flushed, completely out of her depth.

Lining up in front of the tables in the cookery room we listened impatiently as Flossie took us through the rudimentaries of successful biscuit-making. Armed with a large bowl and wooden spoon we set about mixing the dough.

"Yes," I decided triumphantly, forgetting my failed attempts at sponge cake, "today I'll make the best oat biscuits in the history of the school. They'll be my masterpiece!"

After cutting the dough into regulation discs I placed them in the oven.

"Mm, they look marvellous!" I thought.

Sighing with satisfaction I waited my eyes flitting to the oven while I washed up my utensils sniffing appreciatively as the smell of baking biscuits wafted through the room.

Finally, they were ready. Anxiously, I craned my neck as Flossie opened the oven door. Heat blasted my face turning my cheeks bright pink but the biscuits were perfect. Gingerly carrying the tray I placed it on the table to cool eyeing my creation with growing self-admiration for my culinary skills. At last it was time to taste them. Flossie picked one up and delicately bit it: nothing happened. She bit a little harder: still nothing happened. They were rock hard and completely inedible.

"Yew've done it again!" she wailed. How *do* yew manage it?" Devastated, I hung my head in shame as she tried the other girls' biscuits and declared, "Very tasty!"

"Oh well," she said sighing with resignation, "yew might as well take them home."

Wrapping them in grease-proof paper I stuffed them into my satchel with a vengeful thrust hoping they would at least break into small pieces. Nobody could try to eat them if they were broken up. When I arrived home my mother queried,

"What did yew make in cookery today? Where is it?"

"In my satchel," I said reluctantly.

"In your satchel! How can yew bring home food in your satchel with all those books? All right, let's have a look!"

Carefully, I pulled out a very crumpled piece of grease-proof paper and put it on the table. Eyeing it suspiciously my mother opened it to reveal biscuits still perfectly formed.

"Oh, they look lovely," she said picking one up and putting it in her mouth. Slowly her expression changed as she realised that it was rock hard.

"I'd better not have one now or I'll spoil my appetite for dinner. Have yew offered one to Nana and Dad Smith. I'm sure they'd like one."

Clutching the biscuits I dragged over to my grandparents' house, proffered my package and waited apprehensively for their reaction.

"Oh, lovely," said Dad Smith, "I'll have two of those." I stifled a snigger as he tried to bite on the biscuit.

"What are they like?" I said.

"Well, they're fine. Perhaps a *bit* overdone but otherwise – fine. Lovely! I'll save it for later."

Grabbing the remainder of the biscuits I dashed out, called for Anwen, and headed for the stream. Throwing myself down disconsolately near the deepest pool of water I could find I grieved over my culinary failure.

"Oh, stop moaning!" Anwen exclaimed. "Let's have a competition!"

"Let's see who can throw the best skimmer. We've got to count the number of bounces as well."

Sighing, I reached for my biscuits, "Maybe they're not perfect but they make great 'flatties.'"

"Well, I can't cook biscuits but my design skills are fantastic!" I laughed as the first biscuit flew low over the water, skimmed the surface and bounced along until it sank leaving the water rippling. I had cooked the perfect skimmer!

BROKEN-DOWN STARLET

Sitting up on Table Rock I was momentarily distracted by the sound of a small bird that had alighted on the grass and was foraging for food. It was still hot and sultry and I had little inclination to move and break the chain of my thoughts. Sinking back languidly I closed my eyes again to recapture the memories. Sighing, I let myself drift over time until I heard the voices of the boys and girls in Duffryn House. Younger ones at play in the handball court; older ones flirting and walking, hand in hand, round the sweeping lawns when the teachers were not looking. Valentino Vaughan and his girlfriend sneaking off to the 'out of bounds' orchard to engage in their courting rituals while others headed for the 'smoking tree'.

For the first few weeks younger pupils treated prefects with awe and deference often mistaking them for staff especially one tall 'man'; a dark, brooding, Robert Taylor look-alike who reluctantly sported a five o' clock shadow.

"Not had time to shave today Rawlins?" was the usual cry from male staff.

"I shave every morning sir and every night. It just keeps coming back sir!" stuttered Rawlins his handsome face flushing with embarrassment.

"Well young sir, get a sharper razor!"

Prefects were allowed to give lines and enforced school rules with disdain and superiority. Invaluable lessons were learned on school etiquette as they patrolled the grounds reminding us,

"Oi! Gerroff the grass or yew'll get five hundred lines!"

Most of them treated the new 'oners' with care and tried to protect them from the surreptitious initiation ceremonies prevalent

159

amongst the boys. New boys were dangled over banisters by the ankles and shaken vigorously until they screamed,

"Oi, stop it, my 'ead's goin funny. Let go!"

"If we let go of yew, yew'll land on yewer 'ead, yew idiot! Let 'im go then boys, if tha's what 'e wants."

"No!" accompanied by tears of fright.

"Aw, come on mun, we were only playin' about. We wouldn't really hurt yew now would we boys?" as the shaking continued.

Loose change, pens and other 'valuables' dropped out of their pockets to the boys waiting beneath who collected them before they could disappear down the cracks in the floorboards or under the cupboards. Small boys were expected to have clean faces in lessons so older boys obliged newcomers by shoving their heads down the lavatory and pulling the flush.

Many younger pupils were impressed at the primordial strength of a particular master when with one sinewy hand a reprobate, still attached to a chair, found himself lifted into the air. Another male teacher was a dab hand with chalk and could hit a child at forty paces, with incredible accuracy, after marching to the front of the classroom and pirouetting swiftly into a fast, throwing position. Elevation was also achieved by grasping a bunch of hair and levering upwards, painfully slowly, or squeezing an earlobe until it throbbed while lifting upwards at the same time.

Disruptive classroom behaviour was thus quelled very early on in the lives of the 'oners'. As they moved up the school, and their knowledge of subjects such as chemistry increased, their methods of subversion became more sophisticated. Wicked attempts to restrain 'Lullaby' by trapping his gown in the door were inferior to the serious business of manufacturing 'stink bombs' by the 'chem' lads.

"Flippin' 'eck, they've been at it again. Cor, what a pong, it's 'orrible, like sulphur, innit?" was the comment often heard outside the laboratory as pupils and staff covered their noses.

"Wait for it!"

Suddenly, Idris Jones, nose screwed up with distaste, emerged from his elegant, wood-panelled study.

"*Who* is responsible for this outrage?" he hissed, in measured tones, barely concealing his anger. "Whomever the culprit is rest assured that suitable punishment will be meted out for this *disgusting* activity."

Then followed a plea to show some spirit and own up like men or suffer the consequences to the full.

This activity was not for the squeamish or the cowards in our midst. This was for the valiant who scorned the wrath of Idris Jones, at least in theory. In practice it found the culprit cowering with fear, head hanging slack with shame, face flushed with anticipation of the slender cane being gently slapped against a thigh. That, coupled with the threat of public humiliation in morning assembly, dampened the heroic spirit of the boys. Miscreants quietly slunk from behind the heavy, carved doors of the head's study clutching their nether regions and fighting back tears.

"Aw, that 'urt, that did. Dew my bum's on fire mun!"

Following them down the corridor the icy, polished vowels of the head softly warning them,

"Let that be a lesson to you young sirs! Another episode like this and you *will* be expelled. Mark my words! Mark my words well!"

Rarely did the same boy repeat the same misdemeanour. It was left to the ignorant and the uninitiated to risk their luck and their backsides.

Naughty girls were rare, but infinitely more subtle and scheming. Rebellion was confined to experimenting with a shared cigarette in the outside lavatories while one of their cronies stood guard outside trembling with undisguised fear when a member of staff walked nearby. Every morning a member of the female staff stood just inside the door to the girls' cloakroom to scrutinise their uniform, hair, faces and general deportment.

Rarely did a girl escape the eagle eye of Ma Dav or Ma Jam on any deviation from regulation dress and facial adornment. Each and every one of us was terrified of being apprehended during the daily ritual of,

"No red socks, bottle green or white! To the knee in winter miss!"

"Red sashes should be worn around the waist not under your bosom Miss Williams! Really gel you are a trial! Don't slump your shoulders! Stand up straight! Remember your deportment!"

"You gel, are you wearing lipstick?" said Ma Jam in a weary, strained voice as I tried to pass unnoticed.

"No miss, they're my real lips."

Stifling sniggers the rest of the line of girls edged past me. Some of them had bought little lip-shaped, cherry sweets deliberately rubbing them over their mouths creating a garish slash of red.

"Hmph! We'll see about that! Off you go and scrub it off!"

Smirking openly one of the prefects marched behind me to the wash-hand basin and supervised the lip scrubbing. Catching sight of myself in the mirror I grinned inanely at the reflection of vivid, painted lips acquired from cherry sweets and remnants of a large gob-stopper. On the way to school I had sucked through a variety of lurid colours finishing with a bright red that had stained my mouth giving the impression of a very bad make-up job. It was no use. The more I scrubbed the redder my lips.

"Yew'll cop it now!" taunted the prefect in a severe tone.

A flush of anxiety rising up my neck only enhanced the depth of colour on my lips. Marching me firmly back to Ma Jam the prefect reported that I had scrubbed my face well. She was not entirely convinced, but finally accepted my story emphasising,

"You'll be in serious trouble if you *dare* to arrive in school with lips more befitting a cheap, broken-down Hollywood starlet than a grammar school gel."

On wet days, after lunch, we were herded into 'rain rooms' to be set some minor task supervised by prefects. As many as forty of us crammed into a classroom trying to work quietly while the long windows steamed up. Prefects paraded up and down keeping us quiet while boys mouthed rude remarks behind their backs or made 'eyes' at the girls. Miscreants were made to stand in a corner with their hands on their heads or balancing a wastepaper basket until they pleaded to go back to their seats. Some girls hid in the lavatories while others headed for the holly tree and the woods preferring to be cold and uncomfortable outside rather than clammy and miserable inside.

Bottom woods, adjacent to new Cardiff Road, was a magnet for some of the younger boys. In winter rain accumulated into large, black pools with protruding, scraggy, water-logged trees in ghostly silhouette to a backdrop of leaden sky. Paddling on the edge or being pushed amid hoots of laughter into the quagmire left their shoes and socks soaked.

Frantically cleaning shoes, at the sight of a master heading towards them, they stamped their feet to dislodge the mud and rid themselves of wet grass that clung to the bottoms of their trousers.

"Quick, wipe the mud off before 'e sees it!"

"Gimme an 'ankie then, will yew?"

"Have yew been down Bottom Woods?" roared Bomba charging towards the boys with a speed that belied his burly frame.

"N-no sir, honest sir. We were just playin' on the edge and I tripped up and fell in!"

"Are yew wet boy?"

"No sir!"

"Well, get into lessons. Now!"

Squelching back for afternoon classes they stoically suffered their discomfort knowing that 'out of bounds' activities would be followed by severe retribution. With pained expressions on their faces they sat in silent acceptance until the bell rang.

Through the mist of images that crowded my memory as I lay in the long grass came shouts of,

"Keep off the grass! Can't yew read?"

Subdued laughter from staff as they sat in their deckchairs on the front lawn of the house eating Welsh cakes and sipping afternoon tea. Llew 'Bomba' Evans, a brilliant, larger than life character telling one of his tales; stories that were famous for decades. A large, well-built, pugnacious-looking man who had acquired his nick-name because of his mop of unruly curls that reminded us of the son of 'Tarzan'. Gweno Lewis, the German mistress, dignified and elegant; widow of the famous war poet Alun Lewis. Threats of catching head lice sent shivers down our spines when Gweno announced in her well-bred voice,

"Gels, I must inform you that the nit is on the march!"

Robust rugby international, Les Manfield D.F.C., and the bespectacled, quietly-spoken Lullaby, his blandness broken only by his round glasses. Whenever I looked inattentive Milo 'maths' threatened,

"Day dreaming again. Keep your eyes open girl or I'll prop 'em open with matchsticks."

Jolting me back to reality if he caught me daydreaming or gazing through the window across the valley searching for a glimpse of my father's grave in Maesyrarian cemetery. Beaky's meanderings about Mesopotamia, the Tigris, the Euphrates, the Peloponnesian Wars and Philip of Macedonia came drifting down the years as I lay on Table Rock.

Rocky Davies, short, stocky, dark wavy hair and florid complexion, cultivated my love of English. His academic gown was constantly covered in chalk dust, but he wore it with dignity and aplomb even when he waved his arms in some theatrical gesture that displayed the shredded sleeves.

Sitting on his high teacher's desk he enthused about prepositions, adjectival clauses and the importance of developing the skills of précis and parsing of sentences. The style and form of the sonnet, alliteration, onomatopoeia, genre: magical, mysterious words indicating boredom for some and fascination for me. Unlike the 'cello words were music to my ears.

I THOUGHT YOU SAID A PIANO?

Dickie Reynolds, head of music, became a constant irritation in my life after duping me into playing the 'cello. Towards the middle of the spring term we assembled in the library; a beautiful room full of mirrors, wood-panelled walls and crystal chandeliers. Dickie came in and enquired,

"How many of you would like to learn to play the piano?"

As I had some knowledge from my truncated music lessons with Glythyn in Carnetown I quickly put up my hand.

"I've had a few lessons," I ventured.

Seven of us opted for piano and dutifully traipsed behind Dickie to Room Two next door to the headmaster's elegant study. Pushing open the heavy, carved door we saw a beautiful room with panelled walls, a huge wooden fireplace with wall sconces set against the back wall. On one side of the room windows stretched from the ceiling almost to the floor, oak shutters folded back to reveal a glorious view of the grounds.

Dickie busied himself giving three girls violins and another two violas then disappeared through the door instructing,

"Don't touch *anything* until I get back!"

Fay, a tall, dark-haired, angular girl, waited patiently staring down at her long, delicate fingers resting in her lap while I fidgeted and tapped my foot with impatience increasingly anxious to get started.

Dickie finally reappeared with what appeared to be two giant violins and informed us that he had changed his mind about piano lessons. Thrusting the huge instruments at us he declared airily that we would have to play the 'cello instead. Gawping at each other Fay and I protested the unfairness of it.

"But sir, it's huge! How am I going to get it home?"

"On the 'bus, of course," Dickie responded cheerfully. "At least you won't have to carry it into town and catch the train like last year."

"It's not fair!" I moaned at Fay. "Why must we have these monsters?"

Ignoring our protestations he ordered us towards a pair of chairs. Instructing us to sit down he showed us how to position the 'cello,

"Now, place the 'cello between your knees, hold the bow with your right hand and draw it across the strings."

Armed with a bow I drew it slowly across the strings and winced as I heard the most excruciating sound I had ever heard; a combination of an agonising groan and the scraping of metal.

"I'll never learn to play this thing," Fay laughed.

Dickie had other ideas. Fired with enthusiasm he taught us to play, "*Twinkle, Twinkle Little Star*" followed by an obscure Morris dance. A few weeks before St. David's Day he presented us with a piece of Welsh folk music ordering us to practice the tune for at least an hour a night. Shuddering, I realised I would have to take the instrument on the school 'bus. Still, it was marginally better than dragging it through the woods down past St. Margaret's Church, over the bridge and through Mountain Ash.

Laughing groups of children fell silent as they entered Duffryn Woods by the footpath that edged the trees. Walking up past the War memorial and the druid stones, carting their heavy, leather satchels full of textbooks, they noted the changing seasons. Gazing sightlessly over the tranquil woods figures of fallen soldiers, frozen in bronze, graceful in painful death; a generation of lost fathers and protectors. Springtime bluebells casting an indigo shadow on the greenness of the grass. Glowing white snowdrops amongst a carpet of bright, yellow daffodils: morning dew on petals touched by the glint of a white, wintry sun shining through the tall trees to herald our saint's day.

St. David's Day loomed ominously like a carbuncle on the school calendar. Dickie had promised that those of us who were good enough would play our "little tune" during the celebrations. Hoisting the 'cello over my shoulder, battling with sudden gusts of wind that threatened to snatch it from my grasp, I walked up the path at the front of Duffryn House, muttering and complaining, before struggling down the drive towards the main gate.

Stepping up to get on the 'bus I found myself wedged in the doorway unable to move. Struggling with my satchel I pulled furiously to get the instrument on board. It came on to the 'bus with such speed that I lost my footing and fell back into the lap of a boy sitting in the front seat. Guffaws and calls of,

"Ooh! She's sitting on his lap." and "Ooh! I think she fancies him." made me blush bright red.

Finally, I composed myself and dragged the contrivance to the back of the 'bus to the annoyance of the driver who was encapsulated in his little cabin at the front of the bull-nosed vehicle. I was the only pupil on the 'bus with a 'cello. I felt like the only person in the *whole* world who had a 'cello.

Hauling my cargo behind me I squeezed off the 'bus at Doctor's Hill and walked home half carrying, half dragging the heavy, bulky instrument. With a sigh of relief I clattered into the kitchen and propped it up against the wall. The boys eyed it suspiciously, straddled it like a hobby horse then, puffing and blowing, dragged it into the living room.

"Oh!" said my mother proudly, "They've picked yew for the 'cello!"

She came to regret those words. One night as I was rasping out "*Twinkle, Twinkle, Little Star*" for the umpteenth time she said,

"I expect nana and dad would like to hear yew play. Why don't yew go over and show them how good yew are."

My grandparents sat with rapt attention as I played and even sang along with me, but after playing for half an hour Nana Smith suggested,

"Why dwn't yew go into the other room to play. Yew'll have more quiet in there."

The last words I remember about my 'cello playing were,

"Mrs Hughes would love to hear yew. Perhaps she'll let you

practice in her shed with Nia. She can play that musical saw they keep in there."

Fay, my classmate, had taken a liking to the 'cello and continued to play with enthusiasm, but I hated it with a vengeance. Continual pleading with Dickie, coupled with my deliberate lack of aptitude, eventually brought results. Finally, he relented and gave me a violin that I managed reasonably well, but not before doling out a thousand lines of his favourite quote from Tennyson's '*The Passing of Arthur*',

"*What harm undone? deep harm to disobey*
Seeing obedience is the bond of the rule."[1]

Tying three pencils together I made short work of the task writing triple lines simultaneously. They were so untidy that Dickie made me own up to the ruse.

"I *should* put you on daily report for this," he admonished, "but I'll let you off this time for using your initiative. Now *begone* with you before I change my mind."

He flapped his hands to indicate I should leave, but I was already going through the door relieved to have escaped the humiliation of daily report.

[1] p184. Extract from 'The Passing of Arthur',
2 lines from "Tennyson – Seleceted Poems"
edited by Millgate, Michael (1963)
By permission of Oxford University Press

DANNY BOY

Other than death, or being struck with a mysterious, incurable illness, expulsion from grammar school was the worst thing that could happen. One particular lad called Danny had been threatened with a dishonourable discharge from the grammar school on more than one occasion. He was a loose-limbed, sinewy boy who slouched rather than walked. Lurching into the classroom with an inane grin on his face, which made his thick lips only marginally more attractive, he squeezed into his seat with a defiant,

"Mornin' sir," that sounded almost like an insult.

Tousled, dirty blond hair, clothes unkempt and dishevelled he was markedly different from his classmates. His most distinguishing feature was that his shirt collar, on one side, was always hidden beneath his tie belying his claims of examining his appearance in a mirror each morning.

Danny's bleak, home environment was well-known. Everybody felt sorry for him, even the teachers, which was why he reigned as the school joker for so long. Friends and staff had done their utmost to compensate for his lack of parental support, but as the months wore on he became more and more difficult. Academically bright, not vicious or aggressive, but very argumentative seeming intent on aggravating the staff by playing silly, practical jokes or trying to make them or himself the object of ridicule. When a knock came on the door during a lesson it was always Danny who had been summoned to the head's study.

His downfall came one warm afternoon during a French lesson with the pretty, dark-haired mademoiselle who was teaching us how to conjugate verbs while improving her English. Rumour had it that she was also learning the rudiments of the Teutonic languages with the young German student who had taken her under his wing. To give us a break she asked us to write a word of our choice on the blackboard while the others tried to translate. We gained house points for successful answers. After about ten minutes Danny's hand shot up.

"Miss! Miss! I've got one! Knickers!"

"All right cheeldr-r-en. Tr –r anslate. How you say – kn –ee-ee kers in Fr –r ench?"

Somebody translated reasonably well but Danny was not content. He shouted,

"Try corset, or what about brassière miss?"

Mademoiselle fielded these with aplomb and decorum complacently demonstrating her 'worldly' knowledge. Danny sat back looking slightly defeated while the rest of us attempted to settle down. Like the others I had been giggling surreptitiously aghast at his brazen behaviour. It wasn't long before Danny's hand shot up again.

"Yes, Dann – ee. What eez eet?

"Try arse miss. That's a good word to translate."

"Ar–r–rse? Ar–r–rse? What kind of word eez a –r–rse? Would anyone in the class like to tr–ranslate?"

Nobody moved; nobody spoke. We sat frozen to our seats with shock; eyes lowered, desperate not to catch her eye.

"Tom – you know zees word ar–r–rse?"

"No miss," he said trying to hold his exercise book in front of his face his shoulders shaking with silent laughter. She looked at me.

"Per 'aps you know ar–r–rse?"

It was too much. No longer able to control ourselves the room erupted. I couldn't have replied even if I had known the word 'derriere' because of the volume of laughter. It suddenly dawned on mademoiselle that she was the cause of this hilarity.

"Dann–ee, go to Mr. Jones' study at *once!*"

Danny didn't move. He just stared at her laconically, pushed his chair back and put one foot on his desk.

"I we-e-l not tell you again Dann-ee! Go!"

He didn't budge just continued staring and grinning at her.

Mademoiselle's eyes filled with tears as she opened the door. Suddenly, Danny sprang from his seat and lunged at the door pushing it shut.

"Get out of my way, you eempudent boy! Let me out!"

We had never seen this kind of behaviour. Gaping mouths and eyes wide open with shock, not daring to speak, we sat in stunned silence. Danny leaned against the door, folded his arms, crossed his legs and dared her to push him out of the way. She tried to grab the doorknob but he pushed her hand away. For the rest of us the joke was well and truly over. This was the worst stunt he had ever pulled and I think he knew it. There was no going back for Danny.

"Come on Danny, get away from the door. It's not funny anymore," Tom muttered aghast at this unfamiliar behaviour.

The rest of the class just stared, slack-jawed, unable to believe that anyone could be brazen enough to answer back.

Feeling sorry for Mademoiselle Thierry I watched the tears flowing down her face. Cheeks flushed pink with embarrassment and confusion she stood powerless to remove him.

Suddenly, the door was thrust open by an unseen force and there stood the German student, crew-cut bristling atop his six-feet two inch, muscular frame, chiselled features distorted with fury. Danny fell forward with the momentum straight towards mademoiselle who stepped to one side while he fell face down on the floor with a loud thud. Rubbing his arm, he suddenly became aware of his audience. Springing to his feet he looked at the class then at Herr Berg before sloping languidly to the door with his hands thrust deep inside his trouser pockets. As he went out his last words were,

"Ta ra folks! See yew around then!"

He doffed an imaginary cap in a sweeping gesture of defiance, walked out, and was never seen in the school again.

We were still in shock days later when Idris Jones, snowy head bowed sombrely, eyes lowered, stood silently behind the rostrum at the close of morning assembly. Slowly, he looked up sweeping his penetrating gaze over the assembled mass: deep into our eyes as though searching our souls for some glimmer of hope.

171

"*Never, never* in all the years I have taught in this magnificent school have I experienced the kind of behaviour that occurred this week," he said in a low, thin voice.

"It is unbelievable, I say unbelievable!" he expostulated emphasising every syllable in an icy, precise tone. "*Unthinkable*, that a pupil in Mountain Ash Grammar School could behave in such an ungallant, uncivilised manner!"

Diminished by his piercing look I lowered my head shrinking into my blazer ashamed for Danny; ashamed for myself.

"It will not – I repeat – *not* be tolerated! The boy concerned with this unseemly act has been expelled for behaviour unbefitting a gentleman and a grammar school boy. You are dismissed!"

In total silence we filed out from assembly, heads hanging down, not because we felt sorry for Danny, but because all of us were feeling slightly guilty that we had laughed at mademoiselle's predicament because we really liked her. Danny was the main subject of conversation for weeks. He had become the stuff of legend.

DANCING DIVAS

Every morning we trooped into assembly under the eagle eye of staff elevated on the stage. Voices rose to the stirring strains of, '*Holy, Holy, Holy*', '*Jerusalem*', '*Calon Lan*' and the ancient, rousing '*Gaudeamus Igitur*'. At the close of morning assembly we waited with quiet unease to hear who had been put on daily report. White head bent over the rostrum Idris Jones stood silently for a few moments as if in deep contemplation and sadness regarding what he was about to announce. In the mildest of tones he read out the name of the miscreant,

"Peter Wilkins, come to the front please and face the school."

Dragging his feet the malefactor shuffled to the front of the hall and turned to face his fellow pupils.

"You saw fit to misbehave in the crudest way towards a member of the female staff," he said dangerously quietly.

Repeating the warning we always heard on these occasions he changed his tone barking,

"This kind of behaviour will *not* be tolerated. Well, what have you to say for yourself, Mr. Wilkins?"

"Nothing sir."

"Is that *all* you have to say?"

"No sir, I'm sorry sir, *very* sorry sir."

An icy invitation to inform the assembled mass of his 'crime' was followed by Mr. Jones announcing the 'sentence' to be given. Even sixth formers, foolish enough to stray from the straight and narrow path demanded by Idris Jones, were subject to the same treatment. No one giggled or made any comment. Wilkins hung his head desperately regretting sticking out his tongue; regretting even more fervently that Ma Jam had turned round and caught him. An effective punishment, it was rare for the same pupil to be called out twice during a school career

The assembly hall was also used for dancing lessons, St. David's Day concerts and other musical events arranged by Dickie Reynolds. Sometimes we were ushered into the hall to benefit from cultural experiences such as chamber music provided by visiting musicians.

Sitting on wooden, polished, hard-backed chairs, not daring to fidget just in case we were spotted looking bored, we were subjected to Dickie's favourite torture: a quartet of ladies, clones of Hinge and Bracket. Smiling histrionically the pianist played with passionate gestures while the grimacing violinist closed her eyes and swayed theatrically to the melody.

Dancing lessons were marginally better. For weeks before the Christmas party Ma Jam and Ma Dav taught us to waltz, foxtrot and quickstep. We even had a stab at the 'Coronation Tango' dipping exaggeratedly until we lost our balance; clinging frantically to partners while our heads almost brushed the floor. Girls danced with other girls as Ma Jam instructed,

"One, two, three! One, two, three! Gels you must flow with the music! You're not running in the relay! Don't look at your feet!" she shouted as one of the girls became entangled with the feet of her partner and crashed to the floor.

Throwing up her hands in despair, while raising her eyes to the ceiling in silent supplication, she commanded,

"Be seated!"

Sighing thankfully we sank to the polished, parquet floor exhausted and giggling.

On the night of the Christmas party the atmosphere was electric. Academic gowns discarded staff, dressed up in their finery, actually looked as though they were enjoying themselves. With a conspiratorial smile Ma Dav ushered all the girls into the library while Gweno ordered,

"Stand in a straight line gels. Come on now, quickly, no pushing; one behind the other."

Wuffles, a tall man who sported a ginger R.A.F., style

moustache directed the boys through the wide, elaborately carved mahogany door into the Old Hall.

Lord Aberdare's banqueting hall was a magnificent room with very high ceilings master-plastered with intricate coving and ornate, ceiling roses. Huge floor to ceiling windows dominated two sides of the room. Wood panelling covered the other walls above the highly polished, parquet floors where long-dead dancers in their elegant ball gowns had pirouetted into the small hours. In two of the walls were set massive wooden, carved fire-places. Memorials to the young men whose lives had been cut short by two world wars, their names a poignant reminder to their sons and daughters, were set above the fireplace.

Chattering animatedly, excited and nervous, I stood waiting to file out of the library beneath the shimmering, crystal chandeliers; their light reflected in the large mirrors on the wall echoing a more gracious period in history.

Armed with a knife, fork, spoon and cup we emerged, one by one: a girl from the library and a boy from the Old Hall who then became partners for the night. Craning my neck to see who was coming out I counted the bodies hoping for somebody I liked. Two boys emerged. Breathing a sigh of relief I watched a tall, dark-haired boy being guided through the door followed by a pale, red-haired lad.

"Phew! Thank goodness for that!" I thought looking at some of the other girls' partners. "Mm! Not bad, not bad at all!" I mused. "It won't be too much of a hardship to spend the rest of the evening with either of them."

As the boys moved forward I realised that, 'tall, dark and handsome' would meet up with the girl in front of me so I would be with the redhead. Too late, I saw another body in between the two boys concealed because he was so short.

Smiling happily, oblivious to my dismay, 'Bertie', a small, rather fussy boy, came trotting out dressed in black jacket, short grey trousers, knee-length socks, handkerchief dangling from his breast pocket, dickie bow and slicked-down brilliantined hair. My heart sank.

"Oh no," I groaned, "not him!"

"Bad luck!" laughed my friends. "Rather yew than me."

"Oh, ha, ha, very funny!" I snapped through my teeth.

Gazing down at 'Bertie' I realised he was at least a foot shorter than me. His hand in mine he looked like a little boy strolling with his big sister.

"Yew'd better help me out. I'm not staying with him all night! He's a right little fusspot!" I whispered as Bertie' dragged me purposefully down the corridor.

Forced to hold hands we walked along the covered way until we entered the assembly hall. Attempts to prevent him following me around all evening failed. Dancing with a boy a foot shorter than me, whose eyes were dangerously level with my bosom, left me cringing with embarrassment. Looking over his head I mouthed desperate pleas to my friends. Eventually, they managed to wedge him into a corner and agreed to keep him there until I could make my escape to dance with 'tall, dark and handsome' who was waiting impatiently in the wings.

Christmas vanished and with it 'tall, dark and handsome' who faded into obscurity after a few weeks of self adulation; a young man who had the whitest teeth, blackest hair, biggest brain and hardest muscles in the school, or so he claimed. As summer approached I spent more and more time in the 'long grass', roaming the hills above my home or playing tennis on the pine end of Milton Villa.

NOT ANOTHER COMB FROM
BARRY ISLAND?

The full warmth of a mid summer sun seeped pleasantly through my cotton blouse as I skirted St. Margaret's Church, climbed past Matic's shop and up the steep slope of Austin Street.

"Hi!" I called as I spotted Gaynor, a chubby, dark-haired girl who was emerging from her aunt's house.

"Yew up for the holidays then?" she queried.

"I'll be here right through July and most of August."

"Great! We'll go over the tennis courts later on, shall we?"

"Yes, but I'll have to ask my grandmother first. P'raps we could have a bit of a practice before we go."

"Smashing, see yew later then," she cried as she ran off down Granville Terrace and disappeared into Richmond Road.

Milton Villa sat at the junction of Fox Street and Granville Terrace; its whole length, front and back gates, opening onto the latter. Quiet and still except for the sound of chirruping; a sudden rustling as a bird flew out of the foliage; the scampering of some small animal scuttling in the lane across the road.

"It's so peaceful," I observed as I pushed open the gate.

The stillness in the air gave a sense of tranquillity and continuity as I watched the faint breeze lick the leafy corners of the street trees. Sighing contentedly I closed the gate behind me and called out,

"Nana! Nana!

"In here!" she called. "I've been freshening up the crockery," she informed me as she carefully positioned her Royal Albert tea service in the glass-fronted wall cabinets. "We'll have a nice cup of tea in a minute or yew can have a glass of my home-made lemonade."

"Oh, lemonade please nana."

As she chatted animatedly my eyes strayed to the big writing desk on top of which was housed a glass-fronted bookcase with leather-bound volumes; red, burgundy, navy, dark green and black, their titles embossed in gold lettering. I contemplated long afternoons engrossed in their contents.

Even as a small child I had treasured books. Reverently, my hands caressed their texture, loving the feel of the leather, carefully turning the pages, one by one, to drink in the words and colourful illustrations.

"Nose in a book again?" nana laughed. "What are yew reading this time?"

"Mm," I mumbled incoherently lost in the make-believe world of,'*The Boy Who Lost His Temper*' as it disappeared in a puff of yellow cloud to disperse in the air.

Wrapped in a magical world I slid with the children who spent the midnight hour skimming down silver moonbeams: flying through the starry sky experiencing wonderful adventures every night after they had been tucked up in bed. Now '*Northanger Abbey*', '*Wuthering Heights*' and '*Great Expectations*' found me projected back into their time experiencing their joys, triumphs and sufferings; continuing their adventures in my dreams at night.

The sound of my paternal grandfather's voice brought me back to reality.

"Now yew know we're going away in a few days time, dwn't yew? Margaret and Roy are going to look after the house for us."

"I know, I'm staying as well then Tony will have some company. I'll take him for walks."

"Oh, I dwn't know about that. You're a bit young, I think."

"No, I'm not!" I declared indignantly.

"Well, yew'll have to sort that out with Margaret," he remarked as he removed his hat.

Dad Howells was over six feet tall with thick, curly hair on his chest but very little on his head. Completely bald except for some sparse, copper-coloured hair either side. Whenever I went to the seaside I brought back souvenirs; his was always a comb in a leather case.

Proudly I said, "I've bought yew a comb and case from Barry Island."

"Oh, lovely, a comb, just what I wanted," he grinned putting it in his pocket while Nana Howells covered a smile.

With exaggerated actions he sliced the teeth through his bits of fuzz. Patting his jacket he declared,

"I'll keep it in my breast pocket for 'safe-keeping'.

It never occurred to me that he had no use for it. On the following trip I'd buy another one just in case he had lost the previous present. Later, I discovered that the bathroom cabinet held a stock of combs collected from all the seaside resorts from Llandudno to Lynmouth in Devon. From a strong Methodist background, for many years, he wore an abstainers' lapel badge as a silent statement to the community regarding the evils of alcohol.

Following Nana Howells outside I grabbed a trowel to help her weed the bank at the far end of the garden. Very tall for a woman in the 1950s, a statuesque five feet eight inches. Blonde, blue-eyed, high cheek bones and finely-drawn, well-bred features. Rather reserved, some mistakenly thought she was aloof and unapproachable particularly as she did not encourage neighbours to pop in and out at will. This outer façade concealed a warm, empathetic soul with a strong sense of justice and integrity.

"Yew start that side and I'll start over here then we can meet in the middle," she said stabbing at an established root.

"How are yew Mrs Howells?" Mrs Francis called as she pulled herself up and peered over the high side wall. "Beautiful day it is too. Mind yew I dwn't know how long it'll last."

"Definitely too warm to be indoors," Nana Howells replied wiping her glistening forehead with the back of her hand.

"Funny weather though; cold and wet for days then it's too hot and clammy to breathe properly."

"Well, we could do with a drop of rain now Mrs Francis. The ground is as hard as a rock."

Mrs Francis lived next door. Tiny, frail-looking with grey hair, typically Welsh, her Celtic blue eyes darted everywhere. Quick and mercurial her movements were like those of a bird. For the benefit of the tourists her face could be seen smiling out of a thousand postcards all over Wales under the tall, black hats of the women dressed in Lady Llanover's Welsh folk costume.

"We're going away for a couple of weeks Mrs Francis. Margaret and Roy will be here, but I'd appreciate it if yew could keep an eye on things round the back as well."

"No trouble Mrs Howells. And are yew going too cariad?" she enquired glancing at me.

"No, I'll be staying with Margaret until nana comes back."

"Oh well, anything yew want, dwn't be shy; yew just come round."

In the valleys some next door neighbours remained friends all their lives, but it was also quite common for people to address each other formally. It was considered bad manners for children to call adults by their first names. Instead, they often referred to them as 'auntie' and 'uncle'.

Whole families, grandparents, parents, aunts and cousins often lived in the same street. Their child-rearing and housekeeping skills were passed from generation to generation. Unlike today elderly relatives remained within the family fold, a source of love, wisdom and experience.

"I'm going next door to tell gran and gransha about yew," was a familiar cry.

If mam didn't know what was troubling her brood granny usually provided the solution.

Mountain Ash in the 1950s was a prosperous, bustling town with well-stocked shops. When Nana Howells announced,

"I'm going down the 'Mount'. Do yew want to come with me?" I'd rush to fetch the wicker basket with its curved handle.

Excursions over town saw us ambling from shop to shop picking up a joint at Lougher's the butcher or spools of cotton from Pugh's drapery and haberdasher's. 'Mount' had more than one greengrocer's, cake shops, Italian cafés, shoe shops, a gentlemen's tailor and outfitters, the Co-op, Marshall's fish and chips and two banks. The town throbbed and pulsated to the music of its people.

In the little fresh, fish shop that opened onto the pavement I gazed at the lifeless eyes of cod, hake, herrings and kippers surrounded by ice: little pots of cockles, mussels and whelks that turned my stomach.

"Dwn't buy a fish with its head still on," I pleaded.

"All right, top and tail it please," instructed Nana Howells.

Shuddering, I turned away as the fishmonger took his lethal knife and decapitated the fish as easily as slicing through butter.

At the southern end stood the Palace cinema and Workman's Hall stamped with the same architectural style as countless others in the valleys. Distinct communities had grown up separated by the River Cynon. On the west side Darrenlas stretched up from the town its straight streets of neat, terraced houses built on steep hills spilling down the mountainside before spreading outwards to Miskin.

Over the bridge Caegarw was separated by a stream that flowed downhill at the side of Allen Street. On one side mainly terraced houses that opened directly on to the pavement. On the other side semi-detached villas, detached houses and some larger, substantial properties that edged Mountain Ash General Hospital.

Close-knit relationships amongst villagers were the life-blood of the community. This was the custom for many people in the Welsh valleys in the 1950s as it was in other parts of Britain. Everybody knew everyone else's business; their achievements, misfortunes, scandals and quarrels amongst neighbours. But, in times of strife, tragedy or festivity the community pulled together to comfort, support or celebrate.

POOR LITTLE JOEY

Blue skies, the warmth of a hot sun glowing brilliant yellow: days spent walking along Granville Terrace under the street trees covered in verdant foliage. Wandering through the lane with Tony pulling on his outgrown baby reins, struggling to charge ahead, I heard Margaret's anxious voice calling across the road,

"Dwn't go any further than the end of the lane and dwn't let him off the reins! Did yew hear me?"

"Yes, I heard and I won't," I called back trying to keep Tony in check.

Such a strong, sturdy little boy: tall, bright blue eyes, dimpled chin and a mop of golden curls, he was never out of her sight.

"Well, dwn't be long because they'll be off soon," referring to my grandparents.

Margaret was the eldest of my father's three sisters. Tall, slim with high cheekbones inherited from my grandmother. All had an indefinable presence and rather regal bearing that marked them as siblings. A haughtiness of stature that made heads turn when they walked into a room, or when walking through the streets, although they were completely unaware of the impression they made on others. Trevor, his brother, six feet three inches tall, handsome, with the same fine, bone structure and haughty expression as his sisters.

The previous night he had turned up dressed in white tie and tails, complete with silk top hat and cape looking like a Hollywood film star or a guest about to attend a Royal gala.

"Just popped in to wish yew *bon voyage*," he joked.

"We're going on the river not the Atlantic," Nana Howells retorted visibly nervous at the prospect of two weeks on water. "Goodness me. Where are yew off to?" she asked proudly.

"A formal dinner and dance in Swansea. It's going to be a *very* swish affair," Trevor replied picking imaginary bits of lint from his cape.

"Have a good time," we chorused.

"Doesn't he look lovely," Nana Howells murmured as, dashing and elegant, he headed for the door flinging his white, silk scarf over his shoulder.

Tired of struggling with Tony, who wanted to be free of his harness, I decided to knock a few tennis balls against the pine end of the house. Rita came rushing out scolding,

"Nana's Royal Albert almost fell off the shelf then. Yew can look out if it breaks!"

"Is she hitting that ball against the pine-end again? What have I told yew about that?" Nana Howells rejoined impatiently as she emerged from the back door. "I've got enough to do getting ready to travel. Come in *this* minute!"

Reluctantly, I dragged indoors to see Nana Howells hurriedly opening her suitcase.

"*Now* what have yew forgotten, for goodness sake!" my grandfather remonstrated.

"Drat! I forgot to pack my comfortable canvas shoes. I can't go without them, can I?" she protested as she disappeared towards the stairs to fetch them.

Finally, after ensuring they had everything they needed, they left for their fortnight's river cruise from Tewkesbury.

"Margaret, be sure that Roy locks up securely *every* night," Nana Howells instructed.

"Yes, I will."

"And make sure yew dwn't leave the gas cooker on."

"I won't."

"And she's not to go out late on her own," she continued looking at me. "Did yew hear that now?"

"Yes nana."

"And watch Tony doesn't go near Mrs Prosser's, if he's in the garden."

"Yes, all right. Anything else?" Margaret queried with barely concealed exasperation.

"Oh, for goodness sake let's get moving or we'll be lucky to get there before it gets dark," Dad Howells called.

"Come on Valerie, get in the car," he ordered my teenage aunt who was going with them.

Margaret, my grandmother's namesake, breathed a sigh of relief as the car disappeared round the corner into Austin Street.

"Knowing nana they'll be back in a minute to check that I heard all the instructions she gave me."

Giggling, we closed the back gate but not before Margaret had stuck her head out to check one last time that they had actually gone.

"Right, a nice cup of tea I think, is it?" she laughed.

Dry-witted, with a wry sense of humour, she was easy to get along with so I looked forward to an extended stay. Later that evening the telephone rang.

"Hello, Margaret, is that yew?" Nana Howells' voice resonated. "We've arrived, *at last!* Is everything all right?"

"Everything's fine," Margaret assured her, "just enjoy the holiday. Bye!"

"Bye, bye, oh and Margaret dwn't let the girls go frightening Joey to death with all that thumping against the wall."

During the summer months Joey, Nana's pretty pet budgie, resided next to the conservatory door that opened into the garden.

"He'll get plenty of fresh air there, won't yew Joey? Whose a pretty boy then?" Nana would coo as Joey dozed on his perch.

Home-made preserves, chutney and jams filled the tall cupboard set against the opposite outside wall.

"Why are yew putting in that stuff?" I queried.

"Yew have to add pectin or the jam won't set," she explained as she heated the fruit. "Once we've filled all the jars we'll make some toffee, shall we?"

Anticipating the mouth-watering result I watched intently.

"It smells sweet; makes my mouth water," I drooled as she poured golden solution into a flat tin.

Cooled and set into slabs of sticky toffee she broke it up into pieces with a tiny metal hammer.

"Dwn't try to eat such big pieces," she laughed as I crammed a large, triangular portion into my mouth.

"Mm, s'lovely!" I mumbled unintelligibly.

Left to my own devices, while Margaret busied herself about the house, I rattled the wires of Joey's cage.

"Pretty Joey, pretty Joey. Come on, say Joey," I chanted, while the bird totally ignored me.

"Whose a pretty boy then? Silly bird!" I declared whilst Joey resolutely ignored my pleas.

Bored with trying to get the bird to talk I unscrewed my racquet from its wooden press. Guiltily, I sneaked outside for a quick game of wall tennis.

At first I stood close to the wall delicately knocking the ball against the pine end. Gradually, I moved further and further back to lengthen the shots using more force each time.

Thump! Thump! Thump!

Suddenly, I heard a loud scream coming from the conservatory.

"Help! Help!"

My immediate reaction was to run, because I thought the china had come crashing off the shelf, but the shouting continued.

"Somebody, anybody, help!"

Sticking my head rather tentatively around the back door I looked into the garden. There was no-one in sight, but the row was even louder. More screams came from the direction of the conservatory. I crept forward then stopped, transfixed.

Through the glass door I could see Margaret standing with her back to the cabinet. Top and bottom doors were wide open. Jars of stewed prunes, pickled onions and beetroot were flying past her head at great speed smashing on to the floor at her feet. Slipping and sliding in the mess she desperately tried to maintain a footing. The pungent mixture of smells hit my nostrils as I opened the door.

"Quick!" she screamed as her feet started to slide under her. "My feet are slipping in this. I'm going to lose my bal-a-a-nce!"

With that she skidded down the front of the cabinet and landed heavily in a mass of oozing jam and chutney. Grabbing her under the arms I pulled while she tried to get a foothold to force herself back onto her feet. The last jar of jam shot past her head to join the brightly-coloured concoction on the tiles.

"Oh," she complained, "my nether regions hurt. I bet I'll be bruised all over."

Forgetting that her hands were now covered with 'goo' she pushed back the hair from her eyes smearing her face in the process. Suddenly, she wailed,

"Oh no, the blessed budgie's escaped!" Joey had found his way out and was making a break for freedom; flying round and round the room smashing against windows in his search for an opening into the outside world.

"Quick, close the door before he gets out! Try to catch him!" she screamed.

Too late, in a flutter of wings the intrepid bird had flown out through the open door and freedom.

Apparently the cupboard had started to topple over just as Margaret had opened his cage to put in fresh water and birdseed.

"That's put the tin hat on it," she moaned later. "What will Nana say when she gets back: between the chutney and the blessed bird?"

After a hasty conference Margaret and Rita decided that the best plan was to buy another bird to replace Joey. I was sworn to secrecy and threatened with hell-fire and brimstone if I as much as hinted to Nana Howells what had happened to him.

Eventually, we went off to the pet shop down the 'Mount', bought an identical budgie and installed it in Joey's cage.

"Do yew think she'll be able to tell the difference?" I asked.

"No, I shouldn't think so," Rita remarked tentatively. "They all look the same; a budgie's a budgie isn't it?" she remarked uncertainly.

"She'll *never* know the difference," Margaret declared.

A few days later my grandparents arrived home full of stories about their trip on the river.

"I'm glad to see my china's still intact," Nana Howells remarked with a hint of relief. "Were there any problems while we were away?"

"No, except for the chutney and jam and stuff," Margaret ventured.

"What stuff?" Nana Howells demanded.

We told her the story about the chutney, but we all kept quiet about Joey. Every day Nana Howells looked at the bird and remarked,

"Well, I dwn't know Joey, you dwn't look well to me. What's the matter boy? Poor little boy."

Joey always said "poor little boy." It was the only thing he could say, but the bird stayed silent.

Nana was convinced her pet was sick and eventually took it to the vet. She came back with the cage in her hand and an accusatory look on her face. Waiting with bated breath we feigned nonchalance.

"Right you three," she said looking directly at Margaret, Rita and me. The vet had told her something we did *not* know. The replacement Joey was a female bird. Strenuous attempts to convince her about Joey's gender fell on deaf ears.

"P'raps Joey is a girl bird," I offered helpfully.

"Now, dwn't be so silly. I'm not falling for that. They told me in the pet shop that the bird's wattle is the wrong colour for a male budgie."

"What's a 'wattle'?"

"It's the fleshy bit above the beak. I knew there was something different, but I couldn't *quite* put my finger on it."

The game was up and we had no alternative but to tell her the truth. Eventually, we were forgiven but, ironically, the new budgie was sick after all and died just before Christmas. Nana Howells came downstairs one morning and found her dead in her cage. Poor little Joey!

A VILLAGE CHRISTMAS

The metallic click of horses' hooves on stone brought me sharply into focus. I gazed lazily from my bedroom window as they clattered past, sinewy thighs glistening with fine beads of sweat; steaming the hot, musky smell of horse flesh. A cold, crisp, Christmas morning in the valley. Smells of roasted meat and the sweet odour of chocolate wafted up the stairs. Anticipation and joy of the day ahead shone before me like a multi-faceted jewel.

Downstairs the boys were excitedly tearing open their Christmas presents under the tree that was already shedding some of its needles leaving a carpet of muted green around the base. The evocative scent mingled with the warm smell of twinkling fairy lights. Little transparent, Cinderella coaches: red, blue, green, yellow and purple with tiny gold-painted wheels. Hanging from the branches shiny, coloured baubles, chocolate novelties in multi-coloured wrappings and net bags full of golden 'money'.

"Cowboy clothes!" they chorused showing me identical outfits except for the colour of the Stetson's hatbands.

"And six-shooters! Bang! Bang!" Michael shouted. "I got yew first!"

"No yew didn't then. I got yew first!" retorted Roger.

"Look mam, look what Father Christmas brought us; cowboy outfits!" they yelled in unison."

"I bet you're glad yew sent that letter now," I laughed.

On Christmas Eve they had watched intently as their letters to Santa had soared up the chimney propelled by the draft and heat. At bedtime a mince pie and a tot of sherry left high on the mantelpiece above a blazing coal fire.

Outside a light glaze of hoar frost covered the ground. It

gleamed on the dark branches of the trees reflecting the cold, sunlight that shone out of a fading, blue-white sky mottled with dark, ponderous clouds. The sharpness of the air, so cold and pure, with the expectation of heavy snow. It filled my throat cascading like sparkling wine into my lungs forcing me to catch my breath in the rarefied atmosphere.

The sun glanced off the threads of frost running along the road like a silvery, spider's web frozen into intricate patterns of lace. Halting footsteps scrunched on transparent, filmy layers of ice. A little girl, clutching her new doll, peeped from her doorway while her brother launched his model aeroplane over her head and out into the road. Neighbours shouting, 'Happy Christmas!' as they picked their way along the precarious pavements bearing a stack of festively wrapped gifts in their arms. Grabbing my grandparents' Christmas presents I called to my mother,

"I'm going over nana's to give my presents."

"I'll be over myself in a minute now," she replied putting down the basting spoon, her face flushed from the heat of the oven.

Nana and Dad Smith were in the kitchen enjoying a couple of boiled eggs and hot, buttered toast. I almost fell into the room in my eagerness to show them what I'd bought.

"Here's your Christmas presents," I said excitedly as I handed them over.

"Mmm, I wonder what's in here?" queried Dad Smith gently shaking the little box wrapped in paper covered with golden bells and sprigs of holly.

"Open it, open it! Yew too nana, rip it off!" I cried impatiently as she fiddled with the sticky tape.

She opened the box and lifted out marcasite earrings encrusted with amber and emerald-coloured stones.

"Lovely; look Harry they're beautiful."

"I've been saving up sixpences and thrupenny bits all year round in a jam jar," I babbled.

"Oh, just what I wanted," Dad Smith grinned clipping his present on to the pocket of his cardigan.

"It's a tie pin for your tie silly."

"I'm just teasing: dwn't worry I'll definitely be wearing this with my new shirt when we go down to see Peggy and Eric the day after Boxing Day," he declared referring to my mother's sister and her husband who lived in St. Mary Hill near Cowbridge, "*and* I'll show them off to Harry when he comes down." Harry junior, the eldest of their sons and a keen sailor, lived in Swansea where he could indulge in his favourite pastime, sailing his precious boat. He was never happy unless he was on the sea. Even though it was just a hobby he diligently studied and passed all his navigator's examinations so that he could skipper large passenger-carrying craft.

Soon the house filled with family exchanging gifts, sipping sherry from nana's little glasses embossed with mounted huntsmen in flaring, red riding coats. Banter and laughter as each son tried to out-brag the other while the women raised their eyebrows and shook their heads.

"Right, let's go and break open your sherry now Dodo, if yew can find it, that is!" Donald grinned mischievously at my mother.

"Now, yew know I only keep it hidden in the wardrobe so that the boys dwn't drink it thinking it's pop," she retorted sounding slightly miffed.

The clatter of kitchen sounds mingled with laughter, chatter and the music of '*Forces Favourites*'. Nostalgic melodies and merry Christmas songs dedicated with poignant, seasonal messages from service personnel stationed overseas to their missed loved ones at home. Donald raised his glass and said happily,

"Happy Christmas everybody and here's to many more to come."

Glasses clinked and tinkled as they sipped their drinks then thought of another toast until each had contributed something to the day.

"Merry Christmas! Merry Christmas!" called a voice as Aurona May and Nia poked their heads round the back door.

"Look what I've had from Ted," Nia said brandishing a large book. "It's a '*Film Annual*'.

We flicked through the pages admiring the glossy portraits of Clark Gable, John Wayne and Cary Grant.

Aurona May, a petite, black-eyed, dark-haired woman chattered animatedly exchanging stories of Christmas' long gone.

"Remember that Christmas when yew dropped the Christmas cake as yew were takin' it out of the oven?"

"Do yew know it looked the most perfect cake I've ever made," my mother replied. "It was like being in a dream. I could see the cake sliding, almost in slow motion, but I didn't have enough hands to stop it falling."

"And *I* was too slow to catch it!" Aurona May chortled. "All over the floor it went in pieces, oh, and it smelled lovely, didn't it?"

They giggled hysterically prompted by the memory and the effects of the sherry. Just one small glass was enough to set my mother's head spinning.

"The poor dog almost went mad, didn't he Aurona? He must have smelled it from outside 'cause he darted in and started gulping huge chunks, but it was so hot he burnt his tongue. Yelping like mad he was and trying to wolf it down at the same time. I had to pull the silly thing off, didn't I?" she laughed as she looked lovingly at Tammy our corgi.

"Watch him now," she said as she started singing Alma Cogan's "*You Belong to Me.*" Tammy's ears shot up and his head strained back as he accompanied her with a series of long drawn-out howls; a daily ritual that sent him into paroxysms of ecstasy.

Pungent odours of sprouts and cauliflower, simmering in the saucepans on the hob, sent her scurrying to the kitchen. The house fell quiet as family trailed back to their homes nearby. She peered under the rattling lids then stirred the thick gravy made from flour and meat juice.

"I think that's it now," she declared eyeing the chicken. "We've got beef, pork, chipolatas, stuffing, apple sauce, veg.....what have I forgotten? Parsnips and roast potatoes are in the oven, soup's ready......" she tailed off, eyes gazing vacantly into the distance, as she mentally listed the necessities for a successful Christmas dinner.

A final tugging and smoothing of the tablecloth, a knife adjusted here, a condiment there. In the centre of the table a fat, red candle surrounded by sprigs of fresh holly with luscious red berries.

Christmas crackers patterned red and green embossed with shiny golden bells. The boys, in their cowboy outfits, fidgeting in their seats fiddling with the butts of their six-shooters sticking out above stud-encrusted holsters at their hips. Above us trimmings made from crêpe paper their edges cut into fringes: coloured paper, fashioned into oblong hoops, strung into garlands that we had glued together sitting round the kitchen table. A sprig of mistletoe hanging above the door.

Finally, quiet as the meal was served and we thanked the Lord for the food before us. Words of caution before eating the Christmas pudding that concealed little lucky, silver thrupenny bits that we all hoped to find hidden in the dark, fruity mixture. Exclamations of delight as crackers snapped revealing tiny gifts inside.

"Quick, turn on the wireless, it's nearly three o' clock!" my mother exclaimed.

Full and contented we sat back and listened to the young Queen's Speech occasionally shushing the boys until it was finished. They played until weariness carried them off to bed and darkness wrapped itself round the village.

JODPHURS AND STIRRUP CUPS

Nana Smith sat disdainfully sipping a cup of tea beside a roaring coal fire that shot bright red and orange flames dancing up the chimney. From the kitchen women's laughter, mingled with the clink of cups and saucers, drifted into the living room. An air of anticipation hung over the men as they stood clutching their glasses of sherry. Across the road their horses nibbled at patches of sparse, winter grass at the side of the stream; revealed through a light, overnight dusting of snow as they trampled the ground. Sensing the thrill of the chase they shook their manes blowing clouds of steam from their nostrils.

Boxing Day and, as usual, Dad Smith, Emrys and his boyhood friend were riding with the Ystrad Hunt that had been reformed after the Second World War. Resplendent in jodhpurs, wings sticking out below their black coats above their gleaming, riding boots. Velvet hats thrown carelessly onto the sideboard; Dad Smith slapping his riding crop against his leg; Emrys impatient and anxious to be away. Both men short, stocky, but solidly built; my grandfather's blue eyes twinkling in his handsome Celtic-Roman face. Nana Smith shot a disapproving glance at the group.

"I dwn't know why you're going in this weather Harry, especially now it's been snowing."

"That'll be gone in a couple of hours, anyway it's only a bit of a dusting Beatrice. Right then, let's be off," he replied as he sauntered out calling endearments to the horses who raised their heads in acknowledgement.

"Yew can tell he's spent his life on a horse," Nancy, Emrys' wife, giggled as Dad Smith crossed the road in his usual, bandy-legged gait and took his horse's reins.

"Whoa there my beauty!" he said as he mounted.

The horses picked their way down the bank and clattered onto the main road. We watched as they trotted down the tarmac rising and falling in the saddle; the horses swishing their tails and champing at the bit in their eagerness to expel energy.

"Have a good day!" we shouted after them.

"Be careful," Nana Smith called as they rounded the bend and disappeared from sight, "and dwn't be too late back in this weather."

The women reminisced on Christmas' past while the men followed the baying hounds across the snowy hills invigorated by hot toddies. Warmed by a glass of sherry the women chattered and laughed while the children played contentedly with their Christmas toys, except Roger who sulked around my mother complaining,

"I wanted to go; why couldn't I go with them?"

"Because you're too young yet," she replied.

"I can ride as good as they can," he pouted. "I've been in a Gymkhana haven't I?"

"I dwn't care, anyway it's too dangerous," she retorted.

"Well, can I go next year then?"

"Well, maybe," she said half-heartedly fearfully visualising him riding at break-neck speed over the Welsh hillsides.

Mollified, he joined the other children who were sitting on the floor playing snakes and ladders.

"Time for something to eat," my mother declared as she set about creating an enormous 'fry-up' from the remnants of Christmas Day vegetables and potatoes.

Cold chicken, pork and beef garnished with pickled onions, beetroot, red cabbage and bright, yellow Piccalilli.

"Yew've done enough to feed an army," Nancy remarked as she tucked into the succulent meats.

"Anybody for Christmas pudding?" my mother asked as Nana Smith sat back looking as if she couldn't tackle another morsel.

"Oh, not for me, I'm too full as it is."

"I'll have some mam," Michael said.

"And me, and me," chorused the others.

Sated, they gathered round the fire to gossip laughing

uproariously, or giggling mischievously, hands held to mouths and eyes wide at some particularly juicy titbit.

As the day wore on chocolates, nuts and dates appeared. Nana Smith brought out her favourite; a round, wooden box of pink and white Turkish Delight covered with icing sugar. She speared a square of pink with a little wooden fork and delicately inserted it into her mouth.

"Mmm, I love these," she sighed.

"Me too nana; I could eat them all day," I declared munching the glutinous concoction.

As I reached over for another piece my hand slipped knocking the box out of her hands into the air. A flurry of white, icing sugar rose in a cloud and hovered momentarily. In slow motion it descended in a fine mist over her clothes and hands leaving a dusting of white powder on her nose and the arms of the chair. The remainder of the '*Turkish Delight*' sat in her lap in a mess of icing sugar.

"Now look what's happened!" she exclaimed. "I can't eat those now."

"We'll eat 'em for yew nanny," the boys shouted as they dived at her lap.

In seconds all that was left was a lapful of powder and two grinning, white-powdered faces.

As dusk fell the horsemen returned, tired and happy, smelling of whisky, horses and dogs. The table was laden with cold meats, salmon sandwiches made with Shir Gar Welsh butter, cheese, pickles, red cabbage, beetroot, little sausage rolls, mince pies and sherry trifle. In the centre a home-made Christmas cake decorated with a Santa, little houses, reindeer and a tiny Christmas tree set in icing drifts of snow; all wrapped in a red, green and gold cake frill. Under the tree children squabbled over chocolate novelties and pulled the last of the crackers their faces illuminated by twinkling fairy lights.

Appetites satisfied the talking went on until late evening when the singing began. All had fine voices and sang their favourite songs, except Emrys, who never joined in the singing.

"Come on Dodo sing, 'O Mio Babbino Caro," cried Donald after his renditions of 'La Donna Mobile' and a duet of Mario Lanza's, 'Because your Mine.'

Solo renditions were followed by Christmas carols and Welsh hymns with my mother's soprano and Donald's tenor voices taking the lead in 'Calon Lan' and 'David of the White Rock.' As evening cast her final shadows and night wrapped her cloak of darkness round the village Donald sang, 'The Lord's Prayer'. Finally, all fell quiet engrossed in their own memories until, reluctantly, they said their goodbyes and hurried through the darkness to their homes.

Above the divine spirit had flung a handful of stars into the heavens and scattered them across the firmament shining brilliantly like diamonds set in smooth, blue-black velvet; their brightness increased by the clarity of the frosty, night air. Below the street lamps glowed yellow. Christmas trees twinkled with coloured, fairy lights and windows glowed golden into the gloom of the night. Humans beings wrapped in a transient, protective cloak of happiness free from the daily grind of life.

On New Year's Eve the family gathered again to herald the coming year. At midnight the bells of St. Donat's rang out loud and clear across the village with their message of goodwill. The owner of the Thorn Hotel brought out a tray of drinks for people in the surrounding houses to herald the beginning of a new year.

"Happy New Year!" they toasted each other while they listened to the joyous peal of the bells.

A knock on the door brought a neighbour carrying a small lump of coal wanting to be 'first foot'. Some older children ran from door to door calling out,

"Happy New Year!" taking the proffered fruit, sweets or money handed to them.

"Duw, duw! It's those Jenkins' from right up past the woods. Disgraceful! Where are their parents letting them all the way down here and this time of night too," remarked our next door neighbour as she answered the door. "Yew'd think they'd be in bed by now."

"Dwn't worry, they'll be the first down the 'Top Club' in the mornin'," observed her daughter.

On New Year's morning the 'Top Club' opened to dispense gifts to the children of members, most of whom were miners. Each child moved shyly forward to accept a piece of fruit and a sixpence. Fathers, facing the prospect of a long shift underground the next day, stayed for a pint of beer. Mothers hurried home to prepare the first meal of the New Year. Other Christmas's to come; another year to laugh, to weep, to worry and wonder about the future.

WINE-COLOURED WINGS

Christmas and New Year had come and gone in a flurry of activity before dissipating into the chill of winter. Pleading with my eyes, without saying a word, she knew and understood what I wanted when my birthday loomed in February, but to no avail. Looking away slightly discomforted my mother rebuked,

"Dwn't look at me like that: you're not having a bike and that's that! I'd have a heart attack every time yew took it out!"

Having a bicycle of my own was a futile dream since my mother was firmly set against the idea. The results of the scholarship had left me in a state of anticipation dreaming excitedly about this prize as the accolade for passing. Once again my hopes had been dashed when she produced a beautiful gold-plated watch complete with matching bracelet. Marking my achievement with such an expensive gift filled me with pride, but I still hankered after that elusive machine – a bicycle.

Flushed with annoyance and frustration I whinged,

"I'm good at riding a bike, yew know that."

"No, that's my last word on it and that's all there is to it!" she declared emphatically.

"But I'm sensible. I wouldn't do anything stupid now would I? Please, please!" I nagged.

Desperately trying to smother a snigger she reminded me,

"Oh yes, and what about when Mrs Pierce saw yew trying to cross the river down the park on that pipe when yew had been categorically told not to go near the river?"

About a week before one of her cronies had caught me doing a tight-rope walking act on a pipe spanning the River Cynon when I should have been having tea with a school friend. Malice, rather than

198

concern for my safety, found her gleefully reporting it to my mother who was always broadcasting how well-behaved and quiet I was. Her own children were spiteful and ill-mannered; a constant source of irritation to her and gossip for the neighbours, so she revelled in the opportunity to criticise any other child which obviously afforded her some comfort for the inadequacies of her own.

"No!" she said firmly, "Yew heard what I said, no bike!"

Bitterly disappointed I slouched over the road to look for sympathy from my grandparents hoping that I could persuade them to let me borrow Terry's bike.

Terry had a magnificent wine-coloured racing cycle complete with speed gears and drop handlebars. I coveted this machine and spent hours fantasising about racing down roads deserted of cars, alone and free to travel where I pleased, without restriction. The hum of wheels on tarmac; the rush of the wind as I hurtled forward towards an ever-receding horizon that glowed and beckoned to me to learn its undiscovered secrets as my mind reached out longingly to take the silver path of my dreams; soaring up into the brilliant, azure sky like Icarus with wine-coloured wings.

Being the eldest grandchild and very close to my grandparents I usually got what I wanted, but a whole summer and autumn of nagging and begging had proved futile. Still, it was worth another try.

"I can't have a bike," I told Nana Smith despondently. "It's not fair. All my friends have got bikes, haven't they?"

"Well, yew know your mother is nervous about yew on the roads, especially since Roger's accident," Dad Smith said curtly.

"I know that, but I could ride Terry's bike down the back lane. He lets me have a go sometimes."

"Well, I dwn't know about that. Yew know how fussy he is about his bike; doesn't like anyone touching it."

"Please, I'll be really, really careful," I wheedled noting a softening in his attitude.

"Hm! Well as long as yew promise to stay in the lane and not go near the main road. I hope yew are listening to me my girl!" he shouted after me as I headed for the door.

"Yes, I promise!"

Muttering and protesting about safety regulations and assurances from me of extreme care I watched with bated breath as the beautiful machine was wheeled into the lane at the rear of the house. An hour later, flushed with pleasure, I dutifully took the bike back assuring my grandparents that if I was allowed to take it out on future occasions I would obey them implicitly.

After the initial excitement of the first few rides wore off boredom set in as I rode in a dignified manner up and down the lane; up and down the lane. In the ensuing weeks my will power gradually waned. Even the thought of retribution from Nana and Dad Smith could not stem the tide of frustration that swept over me every time the lane cut across an opening in the houses and the road came into view. My friends, riding happily along the highway, laughingly jeered at my predicament.

"Look at 'er ridin' down the lane. Come on mun, come for a ride up the Quarter Mile!"

"I'm not allowed to, I promised!" I shouted back feeling more and more foolish.

"Cowardy, cowardy custard. Aw, what a drip. Come on boys, let's go!" they laughed as they raced up the road.

Resentment and humiliation stung every fibre of my being until one day I could no longer stand the taunts. The temptation for greater speed, on a smooth surface, was too much to bear and I hesitantly rode the bike down the lane and onto the main thoroughfare. Dropping forward to gather speed in order to catch up with my friends a loud voice suddenly boomed,

"Gerroff my bike yew nitwit! Do yew want to get killed?"

Startled, I braked violently before screeching to a shuddering halt almost falling sideways into the gutter as I heard the familiar voice. Terry was running down the road with a menacing look on his face, steaming with indignation; black hair, that was usually sculpted into a fashionable quiff, flopping like a spaniel's ears; eyes flashing with anger, chest thrust forward and puffed with importance ready for the ensuing onslaught.

Dropping the cycle with a loud clatter that enraged him even more I yelled, "Catch me if you can pimples!" and bolted at high speed to find refuge with Nana and Dad Smith. Triumphantly, I realised the barb had pierced his Achilles heel. Prone to teenage acne he was excessively sensitive about his condition having reached an age when girls were becoming increasingly important in his life. Dad Smith suddenly appeared in the doorway as Terry hauled the cycle up the steps into the front garden.

"She's been riding my bike on the road," he seethed.

Dad Smith glared at me,

"I'm disappointed in yew, very disappointed. Yew promised yew wouldn't go on the road and now look what yew've done. Look at me when I speak to yew!" he said angrily.

I couldn't look at him because I was so deeply ashamed; ashamed that I had betrayed his trust. Snivelling, I slunk into the kitchen hoping Nana Smith would sympathise, but she was not impressed.

"Serves your right! Yew should have listened in the first place shouldn't yew?"

Head bowed I vowed never to break a promise to them again.

Still, I felt a sneaking sense of satisfaction that I had wounded Terry's pride. As the baby in the family he often resented the attention I received from my grandparents and sometimes seethed with ill-concealed, boyish jealousy. More akin to an older brother his attitude fluctuated from protective to sibling rivalry. My mother's youngest brother, seventeen years her junior, spoiled and cosseted until I came along and ruined it for him.

On long, winter evenings we sat in front of a roaring coal fire. Terry taught me how to make tanks out of cotton reels, rubber bands and pieces of candle. At other times we placed pictures underneath sheets of bevelled glass, traced the outline then painted the surrounds with black, lacquer paint.

"It doesn't look much good like that, does it?" I complained looking at the clear space in the glass.

"Ah, but wait until yew stick on the bits of foil. It might look messy on the back but from the front it'll be great. See this bit of red with gold dots on it. That'll make a perfect skirt, then we can put some of the blue for her pinny."

"Oh, yes, it's so pretty," I enthused as the picture took shape.

Patterned, silver, gold and multi-coloured sweet wrappings served as pretty dresses and tunics for the figures frozen in glass. Little squares of foil were carefully smoothed until every wrinkle disappeared, honed with a half-crown, or two-shilling piece, until it spread to twice its size to clothe a smiling peasant girl and wrap the contents of her basket.

THE BUCKING MULE

After the incident with the bicycle we came to an amicable agreement. Terry would allow me to ride his other 'bike', but only if I swore a pact which would relegate me to the fire and flames of Hell if I breathed a word to either my grandparents or my mother. I realised his desire for secrecy when I saw the cycle. It was an ancient, mangled wreck without tyres and bare, rust-covered hubs; no chain so it was impossible to pedal.

"How can I ride *that* thing?" I cried. "The handlebars are all wonky!"

"Dwn't worry, yew just have to turn them to the side and it'll work perfectly, see!" Terry exclaimed jumping onto the rickety machine. Leaning to one side he lurched down the lane with the handlebars in a very dangerous position.

They had been knocked out of alignment so in order to move the machine in a straight line they needed to be kept at a perilous angle. The narrow, leather seat, at least what was left of it, was just as hazardous.

"Ouch, that hurt!" I groaned as the seat moved up and down like a bucking mule when I mounted the bike.

There was also a complete absence of any form of braking system.

"The brakes dwn't work mind yew so yew'll have to drag your feet to stop. But be careful now. We dwn't want any accidents do we?" Terry instructed solicitously.

But I didn't care, it was a bike wasn't it! Warming to Terry I basked in the glow of his generosity.

Carefully, I trundled the machine down the back lane behind my grandparents house on to the top of a small rise. Heaving my leg over the crossbar I raised myself onto the seat, adjusted the mangled handlebars, rammed my feet to the ground with as much strength as I could muster, then pushed my legs backwards as vigorously as possible. The effort sent me careering down the slope at considerable speed. The only means of stopping was to hurtle the full length of the lane and shoot up the gradient at the other end.

Steep steps dropped from the path to the back doors of the houses. Without warning, old Mrs Evans stepped through her back door and climbed the steps into the lane,

"What's goin' on 'ere then?" she demanded hands on hips.

"Whoa! Look out, look out, I can't stop!"

"Yew little idiot!" she screeched as she saw me advancing towards her.

For a split second she stood mouth open, eyes wide and startled as I raced down the path.

"I'm surprised at yew behavin' like a lunatic," she remonstrated. "Yewer mother is goin' to 'ear about this, my girl, yew mark my words," she flung at me as she made for the safety of the steps.

Suddenly, her fulsome figure leapt back inside as swiftly as her arthritic limbs and age would allow, simultaneously throwing insults about lunacy and doubtful intelligence as, flushed and wild-eyed with excitement, I came hurtling down the path.

"I've got to practise stopping," I thought wobbling dangerously," because if I dwn't I'll fall off."

I continued down the lane 'braking' with my feet until I felt confident that I could control the bike quite easily stopping before I reached the slope that led to the stream.

It was February, very cold; a hoary frost glistened on the pebbles in the lane radiating silver sparks of white light from the hard, black earth like diamonds set in the coal seams far beneath in the bowels of the valley. The stream was almost overflowing its banks due to recent heavy rainfall. Freezing weather had left patches of frost that clung to the damp grass at the edges of the water. Along the lane silver threads of frost decorated the lifeless foliage giving them a fresh beauty. Sheer excitement, the rarefied atmosphere and pure pleasure of riding my new bike filled me elation.

With my red bobble hat pulled well down over my ears I clanked up and down the lane. The bobble swung furiously from side to side as I careered along oblivious to the fate that awaited me.

"This is easy," I thought smugly.

"A few more 'tries' and I'll be able to ride with my eyes closed."

Suddenly, a voice called from further up the lane,

"Yew'd better come in now, quick!" Terry called urgently. "Mrs Evans said she's going to tell Dad Smith about yew!"

"Aw cripes, I'm a dead duck now! I'll have one more ride, just a little one, then I'll come in."

Dogged by the thought that this was going to be my one and only cycling excursion on Terry's bike, I determined to ride the full length of the lane until I reached the slope at the opposite end.

My downfall was imminent. This way the path narrowed dangerously by the stone-cutter's, turned sharply downwards and led directly onto the main highway. Opposite this sharp bend the stream cascaded down from the mountain to be swallowed up in a culvert that ran under the main road.

Approaching the first gradient I hesitated momentarily at the crest to get my bearings, turned the handlebars to the required angle and shot off the top of the rise. The momentum of the machine increased with every dip in the lane until I could barely control it.

"Terry, I can't stop! Whoa! Whoa!" I shrieked forgetting it was a bike and not a horse.

Realising my predicament I tried to stop by dragging my feet along the ground. Too late! Due to the hazardous 'design' of the cycle I turned the handlebars the wrong way attempting to avoid the main road. I did. The bike shot headlong over the rough road. Suddenly, the front wheel hit a large stone bringing the machine to a jolting halt.

"Argh! Mammy! Mammy!" I screamed in terror as the bike started to nose-dive.

The back wheel reared into the air, suspended perilously for a few breath-catching seconds, before I shot head first over the rusty handlebars landing in the stream with a loud splash and a blood-curdling shriek.

Shivering in the freezing water, tears of frustration, anger, pain and humiliation welling in my eyes, I struggled to dislocate myself from the rusty metal, but I was weighed down by my heavy, winter clothes. As I hauled myself up my foot caught in the spokes of the bike throwing me off-balance and back into the brook. I kicked savagely at the wheels,

"You're going to pay for this Ter', just yew wait and see," I seethed through chattering teeth. "I bet I'll have pneumonia or something. If I die 'cause of this, it'll be your fault," but there was no-one to hear my complaints.

Fortunately, the volume of water had broken my fall preventing me from sustaining serious injury. Some of the sharper stones had dug into my ribs and knees. Pulling myself up miserably, wellies full of water, I squelched towards my mother who had appeared at the front door on hearing my screams. Hand fluttering over her mouth she stood frozen in horror at this abject sight advancing towards her.

"I fell off Terry's bike; it was his fault!" I grizzled.

"What have yew been told about going on his bike?" she admonished.

"It wasn't that one. I promised I wouldn't go on that one again didn't I? It was his other one."

"What other one?"

"The one he keeps in the back garden; the rusty one without brakes."

"Without brakes! Wait 'till I get my hands on him!"

"He did it on purpose to make me look stupid! Wait 'till I tell nana and dad about him. He'll cop it now!" I grizzled as my mother charged over the road to confront Terry.

My much-loved ramshackle bike was smashed to pieces with an old axe ready to be carted away by the rag and bone man when he came on his annual summer rounds. I hated the rag and bone man!

A GOOD INNINGS

Days later I was taken ill in John Evans' shop at the top of West Street. As usual I had trailed along behind Nana Smith to help her choose her groceries. Standing nonchalantly in the middle of the store, taking note of the tins of biscuits and sacks of potatoes, my eyes lighted upon a side of streaky bacon on the counter alongside huge slabs of cheese and bright, yellow butter. Just as the assistant cut through the butter and slapped it on to a piece of greaseproof paper the room began to swim before my eyes. Mountains of butter, tins of vegetables and glass jars swirled around the room. From a distance I could hear someone saying urgently,

"What's the matter with yewer grand-daughter Mrs Smith? She's gone a funny colour, 'aven't she?"

My head felt like cotton wool as I started to sway from side to side. Overcome by nausea I desperately tried to stay upright. Through the babble of disconnected voices, that ebbed and flowed like a distant signal from space, I heard Nana Smith say anxiously,

"What's the matter? Are yew all right?"

Nana Smith had her arms around me trying to prevent me from falling down, but I was already much taller than her diminutive figure. Suddenly, Evans the Shop shouted,

"She's going! Look out!"

With that I gave a mighty heave and vomited all over the scrubbed, wooden floor. Feeling myself falling slowly, uncontrollably, as though I were in the middle of a dream; I felt the coarse wooden floorboards as they came up to meet me.

In the background I could hear people talking and Nana Smith urging me to be still whilst apologising to the manager and the customers.

"I'm very sorry Mr. Evans. It's not like her to be sick like that. It was so sudden. She hasn't even been ill. I'll take her home then I'll come back and clean up the mess," she said anxiously.

"Now dwn't yew worry Mrs Smith. It couldn't be helped now, could it? Yew just go off home and I'll see to everything. These things happen yew know."

"Thank yew Mr. Evans. It's very good of yew."

Woozily, I watched as sawdust was thrown over the contents of my stomach which made me feel sick again.

"It's a bit of a mess innit?" Mrs Jones added heading for the door. "I'll come back later when yew've cleaned up. Bit of a weak stomach see."

"Dwn't try to take 'er on your own now. Grab 'er under one arm and I'll take the other one," urged Mrs Moses, one of the neighbours.

Eventually, I managed to stay upright long enough for Nana Smith and Mrs Moses to walk me the two hundred yards to my home.

"Oh, my God, what's wrong?" my mother fretted eyelashes fluttering with anxiety.

"She's been sick in Evans' the Shop, all over the floor. Gushed out like a waterfall it did. I was worried to death."

"Lie on the sofa 'till yew feel a bit better then we'll get yew undressed and up to bed before the doctor comes," my mother instructed.

"Yes, it's best to get the doctor straight away."

When Dr. Nora arrived she took one look at me and my eyeballs and declared,

"Jaundice, keep her in bed for a week and make sure she takes this medicine," she instructed thrusting a prescription slip at my mother.

"She fell in the stream last week, got soaking wet to the skin. That's what's did it, I expect," offered my mother.

Dr. Nora laughed,

"Nonsense, now yew know that! And what were yew doing falling in the stream then?"

"Fell off my bike," I whispered feeling nausea rising again.

"She was told not go on the bike, but she wouldn't listen would she?" my mother added quickly looking as though everything was her fault.

"Dwn't worry, she'll be right as rain in a couple of weeks," Dr. Nora shot back as she exited the front door.

"Hmph!" Nana Smith remonstrated. "Perhaps yew'll listen in future, my girl."

Nothing I said could convince my mother or my grandparents that my 'yellow jaundice' had absolutely no connection with my untimely plunge into the icy waters of the stream.

I lay in bed convinced that I was going to die. I wondered what it would be like. Would all the family gather round my bed and sob into their handkerchiefs, or would I die while I was alone in the room?

"I dwn't want to be on my own up here," I moaned at my mother as she went downstairs to check on her cooking.

"I won't be two minutes now and I'll be back. Cwtch up, close your eyes and lie quietly for a bit."

Feeling sick and feverish, head full of cotton wool, I drifted in and out of sleep.

My mother came into the room, an anguished scream of horror pouring from her lips as she found me stone cold. Crying hysterically she ran out of the house and screamed across the road to Tommy the Fruit who was on his daily rounds

"Tommy come quick, I think she's dead!" she screamed wringing her hands in anguish.

Through a swirling mist he ran into my bedroom and bent over me to touch my forehead recoiling at the sight of my wide-open eyes. In a cold sweat I awoke from my nightmare arms and legs thrashing feverishly at the blankets but very much alive.

Still, I was frightened and depressed. Outside the wind howled. It rattled the sash windows, lifted the lids of the dustbins and moaned and sighed through the grey-slated rooftops. The skies were black and ponderous and the rain lashed the window-panes like a frenzied poltergeist that had been banished from the house by exorcism, but was making one final attempt to gain a foothold.

"Perhaps it's the 'Grim Reaper' I read about in that horror

comic," I shuddered. After smuggling it into the house I had read it by torchlight, underneath the blankets, in case I was caught red-handed. Had he decided it was time to fetch me for my journey through the infinite blackness of oblivion.

Whispered conversations floated up the stairs as I strained my ears to catch a phrase or a word; anything that could be remotely connected with me. I heard someone say,

"Yes, she's at rock-bottom; not an ounce of strength left in her body. It won't be long now."

Fear broke out in an icy sweat over my whole body. Heart racing, blood pounding in my ears, I waited for the next grim instalment in the saga, my breath escaping in short, sharp gasps until I heard the words of reprieve floating up the stairs.

"Poor old soul! Still she's had a good innings; must be all of eighty-five I should think."

"Thank God, they're not talking about me," I reflected as I sank back into the pillows.

Mentally, I counted the number of years I had left if I lived to be eighty-five and broke out in fresh horror as I acknowledged, for the first time, the inevitability of death.

For two weeks I had lain in bed, face ashen and eyeballs pale, sickly yellow. Dr. Nora had told my mother to keep me in bed until she, or somebody else, visited again to check on my progress.

On her next visit she took one look at my ghastly complexion before promptly instructing my mother to keep me on a fat-free diet.

"She shouldn't be eating anything with fat in it. It'll just make her feel sick. I'll give yew a list of foods she can eat."

Naked panic sprang into her eyes as she listened to her instructions with an excitable, worried expression convinced that she may have caused me some irreparable damage.

Dr. Nora patted her arm reassuringly,

"No need to worry. She'll soon be better and out and about in no time at all."

Turning to me she said firmly,

"And yew should be up on your feet by now my girl getting some fresh air."

After endless assurances that she was in no way to blame Dr. Nora asked her to pick up a diet sheet from the surgery consisting of low-fat foods. Immediately, Nana Smith took charge giving orders about suitable foods, the efficacy of isinglass and the necessity for a 'good clearing out' with a large dose of syrup of figs.

They fussed and clucked all that day until the diet sheet was finally produced. Unfortunately, they had already spent a small fortune buying the most expensive foods on the market in an effort to build me up. None of them had helped; they had made my condition regress. Now I was forced to drink tea without milk and soups made from vegetables only: in short I was not allowed fats of any kind.

"It's like eating dry lino," I complained as I chewed on a piece of unbuttered toast. "Can't I have just a thin coating of Shir Gar on it?"

"Yew heard what the doctor said, didn't yew?" Nana Smith retorted in a firm voice.

Vehement protestations at this barbaric treatment of my sensitive taste-buds brought little relief. I was inevitably greeted with the same chorus.

"Eat it, it'll do yew good!"

Sometimes Dad Smith came over to sit with me and told me stories from his youth when he lived in the Old Duke, a coaching inn that had been converted into a large house. Tales with moralistic endings were his favourite.

"My mother, your great-grandmother, was very strict. 1914 it was, just before I went into the war. After I learned to drive she sometimes let us borrow her car to drive around Pontypridd on a Sunday morning."

For a few moments he stared sightlessly through the window lost in pleasant memories.

"It was lovely; a big open-topped car. Richard (uncle Dickie) and Aaron, my brothers, used to sit up on the back seat waving like royalty as we drove past people. We thought we were *very* grand, but when she found out she took the car off us to teach us a lesson. The following Sunday we had to go into town with the horse and trap instead; 'That'll teach yew to show off,'" she said.

Satisfied that I had understood his message about 'pride coming before a fall' he urged,

"Now girl, don't fret and fuss. Yew must do what your mother and your Nana tell yew. It's for your own good. Listen to the doctor; she knows what she's talking about yew know."

Dr. Battram, and the young David Anthony, had a surgery in the front room of a house in Walter's Street while a new doctor had joined Dr. Nora's practice in rooms behind her home in Edward's Street. The side of the surgery was situated on the steep slope of Ynysmeirig Road affectionately known as Doctors' Hill because a surgery had been there for decades; the name has persisted to this day. Dr. Nora's father had originally run the practice along with her husband, but both had passed away years before leaving her to cope with a huge patient list.

To reach the waiting room one had to walk up the path at the side of her house to be greeted by a stark room painted in institutional cream, green and brown. A visit to the surgery could take up most of the evening as there was no appointments' system, but everyone would be seen even if the doctors had to stay there all night. After I had recovered from jaundice I made the dreaded visit to the doctor's for a check-up knowing that it would be a long evening.

"Packed tonight 'buttie' innit?" Islwyn Harris, commented as he walked into the crowded waiting room. Islwyn proudly sported the uniform of Great Western Railways.

"Aye, we're 'ere for the duration tonight mun," replied Gethin Bowen, a wizened, elderly miner who had worked at the colliery face since he was a boy.

"Well, I've blown my last whistle this week. Off now 'till Monday. Oi, we could be still 'ere by then," he laughed.

"Aye, right enough mind," Gethin countered with a phlegmy cough that turned my stomach. "I'm sick of bloody waitin' mun. I've been 'ere over an hour already. I'll take bloody root in a minute!"

Everybody laughed except the women with children who looked disapprovingly at Gethin.

"Tut, tut, mind yewer language in front of the children," Mrs Craddock said indignantly.

"Sorry missus, forgot myself for a minute then mun."

She gathered her arms up under her bosom ready for the final word,

"Well, all right then and yew can stop laughing too Rhys," she remonstrated with her son.

Silence followed except for the occasional sniff, cough or the restless fidgeting of children.

Patients sat huddled against the walls of the cramped room and whiled away the hours exchanging symptoms, praising or complaining about the doctors or just simply having a laugh. In such confined quarters it was impossible not to eavesdrop on their conversations.

"Terrible backache I've 'ad mun, ever since I carried that wardrobe upstairs for the missus," complained a weedy-looking man who looked totally incapable of lifting a teacup let alone a wardrobe.

Mrs Craddock leaned over conspiratorially to Mrs Morris her arms still folded and whispered,

"She's 'ad everything taken away, very sudden like."

"*Everything*?" Mrs Morris queried in a shocked voice.

"*Everything*; she told me 'erself, didn't she?" she said importantly drawing her bosom up even higher.

"Awful mind, innit, a young woman like that still in 'er prime?"

"Aye and that bug....beggar she's married to's got a lot to answer for as well," reproved Mrs Craddock almost forgetting her criticism of old Gethin. "Now there's another a story for yew," she intimated as I passed her to go in to see the doctor.

Always known as Dr. Nora she was short with the leathery complexion symptomatic of a heavy smoker, a brusque manner and heart of gold. Her first words if I coughed were always,

"Yew haven't taken up smoking have yew?" accompanied by a penetrating gaze.

"No, Dr. Nora!"

"Well, dwn't because it's very bad for yew."

"She wouldn't smoke, *would yew*?" my mother said smugly.

"Spread your hands out and let's have a look at your fingers."

After examining my hands for nicotine stains, without finding any incriminating evidence, she turned back to the papers on her desk.

"Hmph! Well, remember what I said, it's bad for yew!" she emphasised with a deep, racking cough.

As she talked the cigarette in her mouth bobbed up and down while the ash trembled precariously, threatening to drop if she waggled it too strenuously. It was a constant source of fascination to me that she could retain a greater length of ash than cigarette. During consultations it was quite normal to see her puffing away surrounded by a blue haze of smoke.

The surgery was the vital centre of the community and part of the social fabric of Abercynon. Unlike today, Dr. Nora knew all the families and called most of them by their first names, because she had known them since birth. Patients felt a certain sense of continuity knowing that their doctor had always been part of village life and knew generations of their relations. All the doctors lived in Abercynon, including the new arrival, which was a welcome relief for Dr. Nora and her patients.

"There's a new locum starting in the surgery, so I'm told," Aurona May related.

"Yes, so I've heard. Where's he from then?" my mother queried.

"Dwn't know, nobody seems to know but there's a lot of rumours goin' round about 'im."

"What kind of rumours, Aurona?"

"They reckon he's separated from his wife and 'e used to drink as well."

"Drinks?"

"Yes, but he's supposed to be reformed; doesn't drink anymore, at least so they say."

"Dwn't like the sound of that, do yew?"

"Well, per'aps it's not true. Yew know what people are like."

"Who told yew he drinks?"

"Maisie Jenkins, yew know Maisie Brooks that was."

"Oh, *now* I know who yew mean, Maisie Mouth. Yew can't

believe a *word* she says. I'd take it all with a pinch of salt if I were yew Aurona."

"Anyway, the surgery'll be packed next week just to 'ave a look at 'im," she laughed.

Like most rumours in the village it had been embroidered and re-embroidered as it passed from one to another until it bore little resemblance to the truth. The gossip proved to be grossly inaccurate. Everybody loved the paternal new locum and wouldn't have a word said about him. Silver-grey hair, twinkling blue eyes, kind and homely; a real old-fashioned family doctor who took time to listen and rarely rushed a consultation even if there was a crowd in the waiting room. He did not own a car and often had a lift to his house calls from Dr. Nora. If he was too long inside she honked her horn impatiently until he appeared.

"I'd better get along or she'll keep on tooting away," he'd laugh congenially looking longingly at the hissing kettle.

Another blast of the horn from outside saw him dashing for the door exclaiming,

"Good grief woman, I'm *coming!*"

Sometimes, if he was waiting to be picked up, he would have a cup of tea and chat about his children.

Apparently, when his son was around nine years old he caught him smoking a cigarette and decided to teach him a lesson. He related how he had given his son a very large cigar remarking casually,

"Well son if you're a man now we might as well share a smoke."

"Thanks dad." the lad rejoined looking decidedly uncomfortable with this unexpected approach.

Carefully, he lit the cigar for him and they sat opposite each other, having a man to man talk, while his son puffed at the cigar with apparent enjoyment.Disappointed he thought,

"This isn't going to work."

When the boy had smoked a third of the cigar he produced a bottle of whisky.

"Well, as we're having such a good time we might as well have a drink. Just a small one though."

He smiled as he poured a tot of the amber fluid into a glass and handed it to his son. As he watched the boy gradually began to look uncomfortable but continued to puff on the cigar and sip at the spirit.

For a few moments he thought his plan had misfired and regretted his actions. Suddenly, his son got up, very slowly, still with the cigar in his mouth. His father caught him just as he staggered to the bathroom to be violently sick.

"Never touched tobacco again," he remarked looking at me with a mischievous glint in his eyes indicating that this should be a lesson for me should I ever attempt to smoke. We never discovered whether his stories were true but they always had a moralistic ending. Like Dad Smith, he loved telling tales that contained a moral lesson for his young patients. His sojourn in Abercynon was brief but memorable. We were all sad, especially the children, when he announced that he was moving to another part of the country.

DWN'T CALL ME DARLING!

Fully recovered from jaundice my mother took me to the 'pictures' in the Workman's Hall to see Desi Anarz and Lucille Ball in, '*The Long, Long Trailer*': a story about a long-suffering man and his empty-headed, red-haired wife who get into all kinds of predicaments as they tour America with their caravan. After putting the boys to bed my mother instructed my stepfather,

"Dwn't forget to check on them regularly, especially Roger. Yew know what he's like if he thinks I've gone out."

In the gathering dusk the scent of spring lingered on damp air as we walked the couple of hundred yards to the cinema at the end of our road chatting to people on the way. With the cinema so close, full of neighbours from surrounding streets, it was like watching a private showing of the film with a crowd of friends.

"It's only just gone seven so we should make 'second house,'" my mother said. "With any luck the 'short' won't have started yet."

Roger had suffered a fractured skull, the result of an accident caused by his adventurous nature, when he was around three years old. The slightest grimace of discomfort brought my mother to a standstill to cuddle and cosset him for hours on end. Wherever she went she took him with her. At home he sat on her lap, arms around her neck, with a pleading look on his face. By now, skilled at getting his own way, he would say in a pitiful voice,

"Yew'll have to take *me* with yew 'cause I might have an accident." a remark that brought naked panic into my mother's eyes.

In the ensuing years she fretted constantly issuing strict instructions about bed-times and checking on him regularly if we went out for the evening.

"Right then," she called to me, "if we hurry up we'll be there just before the start."

We hurried off past Doctor's Hill towards the cinema arriving just in time to see the end of the Pathé News which preceded the 'short' film; usually a black and white 'B' rate picture.

"I hope there's room in the 'one and sixes' upstairs," she said hopefully to Vera Bendle who dispensed tickets through the little window of her booth in the foyer.

"No, yew're unlucky tonight, sorry," Vera apologised.

"There's a couple left in the stalls fourth row from the back downstairs," said the usher, a well-known villager, who had appeared at the door behind the booth.

"One and a half then, please," she requested as I made for the door.

Neither of us could sit in the cheap seats at the front, because looking up at the screen made my mother dizzy and gave me a blinding headache.

As the double doors opened and let in the light people in the back rows turned around to see who was coming in while youngsters in the back row, previously engaged in amorous activities, sat bolt upright trying to look engrossed in the film. The usher waved his torch indicating the middle of the row. Everyone got up muttering and hanging on to the contents of their laps; grabbing at sweets, cigarettes, coats and hats.

"I hope the boys aren't playing up," my mother remarked as we settled ourselves comfortably into the plush seats.

"We've only been out about ten minutes!" I exclaimed.

We had been relaxed in our seats for about three-quarters of an hour when I heard a loud hissing sound.

"Shwsh!" said a voice out of the darkness.

"Eisht now will yew?" from another as the hissing continued intermittently.

I nudged my mother but she was engrossed in the film. Looking around for the source of the noise all I could see were the blurred faces of the audience. Glowing cigarettes pierced the darkness of the auditorium through a haze of blue smoke appearing in more rapid sequence as the tension on screen mounted.

"Can't be, I'm imagining it," I thought to myself as I turned around to enjoy the film.

A few minutes passed and I heard the hissing again.

"Psst! Psst!" then "Psst! Psst! Mammy, it's me! I want yew!"

Recognising the voice I groaned to myself realising that he had sneaked out after being put to bed.

"It's Roger, I bet!"

My mother was by now fidgeting and feeling the back of her neck. Turning to me she remarked,

"I must be imagining it, but I could have sworn I heard Roger's voice calling me. P'rhaps we should go home? Maybe there's something wrong? Do yew know the hairs on my neck are standing on end."

Nudging her elbow I pointed to the end of the row where Roger was crouching with his hands up to his face attempting to muffle his voice as he tried to attract her attention. Her hand fluttered to her face and she covered her mouth nervously.

"What's he doing here now?"

She beckoned to him to come and sit in the vacant seat next to me. As he dropped into the seat she hissed at him,

"You're going to get a good smacking when I get yew home." An idle threat because my mother never smacked us. "How did yew get out without your father knowing?"

"I sneaked down the stairs when he was listening to the wireless, mammy."

"Yew *naughty* boy! I can't go out for five minutes without yew following me, *can* I?"

"Sorry mammy," Roger apologised looking contrite.

"Sorry, yew'll be sorry when I get yew home my boy! Come to think of it how did yew get in?"

"Mr Chocs let me in. Yew know Mr. Tommy Chocs, the one who brings round the tray of chocolates to eat when we watch the pictures."

"I hope yew didn't call him Mr. Chocs, that's his nickname!"

After avoiding the eagle eye of Vera in the ticket booth he had sneaked in through a side door knowing that one of the ushers, who were all villagers, would recognise who he was and let him in.

Apologising profusely, as she spotted a neighbour's daughter leaving the seat in front, she edged her way to the end of our row.

"Winifred," she whispered, "will yew call in and tell my husband that Roger is in the 'pictures' with us. Little monkey slipped out, didn't he?"

"Yes all right," Winifred laughed as she made her way up the aisle.

"Yew'd better sit there and be quiet, if yew know what's good for yew," my mother said testily. "I've been waiting to see this film for ages."

For a while he sat dutifully staring at the screen but he soon became restless. Leaning over me he uttered in a half whisper. "Mammy, I want to sit by yew."

"No, stay where yew are or yew'll disturb people again."

"But, I'll be good, promise."

He struggled past my legs and tried to squeeze onto the side of my seat. Exasperated by his insistence I complained,

"Oh, for goodness sake, all right!" changing seats with him.

"Hmph! I'm certainly not 'cwtching' yew now after being so badly behaved," she said as he snuggled up possessively claiming her full attention.

Lily Legge, the ice-cream lady, paraded up and down the centre aisle her face glowing from the light of her illuminated tray. Tantalisingly, glimpses of fruit drinks, lollipops, choc ices, tubs of vanilla ice-cream with little wooden spoons appeared briefly in the darkness. As she came nearer to our row Roger whispered,

"I'd really like an ice-cream, please?"

"No, yew dwn't deserve one after what yew've done," said my mother crossly.

He continued to nag until she gave in and bought him a choc-ice. That kept him occupied until he decided he was thirsty after the ice-cream. Clutching his throat and groaning with feigned dryness he gasped,

"Aw, my throat's dry now. I'm going to choke if I dwn't have a drink."

"Well, yew'll have to choke then, won't yew. Yew've just had an ice-cream. Now shwsh so I can hear the film."

Lilly Legge walked in the direction of our row looking around for potential sales.

"There's the ice-cream lady now mammy. I'm gasping for a drink now to clear my throat. Ple-e-ase mammy? Quick, before she goes!"

"Oh, for goodness sake, here, and try not to disturb people, will yew?" she said handing him a coin.

Roger scrambled past legs and upturned seats and leaned over to purchase a Kia ora orange drink. Much to the annoyance of the audience he squeezed past again, clutching his prize, stepping on a few toes on his way.

"Will yew be quiet with that drink!" my mother hissed as Roger sucked on his straw to get at the last dregs from the bottom of the carton.

Finally, he settled down and eventually, bored with the film, fell asleep hanging on to my mother's arm whilst leaning heavily against her shoulder. She could never stay angry with him for long and he knew it.

"Look at him," she whispered smiling down at his sleeping face.

"He *was* naughty, but he's being good now not like that little monster down there."

Three rows in front of us a stocky boy of about ten, a classmate of Roger's, had been constantly bobbing up and down throughout the film to the annoyance of people around him.

Passing up and down the rows the usher shone his torch furiously on the boy and uttered a loud,

"Eisht now will yew?"

A hand came up, silhouetted against the screen in the darkness, and the boy was hastily yanked into his seat. At the most interesting part of the film he stood up again and declared in a loud voice,

"I want to pee Mam!"

Looking round in embarrassment his mother motioned for him to go out along the row. He pushed and shoved along forcing people to stand up to let him pass. There were cries of,

"Sit down! Mind your 'ead mun, we can't see!"

Muttering unintelligibly he slouched off to the relief of those anxious to continue watching the film.

About ten minutes later he came back in, looked around uncertainly, then walked up and down the aisle for a few minutes looking for his row. Obviously lost he was getting more and more distressed by the minute. Looking around frantically he bawled,

"Mam! Mam! I can't see yew Mam!"

Crying and snivelling loudly he stood in the aisle while the usher shone his torch over the faces of the audience. From one of the rows a disembodied woman's voice, belonging to a pillar of the Congregational Church, exclaimed in an affected, genteel tone,

"Richard, Richard darling, over here!"

The usher guided his torch to the mother who stood up slightly so that he could see her.

Spotting her smiling and beckoning to him he screamed,

"Dwn't call me darlin' yew — yew silly cow!"

As he tried to force his way into the row she grabbed him by the scruff of the neck and pushed him back out.

"Just wait 'till I get yew home and I tell yewer father," she hissed through her teeth forgetting her perfect pronunciation. Complaining loudly about house rules the usher waved his torch frantically muttering,

"Now then! Now then! Let's have some eisht please!"

"Aw, shwsh yewerself yew stupid buggar!" blabbered the boy as his mother dragged him kicking and screaming through the door."

"Well, I never!" said the woman in the row in front. "What kind of language is that for a little boy especially from 'ers with 'er airs and graces? Put yewer 'ands over yewer ears yew," she said to Mary, her teenage daughter. "I'd give 'im a good wallop if 'e belonged to me and no short shrift!"

"Oh!" said my mother looking at Roger sleeping peacefully.

"He may have sneaked out of the house, but it was only to be with me, after all. He's an angel compared to *that* one that just went out."

As usual Roger's hold over my mother was firm and absolute. He had received the expected pardon.

"Well, at least Michael hasn't followed suit," she whispered thankfully, "he'd never sneak out like that."

MYSTERY BOY

The heat hit me as I pushed open the double doors of the Palace Cinema in Margaret Street. Outside the summer sky was still a bright blue as people queued down past Shepherd's fish and chip shop for 'second house'. My mother and I had gone to 'first house' but missed the beginning of the short film so we stayed on to see what we had missed after the main feature; a futile pastime since we already knew the end of the story. We came out onto the street screwing up our eyes against a still brilliant, red sun now established in the west.

"Phew, it's still hot!" I complained fanning my face. "I could do with a cold drink."

I sniffed the air. Even on a warm evening the smell emanating from Shep's next door was too tantalising to ignore. Relishing the thought of his fat, succulent chips we decided to take some home for the boys. We joined the queue that had spilled out onto the pavement to find that Shep had only just put in a batch of chips to fry.

"We'll have to wait *ages* now and we're right at the end of the queue," my mother fretted. It'll be too late for the boys to have any now. They'll be in bed by the time we get back."

Glancing across the road I nudged her elbow.

"Oh no they won't. Look, I wonder where they're off to?"

On the opposite pavement my stepfather was ambling along with the boys in tow.

"Now where on earth is he going with them at this time? Keep our place in the line. I'm going to find out what they're up to."

She darted through the door, caught up with them outside Kitts' greengrocers, held a hurried conversation then rushed up the street to squeeze back into the queue.

"They're going down to Joe the Café for some pop of all things, at this time of night." She sighed with exasperation as the front of the waiting line shuffled forward a few inches nearer the gleaming counter.

After a frustrating wait we watched as Shep filled two large, greaseproof bags with chips, folded them into a sheet of white paper then wrapped them in newspaper to keep them hot.

"At last!" my mother exclaimed looking at her watch. "Look at the time!"

Arriving home, just after eight-thirty, we found my stepfather and the boys still hadn't returned.

"That's odd," said my mother. "I told him to make certain that he went straight home to put the boys to bed as soon as they'd been to Joe's. Wait until he gets in. Honestly, you can't ask him to do anything right."

Just after nine o'clock he returned with Roger, but there was no sign of Michael.

"Where's Mikey?" said my mother using the pet name he hated.

Nobody was allowed to abbreviate his name; only my mother called him Mikey.

"I dwn't know!" said Leonard.

"What do yew mean yew dwn't know? They should have been in bed by now." said my mother querulously.

"As I told yew earlier, it was so warm they couldn't sleep so I took them for a little walk down Joe the Bracchi's to get some pop. He was stragglin' behind me walkin' up past the Palace just a few minutes ago, right where we saw yew queuing for chips. Seconds later I looked back, no sign of Michael: there one minute and gone the next. It all happened in a flash. I've searched everywhere!"

Michael was the youngest, very quiet and the apple of his father's eye. An obedient child, it was completely uncharacteristic of him to wander off.

Glaring at Leonard my mother exclaimed in an anguished tone,

"Well, dwn't just stand there! We'll have to go straight out and look for him! God only knows where he is! What if he's been snatched by somebody?"

We went over to my grandparent's house, but they hadn't seen him so we asked various relatives in the area. They all came out to join in the search but he was nowhere to be seen. Panic-stricken my mother cried,

"What if he's fallen in the river or tried to cross the railway line and been hit by a train? He should have been in his pyjamas ready for bed like I told yew! We'll have to fetch the police!"

"It's only been a few minutes, stop over-reactin' will yew? He can't have gone far. Sooner or later the boy'll come through the door. Probably comin' up Doctor's Hill right now," Leonard said trying to calm her down.

"Well, I'm not taking any chances. I'm going down to the station now *not* sooner or later!"

We made our way down Doctor's Hill towards the shops searching down gullys and doorways without seeing a glimpse of him. The local bobby, already alerted by Dad Smith, met us halfway up Margaret Street.

"Calm down now; he can't 'ave gone far," he soothed eyeing my mother who was crying hysterically. "Besides, he's not a baby, he's a sensible lad. He's been in the primary school a few years now so he walks down past Doctor's Hill every day on his way to school, doesn't he? Dwn't worry now."

"Dwn't worry? Dwn't worry? Look at the time!"

"Oh, but it's not even dark out yet, is it?"

"I dwn't care, he's been missing hours," she wailed greatly exaggerating the length of time.

"About fifteen minutes, I reckon, even less than that," my stepfather interrupted. "He was with me until after nine o' clock."

"He could be lying somewhere injured or ....!"

She couldn't put into words what she was thinking, but fidgeted with her cardigan buttons. Mouth twitching and eyelids blinking furiously, a sure sign that she was near hysteria, she darted towards the front door sensing some movement.

As she flung the door open Michael hurtled through it and ran up the stairs as if pursued by demons, my mother running after him demanding to know where he had been. Obviously scared, he cowered on the bed not saying a word.

"Where've yew been? Are yew hurt?" but he remained silent.

"Has anybody touched yew; hurt yew in any way?"

"What way mammy?"

Well, yew know, in *that* way?"

"No, mammy, honest, honest!" cried Michael looking confused.

"Are yew positive? Tell me!"

"Positive mammy. I just went back down by Ernie James' to look at the bikes in the window."

"On your own! Yew naughty boy, I ought to give yew a good smacking! I've been worried to death! Haven't I told yew never to go anywhere on your own," she wept 'cwtching' him to her.

Curling into a ball he just huddled there with a frightened look on his face, brown eyes liquid with tears. She decided not to question him any further, but to let him have a good night's sleep. The following morning, assured that he had not been harmed in any way, she finally closed the book on the episode with severe warnings about what happened to little boys who wandered off on their own.

Passing the newsagent's the following week, I overheard two elderly women chattering animatedly as they came out.

"Did yew 'ere about that boy who was locked in the Palace Mrs Griffiths? Funny though innit? Nobody seems to know who 'e was 'cause when they let 'im out he ran away as if the bogey man was after 'im."

Laughing uncontrollably I realised that Mikey Boy had a lot of explaining to do if he was to get away with this little escapade.

Relating the story to my mother she called up the stairs,

"Michael!"

Having overheard the conversation he was not in a hurry to make an appearance especially when she called him Michael instead of Mikey.

"Downstairs, n*ow*!" demanded my mother.

Sheepishly, he came into the kitchen with lowered eyes, his head hanging on his chest.

"Are yew this boy everybody's talking about? Well, answer me!" she said before he had chance to respond.

"Yes mammy."

"Why did yew go in the Palace?"

"I thought yew'd gone back in there. I was going to wait outside until yew came out, but the 'picture' hadn't finished so Mr. Johns, the usher man; yew know Mr. Johns from down the road, well he let me go in to wait for yew."

"Trust yew to do a daft thing like that, making us all look like idiots and worrying us to death. I dwn't know where to put my face! I bet they think we're all 'twp' looking everywhere for yew like that! Oh, I ought to smack your bottom for this my boy!" she cried angrily issuing her usual idle threat.

"Sorry mammy. I won't do it again, honest I won't. Roger always follows yew so I did too."

"Well, the least said the better now," she sighed resignedly, "but I'm not going to the 'pictures' again unless I take them with me. I can't *believe* yew let him manage to sneak out as well." she glared at Leonard.

Nobody knew it was Michael, but she didn't go out of the house for days until the story had been replaced by something more interesting than a boy locked in a picture house.

Unlike Roger, who had quickly made his presence known to her, Michael had just gone into the Palace and sat down a few rows behind where we had been sitting. The usher, who thought my mother was still in the cinema, had put him to wait telling him to watch for her when the lights went up. Lulled by the darkness and warmth he had curled up and eventually dropped off to sleep. Waking up in a deserted cinema, enveloped in darkness, had badly frightened him. Somehow he had found his way to the latticed, metal grid beyond the cinema door. Shocked to find he was locked in he panicked, frantically shaking the gates to attract the attention of passers by. When the gates were opened he lunged down the steps, raced up towards Doctor's Hill and hared the two hundred yards to home, scared out of his wits.

DEFINITELY NO SHENANIGANS!

Going to the 'pictures' was the main form of entertainment for most villagers. Conveniently, they showed two different feature films every week along with a 'short' and Pathé News. The Workmen's Hall had been built from weekly contributions from the miners in an impressive, architectural style indigenous to the Welsh Valleys. It housed a plush balconied cinema, well-stocked library, billiards' hall and committee rooms. Behind the cinema screen was a huge stage; venue for the annual pantomime and operettas produced and directed by Tom Davies, his wife and their daughter, Paddy. Everybody in the village trooped to the 'Hall' to see these colourful shows with a cast made up of adults and children.

Girls who trained in tap dancing lessons, with the local dance teacher, displayed their skills dressed in sequined costumes like mini showgirls. The cast costumes were superb and would have graced any London stage.

"All my friends in school are learning to tap dance," I had told my mother when I was still in Carnetown Juniors. "Can I go with them?"

"I know what yew'll do if yew have to dance in front of anybody; yew'll sit on the side and come over all shy like yew did with piano lessons."

I cringed knowing I had forfeited my piano lessons with Glythyn because she insisted on group tutoring.

"This is different because we'll all be dancing together," I pressed.

"All right, yew can join but I'd better not be wasting my money again!"

Eager to master the art of tap-dancing I tripped off to my first lesson full of enthusiasm. It didn't last long. After the initial euphoria wore off I spent a few miserable weeks painfully aware of every pair of eyes that watched the performance. Head and shoulders taller than most of them I felt big and clumsy by the side of these dainty, petite girls.

"Come on now, yew'll have to get up. Yew can't dance sitting down!" ordered the instructor.

I hung my head still clack-clacking my tap shoes on the floor from the safety of my chair.

"Now, dwn't be shy there's a good girl." she soothed as she dragged me onto the floor.

"But I feel stupid and everyone's looking at me," I whined

"That's the whole idea of learning so people can watch *yew* dance. Yew're very light on yewer feet *and* yew've got a good carriage. Dear, dear, yew have the makings of a very good dancer if yew'd only *try* girl!"

Raising her eyes to the ceiling she mouthed the movements as I deliberately thumped the boards in an extremely ungainly manner. After six weeks she contacted my mother and told her she was wasting her money. Breathing a huge sigh of relief I silently thanked God for this timely intervention. After the fuss I had made about joining the classes it was important that she thought I lacked the skill rather than a lack of enthusiasm.

On rare occasions the 'Hall' opened its doors in the morning for a special showing of cartoons or some educational film that we had also enjoyed whilst still in junior school.

Lined up in assembly we waited for the headmaster's daily announcements,

"As yew already know today Standard Five will be going to the Workman's Hall cinema to see an educational film."

We shuffled impatiently longing to be on our way as Mr. Bevan continued,

"If I have any reports about bad behaviour from Carnetown School pupils yew'll not be allowed to go again. Is that understood?"

"Yes, Mr. Bevan," we chorused in unison.

"Well, I hope yew enjoy the morning."

Accompanied by staff we marched, two by two, to the cinema.

"Hold hands with your partner," Dougie Davies instructed, "and keep well on to the pavement."

We skipped along in a long crocodile, chattering animatedly, filled with excitement at the prospect of a morning in the 'flicks' instead of mental arithmetic and composition writing.

Once a week my grandparents took me to the 'Hall' and we sat in the 'barrier'; a wide aisle that stretched horizontally across the auditorium about half way from the back affording generous leg room. This space separated the expensive stalls from the cheap seats that started with the 'thrupennies' and ended with the 'ninepennies'. From the 'barrier' up the price of a ticket rose to a shilling with the most expensive 1s and 6d seats upstairs. In winter it was warm and cosy because of the wide, round central heating pipes that ran along the wall behind the last row of cheap seats warming the first row of the more exclusive seats.

Vera Bendle, the ticket lady, smiled at us from behind her little glass window.

Dad Smith put a ten shilling note on the counter.

"Two and a half in the barrier please."

Contemplating the delicious warmth, after the chill air of a cold winter's night, my spirits soared or plunged depending on whether there was room. When Vera announced,

" Sorry, the 'barrier' sold out early tonight!" we trooped upstairs to the most expensive seats, because Nana Smith would not sit in the rear stalls. Sniffing indignantly she complained,

"I'm not sitting in the back rows with all those courting couples and their disgusting goings on. Kissing and hands all over each other with no respect for decent people. I'm *not* putting up with their shenanigans and that's that!"

And '*that*' was definitely '*that*'. Before anybody could protest she was half way up the stairs dragging me with her while Dad Smith waited for Vera to give him the tickets.

After the film ended the audience spilled from the 'Hall' onto

Mountain Ash Road clutching their coats around them to stave off the cold. Boys in lace-up, black boots and balaclavas, long, grey, knee-length socks stretched over their freezing knees sliding along the glittering ice.

"Stop that now before yew fall and break something." a mother shouted at her son as, with a yelp of pain, he fell hard on his backside.

Mothers in heavy coats, colourful head scarves knotted under their chins, woollen mufflers pulled over their mouths. Old ladies in ankle-length, fur-trimmed, suede bootees with zips up the front, hats clamped firmly over their ears. For extra warmth socks worn over their stockings rolled down to meet the tops of their boots. Men in conservative suits, waistcoats and trilby hats cautioned,

"Watch the ice, love!"

Tittering like school girls they stepped delicately on the frozen pavement hanging on to their husbands' arms for support as they slipped on an icy patch. Old Johnny, in fingerless gloves, slapped his arms vigorously against his sides to stave off the cold. Huddled in his khaki, army greatcoat, salvaged from the Second World War, he trudged home warm with memories.

Like scurrying ants, families and little groups of neighbours dispersed. A small boy shouted,

"See yew in school tomorrow then. I've got a huge 'pop alley'. Bring yewer marbles with yew!"

"Come on, I'm freezin', stop laggin' behind will yew?" complained his elder sister as she dragged him, still looking over his shoulder, towards Aberdare Road and Carnetown.

Holding onto the wall for support others took tiny, mincing steps as they carefully negotiated the hazardous, steep hill at the side of the 'Spy' Hotel making their way towards Herbert Street and surrounding areas. Others braced themselves for a walk down Doctor's Hill and over to Glancynon unable to resist the smell of fish and chips as they passed Sprague's, or the thought of a hot Vimto in Joe's or Carpanini's bracchis.

Cold air hit the inside of my mouth causing an uncomfortable ache in my front teeth. Quickly, I pulled my red and green school scarf up over my mouth for protection. Even the inside of my nostrils felt icy. I breathed through thick wool coughing suddenly as I caught a strand of lint in my mouth.

"Fancy some chips?" I said sniffing at the freezing air whilst looking expectantly at my mother.

"No, not tonight, it's too cold to walk down Doctor's Hill."

"Why? Anwen's mother's going down for some. I can go with them can't I?"

"No, you're coming home with us now. Anyway the pavements are treacherous. We'll have something hot when we get in."

Shoulders taut with cold I huddled inside my duffle-coat, thrusting my gloved hands into the pockets for extra warmth.

The crowd gradually dispersed as we trudged home to the north end of Mountain Ash Road.

"Goodnight both," called a shivering woman. Only her voice was recognisable as she passed us swathed in winter warmers.

"Goodnight now," Nana and Dad Smith called back as they gratefully opened the front door to a blast of warm air, the promise of hot, buttered toast and a pot of steaming cocoa.

I'SE 'IM

Like others in the valley the Workmen's Hall dominated the landscape. Situated at the top of a steep hill, its grand entrance on Mountain Ash Road, it was the focal point of the village and could be clearly seen from the other side of the valley. Visits to the 'flicks' became a twice-weekly ritual between forays into the dark-polished, wooden bookshelves that lined the library walls. Protected by glass doors they contained tomes of every description; books that quenched the miners' thirst for knowledge and education.

The back of the building dropped into Edwards Street, at the side of Stony Hill, where Dick the Hall's sweet shop was situated. Dick was a small, rotund man who always wore a khaki-brown, work coat over collar and tie when working in the shop.

Peering over the top of the high counter Dick asked the little boy in front of me,

"What would yew like today then?"

"What 'ave yew got for thruppence, please Mr. Williams?"

"Well, let's see now," he replied, hands on hips, surveying the packed shelves.

"What about an everlasting strip or some toffees?"

Unable to decide the lad shuffled from foot to foot asking his pal,

"What're yew gonnw 'ave?"

Boxes of Milk Maid toffees, coconut mushrooms, liquorice comfits, Clarnico Creams and Raspberry Ruffles: tubes of Parma Violets, Trebor Mints, wads of pink, bubble gum and gob stoppers covering the counter made choices excruciatingly difficult.

"Yew'll 'ave to make up yewer mind quick or the 'picture' will be over before yew get there," Dick laughed.

"I'm gonnw 'ave some of those 'ard American gums, I am," his friend said resolutely, "and I might 'ave some 'torpedoes' as well. Yew can suck all the colour off those."

At last, with 'first house' looming, they scuttled out of Dick's clutching their cone-shaped bags of sweets.

Anwen and I gazed at the large, gleaming, glass jars lining the shelves crammed full of sherbet lemons, pear drops, nutty cluster, sugared almonds, striped humbugs, aniseed balls, curly barley sugar sticks and liquorice root.

"I'm gonnw 'ave some liquorice root," Anwen said

"I dwn't like it very much do yew? It's awful after a bit, all stringy and nasty," I replied.

"Oh, aye, but it lasts for ages dwn't it?"

Liquorice root looked like thin pieces of brown twig, very hard with a bitter-sweet taste that was thoroughly unpleasant. After chewing and sucking it for a while it separated into sinewy strands that stuck in one's teeth.

Apart from sweets and pop Dick the Hall also sold cigarettes, cigars and tobacco. Behind the counter, on one side, were stacked packets of Craven A, Woodbines, Senior Service, Gold Flake, elegant, flat, red boxes of Du Maurier, round tins of mahogany tobacco and 'twist' that children often mistook for liquorice. Miners bought the black, round lengths of 'twist,' made from tobacco, to chew underground because they were not allowed to take cigarettes down the pit.

Pockets filled with liquorice roots and two ounces of my favourite Raspberry Ruffles, to take away the taste, we climbed laboriously up the steepness of 'Spy' hill at the side of 'The Hall'.

"I'm not going in the very front in the 'thrupennies' or the 'fivepennies' any more," I asserted. "It'll have to be the 'ninepennies' or I'll get a headache again."

"Aw, trust yew like. I'd 'ave tuppence left for chips if we went in the 'fivepennies'," moaned Anwen.

Armed with a shilling we usually managed to see a film, buy sweets and have enough left for chips on the way home. For a penny John Evans the Shop gave us a bag of apples with the bruised bits cut off.

The auditorium in the 'Hall' was flat which meant children in the 'thrupennies' were right in front of the screen. Every time anyone stood up they were silhouetted against the moving pictures which brought cries of,

"Make those kids down the front sit down mun. They're blockin' the view!"

Younger boys, excited by the action, interacted with the storyline standing up pointing make-believe six-shooters at the baddies while the girls screamed,

"Look out, there's one behind yew!" then covered their eyes as an arrow went whizzing over the sheriff's head.

A young man with learning difficulties could be found in the Workman's Hall every time a Western was showing. Relishing the shoot-outs and the Red Indian attacks he was completely oblivious to the rest of the audience. He was nicknamed 'Ah Foo', because all through the film he shoved his hand against his nose chanting,

"Ah Foo! Ah Foo!" as if he were sneezing.

The dramatic entrance of the gunslinger saw him bouncing up in his seat screaming,

"Ise 'im! Ise 'im!" (I'm him) whilst simultaneously grabbing his imaginary guns from their holsters and firing wildly at the screen. Shouts of,

" 'Ah Foo's' at it again. Aw, sit down mun," from adults at the back had very little effect. When he stood on his seat to swing round and 'fire' at the audience the usher waved his torch frantically ordering,

"Oi, yew over by there, sit down!"

But 'Ah Foo' continued to 'kill' the audience lost in the excitement of bullets and tomahawks flying around his head.

Thwarted, the usher waggled his torch even more frantically whilst barging his way into the row of seats to deal with the culprit.

"Aw, leave 'im alone mister," his snotty-nosed companion protested. "'E's not doin' any 'arm mun, is 'e?"

"Yew mind yewer lip now or yew'll be out with 'im as well son," threatened the usher tripping over feet as he lunged for 'Ah Foo' and grabbed for his coat collar.

'Ah Foo' deftly avoided the grasping hands and pushed through the row to another seat where he took up his gunslinger's stance again.

"Now, come on lad, that's enough of yewer nonsense," Joe the usher cajoled. "Come and sit down tidy mun and yew can stay 'ere."

'Ah Foo' swung round pointed his 'gun' at Joe and 'fired' at him with a loud,

"Bang! Bang! Yewer dead 'butt'."

"Yew'll be bloody dead in a minute if I get my 'ands on yew!"

'Ah Foo' clambered from row to row pushing up empty seats as he went occasionally disappearing and reappearing in another row.

"Yew're a bloody nuisance disturbin' everybody mun," shouted the usher beside himself with impotent fury.

By this time the audience was enjoying the 'show' as much as the film, straining their heads to get a better view of the action. Suddenly 'Ah Foo' lunged from one of the rows directly in front of the screen into the central aisle. For a split second he stopped dead, raised his gun, aimed for the screen and yelled,

'Ise 'im! Ise 'im!" before bolting towards the exit with the usher in close pursuit shouting,

"Yew're banned boy: yew're banned!"

STANDING ROOM ONLY

Unlike the flat, lower auditorium in the Workman's Hall the Palace had a single floor that sloped down towards the screen. Summer and winter saw queues trailing down Margaret Street when there was a good film showing. In winter women huddled against the cold wrapping scarves up over their mouths while men pulled down trilbies or flat caps to meet their collars. The mouth-watering smell of chips wafted out of Shepherd's fish shop to tantalise the taste buds as they resolutely withstood the cold.

"Aw, smell them chips. I could do with a bag o' them," muttered a burly miner.

"Yew've just 'ad yewer dinner. Yew'd swear yew were 'alf starved the way yew carry on," said his wife with disgust.

"Aye, but the smell's enough innit mun?" he said wistfully.

People usually went to Shep's when they went to the Palace and Sprague's after a night in the Workmen's Hall

Mr. Sprague, an anaemic-looking man in a spotless, white coat, ran a scrupulously clean establishment. Very thin, putty-coloured face, black-brilliantined hair combed straight back off his forehead, shaved high at the sides leaving a path of hair down the middle of his head. I couldn't take my eyes off the huge goitre in his neck that made me feel rather squeamish when I thought about him handling the food.

"Look at the lump in 'is neck," I whispered to Anwen.

"Aw, 'e's always 'ad that mun."

"I know that but I'm sure it's bigger than it was last time we came in."

Every time I ordered chips it looked bigger and more threatening to my digestive system.

"Yes, what can I do for yew my dear?" Spraguey asked.

As he spoke the goitre moved up and down like an extra-large Adam's Apple.

"Tuppenny bag of chips please Mr. Sprague."

"Salt and vinegar?"

"Just a bit of salt and lots of vinegar please."

I watched in anticipation as he shook the bottle vigorously over my chips. Malted, brown vinegar travelled into the corner of the grease-proof bag and eventually soaked through to soften the outer wrapping of newspaper. Spraguey's chips were long, limp and insipid-looking; drained of colour just like the man himself, but they tasted wonderful.

Under his bibbed apron Shep wore baggy trousers held up by wide braces and shirtsleeves rolled up to his elbows. His wife was short, plump and pink with a ready smile for the customers. Generous helpings of Shep's chips were fat, golden and crisp, much dryer in texture than Sprague's, but equally as appetising. To a small child straining on tip-toe to look over the counter Shep, a Tommy Cooper look-a-like, was big and jovial. Tall, portly with dark, wavy hair and a face constantly flushed from the heat of the fryers.

"Another couple of minutes and they'll be ready," was the usual response. He stacked old newspapers in a pile at the side of the counter ready to wrap around the greaseproof bags.

"Anybody want some 'bits'? he smiled.

"Me! Me!" chorused the children while the adults added politely,

"Wouldn't mind a few myself Shep if there's any goin'."

"Plenty left mun," he added as he scooped pieces of broken, golden batter into a bag and handed it over the counter to the little girl straining to see over the top of the counter.

Shep had a captive clientele who could not resist the smell of chips wafting from the cinema next door as they emptied out at the end of the 'picture' show. Often older children sneaked out in the middle of a film, bought two 'pennorth' of chips, sneaked back in again and secretly ate them in the darkness of the auditorium to the annoyance and longing of the audience.

Dressed in tweed jacket, flat cap and white, silk scarf knotted at his throat the usher shone his torch into the row and demanded,

"Oi, is anybody eatin' chips over by there?"

"No chips in' ere 'buttie' worse luck!" laughed one of the occupants of the row.

"Turn that flamin' torch off will yew?" hissed another as the beam illuminated his face.

"Well somebody's eatin' chips. I can smell 'em strong."

"I can smell 'em too," complained a woman whose head was swathed in a turban.

Catching sight of a lad surreptitiously trying to conceal his bag of chips the usher ordered imperiously,

"Right yew, out of there now. Yew're stinkin' the whole place out mun."

"But I've finished 'em now," complained the boy stuffing the last chip into his mouth.

"Well, yew're goin' out an' that's that!" retorted the usher muttering under his breath. "Cheeky little buggar!"

Periodically, one of the ushers ventured outside, studied the queue then announced officiously,

"Single seat vacancy only!" allowing a lone person to jump the queue.

Others waited patiently until a pair of seats became available or another announcement declared,

"Room for two in separate seats!"

"Come on Mavis," urged a stocky, little man in a 'British Warm' overcoat as he moved forward.

"I'm *not* sittin' on my own. We came together and we'll sit together arright?" she declared.

Folding her arms in a 'don't you dare manhandle me' stance she resisted his efforts to move her out of the queue.

"Arright! Arright! If that's the way yew feel, but dwn't blame *me* if we're standin' out 'ere all night!"

The usher emerged once again declaring laconically,

"Full house, standin' room only for the rest of the night."

Standing room only did not deter people. They lined the side aisles or stood looking over the barrier that screened the seats from those entering the theatre. On winter nights, tired of standing, they cautiously lowered themselves onto the scalding, central heating pipes lining the walls of the sloping aisles.

"Look out, Tommy Torch is comin' over," whispered Anwen sitting next to me.

She squirmed uncomfortably from buttock to buttock, scorching each in turn, then tried sitting on her hands. In seconds she wrenched her hands free and blew on them vigorously.

"Aw, tha's too warm for me. I'll 'ave blisters in a minute."

"No sittin' on the pipes," ordered a bodiless voice out of the darkness followed by the beam of a flashlight.

Shadowy figures bobbed up quickly, waited for the usher to move on, then dropped thankfully back onto the pipes.

"Aw, I dwn't think I can stand this much longer mun," muttered a skinny-looking youth jumping up whilst clutching his overheated backside.

"Stop moanin' mun. Yew've been at it all night. Sit on yewer 'ands for a bit," his companion replied.

All along the row people shot off the pipes like a game of musical chairs, sat on their hands for a while to cool their bottoms, then sank down gratefully again to toast their buttocks red a second time.

As the lights dimmed the magic began with Abbot and Costello, 'The Three Stooges' or 'The Little Rascals'. Sometimes it would be Gene Autry, Hopalong Cassidy or Roy Rogers and Dale Evans singing a ballad as they rode their horses into the sunset. The 'baddies' never succeeded in their evil endeavours because they were dead, in jail or converted to honesty and decency by the 'goodies' before the end of the film.

Excitement broke loose in Abercynon when the Palace posters announced the showing of a revolutionary type of film.

"We're going to the 'pictures' tonight," my mother declared, "to see that new 3D film."

"Why do they call it a 3D film?" I asked curiously.

"Because it means three-dimensional," replied my mother.

"Yes, but what does it mean?"

240

"Well, instead of everything looking flat like a photograph things look like real life. It's supposed to make the audience feel as if they're actually in the film. They give out special glasses, either red and green or red and blue."

That night a queue of people stretched from the Palace almost down the whole length of Margaret Street, their curiosity increasing by the minute.

"I 'eard the usher say it's a'f-f-fofenom' or something," stuttered the little boy behind us.

"A phenomenon, yew nitwit!" said his older sister.

"Yew think yew know everything yew do, dwn't yew?" he retorted.

"Well she has matriculated, hasn't she?" her mother boasted loudly enough to inform the whole queue.

"What's that then, she been ill?" smirked a skinny woman huddled into a group further up the line.

"Aw, now dwn't start 'er off again, will yew. She takes the bait quicker than a trout," muttered her husband tetchily, fed-up with queuing.

"Old trout yew mean!" cackled the skinny woman. "She thinks 'er girl is the only one who ever matriculated. Both our boys 'ave but yew dwn't see me going on about it night and day like 'er."

Before the banter could develop further the ushers appeared and hauled back the folding metal gates. Chattering animatedly the queue surged forward up the marble steps.

"No pushin'; one at a time for tickets please!" shouted Tommy Torch making a feeble attempt to prevent the crowd rushing the ticket booth.

The ushers handed out pairs of cardboard eye-glasses with the tickets.

"I can't see anything through these," I complained fiddling with the glasses, looking first through the red lens then the blue.

"Not worth the money mun," moaned Little Dai sidling past my mother.

"Yew won't see anything proper until the film starts," Tommy Torch muttered impatiently. "Now move along there."

Comfortably settled, half way up the auditorium, we waited with growing excitement for the film to start. Suddenly, a blaze of blurred colour came from the screen. Cars, people, buildings were layered in shades of blue and red.

"Everything's blurred. I can't see a thing," I grumbled.

"That's what the glasses are for; put them on and yew'll see the difference," my mother urged.

"Gosh, it's fantastic!" I cried as I entered a new kind of reality.

I was in a different world. Children laughed with delight as they ducked to avoid a thrown chair or bottle that appeared to whiz over their heads. Gasping with fright the audience froze as an express train thundered towards them out of the screen threatening to mow them down on the spot.

"Look out!" screamed a disembodied voice as the train appeared to roar straight past us. We loved every minute of it. Once we were accustomed to this new film genre we clamoured for more but 3D was a rare treat.

Crowds also flocked to the cinema to see the new Technicolor films like '*Quo Vadis*' and the first cinemascope production of '*The Robe*' that had been released in 1953, although by the time they reached Abercynon they were often no longer new releases. 1950s tear-jerkers like Lana Turner's '*Imitation of Life*' brought muffled sobs from the women and surreptitious sniffling from the men. A weeping woman, totally engrossed in the film, muttered,

"How could she do that to 'er own mother?" as Lana Turner's black housekeeper and friend took the full force of her daughter's anger.

After the harrowing final scenes, when her daughter ran crying after the hearse carrying her dead mother, flat-capped, part-time ushers, who toiled down the pit during daylight hours, pretended to blow their noses with large, white handkerchiefs as the lights came on and they guided the audience towards the exits.

THE PILLARS OF FEMALE SOCIETY

On Sundays pubs in Wales were closed and only opened during week days until ten o' clock. The Victorian architecture of the Thorn Hotel dominated Mountain Ash Road. Quiet and friendly, it was a community meeting place where miners from the surrounding streets gathered on a Saturday night to wash away the coal dust in their throats.

A huge, pillared porch dominated the double-fronted entrance that led into a foyer from which a wide staircase ascended to the function room and guest quarters. On Saturday nights the sound of communal singing, in the main lounge, rang out into the street. After a few choruses of, '*It's a Long Way to Tipperary*' and '*Pack Up Your Troubles*' the strains of a lone soprano singing, '*We'll Meet Again*' hushed the room. Overcome by nostalgia men sipped their pints and raised their glasses to fallen comrades their eyes misting with memories.

Later, the rousing sound of '*Sospan Fach*', '*Canon Lan*' and '*Cwm Rhondda*' filled the air, but as the night wore on elation turned to melancholy. Tears filled their eyes as, mournfully, they intoned the words of '*Myfanwy*' before rushing to the bar for 'last orders'.

Pint in one hand, an elbow resting on the piano, old Georgie pushed his Dai cap to the back of his head carefully sipping his beer as he waved his arms in time to the music urging just one last song from the dwindling crowd.

"Right 'buttie'; time for one more then Tommy?" queried Jack Dung who always wore immaculately laundered white shirts. Jack had acquired his nickname because of his fondness for picking up horse manure, to fertilise his garden, every time the Co-op or Stan the Milk did their rounds.

"Sorry 'last orders' was five minutes ago."

"Time gentlemen please!" Tom shouted ringing the bell to indicate it was ten o' clock.

"We've got time for '*Hen Wlad Fy Nhadau*' mun Tom," Georgie implored.

"Aye, all right then, but not too many choruses now or we'll be here all night."

Couples in the small, mixed lounge across the foyer rose to their feet at 'stop tap' to join in the Welsh national anthem. Their powerful voices rang out over the rooftops of Abercynon. They sang with passion, with love, and an all-consuming pride in their country.

Finally, they trooped out from the warmth of the hotel, a golden pool of light spilling through the open doors onto the pavement. Arm in arm couples headed quickly for home, chattering animatedly, heads close together discussing bits of gossip picked up during the evening. Miners lingered outside, hands thrust into trouser pockets, deep in conversation about work or politics; putting the world to rights. Others darted home knowing their wives would be peering round the front door, or huddled with a neighbour by the garden wall, cardigans draped round their shoulders.

"Look at 'im now, tipsy as usual!" declared Mrs Griffiths as an inebriated man swayed up the pavement.

"Aye, but 'e's 'armless enough in 'e. Wouldn't 'urt a fly he wouldn't, and believe me 'e's got somethin' to put up with with 'er mind," remarked Mrs Brice knowingly. "Nag! Nag! Nag! I've 'eard 'er up the back garden. Poor beggar, 'e never gets a minute's peace."

"Aye, yew're right, probably only bit of pleasure 'e gets."

"She's a funny one though with 'er airs and graces; thinks she's chocolate. Yew know I 'eard she makes 'im sit on newspaper to keep the chair covers clean even after 'e's 'ad a bath after the pit."

"Poor beggar."

As their husbands came into sight they quickly disappeared inside to put the kettle on the fire. Their husbands found them righteously knitting or making a rag mat from discarded garments: Sunday's apple tart, baking in the big, black-leaded oven, wafting mouth-watering smells throughout the warm kitchen.

Valleys women did not frequent pubs alone unless they were

very elderly or accompanying an older relative. Old ladies gathered on a winter's evening to exchange gossip in the 'Jug and Bottle', a small room at the side of the pub. Men were barred from this female sanctuary. Similarly, women did not go into the public bar unless they were prepared to risk their reputations and be cast out as fallen women to be ostracised by the upright wives of the world. The pillars of female society discussed the waywardness of these women shaking their heads over the kind of men who would put up with, "that sort of 'loose' behaviour"; allowing their wives to flaunt themselves like hussies and drink like men.

Over the years the walls of the 'Jug and Bottle' must have soaked up the biggest scandals in Abercynon as old ladies gossiped and giggled and pronounced judgement on those who had wandered from the path of respectability.

"Did yew 'ear about 'im down the road," whispered a diminutive octogenarian with thin, wispy, white hair. She was about to elaborate when one of the local lads stuck his head round the door.

"Can yew ask Mr. Evans for a packet of Smith's crisps, and five Woodbines for Mam please?" he wheedled picking up his ears to listen to the conversation.

"I'll get the crisps but yew're not getting any cigarettes. I wasn't born yesterday," she declared sagely.

Old Bopa put her finger to her lips as one of the ladies bent forward to join in the gossip,

"Eisht now! Wait 'till the boy's gone. His ears are flappin' like an elephant."

"Oh, yew know who I mean anyway, dwn't yew?" she intimated not wanting to pronounce the miscreant's name.

She nudged Bopa who clucked her tongue and nodded back knowingly.

"Well, disgustin' I call it, dwn't yew?"

"I've never 'eard the like of it in my life!" declared a stout matron folding her arms over her ample bosom. "There's more to that than meets the eye, yew mark my words. It'll all come out in the end. They reckon 'e's got a woman in Ponty. Big in the way they say; about seven months gone. They say 'is wife chased 'im down the gully and nearly killed 'im when she 'it 'im with a shovel. Nasty gash in 'is 'ead. It was a miracle they said, that 'e didn't die. Mind yew serves the silly beggar's right innit?"she smirked.

"We shouldn't laugh but yew can't 'elp it, can yew? Two black eyes 'e's got as well they say," laughed Old Bopa.

'They' being those elusive, unidentified characters who gleefully transmitted scandal throughout the village: stopping in Margaret Street to whisper behind hands or huddling in Joe's café sipping a glass of hot Vimto. Raised eyebrows, handkerchiefs brought delicately to their mouths as they savoured the juiciest bits of gossip. Each time a story was repeated another dimension was added until it became the stuff of fiction rather than fact. Names were superfluous in their gossip since it had already been passed from house to house via the front steps or the garden wall.

Besides Bopa, old Mrs Wiltshire and Mrs Jones Ginger, so-called because of her carrot-red hair in her youth, frequented this respectable watering hole for ladies. The door to the 'Jug and Bottle' opened directly onto the pavement so that elderly ladies could go straight in without having to enter the public house. Bench-style seats ranged around the walls of a tiny room with a hatch in the wall leading to the bar. Knocking discreetly on the closed, hatch door the ladies waited for the barman to open it.

"Two Mackeson's, a shandy and a small, sweet sherry please Tommy," from Old Bopa.

Swiftly, the hatch was closed again so that they were concealed from the view of men lining the bar. When their drinks were ready the door slid back, Tom pushed their drinks through the hatch and closed it again leaving them in complete privacy.

Dark, winter evenings always drew them to this snug, warm hideout where they could safely exchange gossip about the latest scandals or talk about their families.

"Our Robert's doin' well. Yew know my grandson livin' in Aberdare. 'E's in grammar school now," intimated a quiet woman huddled in the corner.

Grammar schools in the 1950s provided a ladder of social

mobility for the children of miners many of whom became doctors and teachers. Some miners were remarkably well-educated, not always from formal schooling, but because they were innately intelligent, well read and participated in cultural pursuits such as music and poetry.

"Goin' on to college when 'e leaves school," she continued proudly.

"Oh, that's good, our Ellen's doin' well too. She's finished 'er training to be a teacher. Yew can tell she's been to university. Speaks very nicely yew know," bragged the stout matron.

"Well, I'm not one to boast, mind yew, but they all say Robert's *very* clever; that 'e'll go a long way," retorted her companion determined not to be outdone.

As the evening progressed the talking became more intense and even more conspiratorial. At 'stop tap' they looked at each other in amazement wondering where the time had gone. A head peeped around the heavy door to see who was outside before the ladies emerged. Elderly widows, living in the neighbouring streets, scurried home together while others tapped on the hatch to inform Tom that they were ready to be collected by their husbands. Leaving their workmates behind the men emerged from the bar after quaffing a welcome pint of beer to moisten their throats after being underground all day.

CAROL'S KITTENS

Tom Evans, the licensee of the Thorn Hotel, had a daughter, Carol, a bonny girl about a year older than me. She hated her short, naturally curly hair, because it would not go into the 1950s pony-tail style. We spent long hours together exploring the rambling building or peeping round the door of the gym upstairs to watch Dai Dower training for one of his fights. Crossing the rope over his hands and skipping at such speed that his feet seemed suspended above the ground.

The attic fired our imagination as we tentatively crept inside tip-toeing over the creaking floorboards. There was something disturbing about it. I felt afraid for no particular reason. Lots of old boxes lay about the floor filled with discarded clothes that smelled musty and damp, some spilling out of their broken containers. Yellowing newspapers littered one corner. A one-eyed, china doll, with a cracked face, smiled crookedly at us while a headless, tailor's dummy stood leaning drunkenly against a threadbare armchair.

Out of the corner of my eye I spotted something, glowing white and supernatural, against the far wall. Catching my breath in terror I stared at the apparition my heart palpitating uncomfortably in my chest.

"Oh, my God, there's a ghost! Look, over there by the wall!"

I felt the hairs on the back of my neck prickle and rise. My first instinct was to run. Carol just laughed and said,

"It's only a statue. Yew didn't really think it was a ghost did yew?"

"Oh gosh," I gasped clutching my chest, "it frightened me to death!"

Still trembling I moved cautiously towards the 'ghost' and poked it gently. A full-length statue in white, gleaming alabaster; it looked as though it should have been at the head of a grave.

Carol frightened me further by relating gory tales of a murder which supposedly had happened in the Thorn and the ghost that haunted the building. I never discovered whether this was true, but some rooms always felt as though we were intruding into another realm of reality. The place undoubtedly had a history of tragedy given the various stories that were told by elderly residents in the village.

"Come on, let's get out of here," I urged. "This place gives me the 'heebie jeebies'.

I gave an involuntary shiver as we left the attic and the 'ghost' behind. Little did we know that in a few short years fate would scythe its way through the Thorn Hotel again.

One winter's night, when Carol and I were playing Ludo in the upstairs living room, she asked,

"Do yew fancy some lemonade?"

Feeling thirsty I readily agreed so she went downstairs to fetch some. Minutes later she burst through the door crying uncontrollably. Between sobs she blurted out incoherently,

"D-dad's not in the b-bar. C-come quick, my c-cat, the k-kittens, the k-kittens, in the c-cellar.

With me close at her heels we stumbled down the steps to the cellar. Her tabby cat was lying curled up on an old piece of blanket in a basket. My sigh of relief turned to horror when I saw what was inside it. The cat was surrounded by seven, newly-born kittens all with their heads bitten off. The heads were lying in various parts of the basket while their dismembered bodies sprawled in nightmarish poses. The animal was licking the tiny, headless creatures clean. Carol screamed at me,

"She's bitten off their 'eads! How can their mother bite off their 'eads?"

She was still crying uncontrollably so I went in search of her father. Not allowed anywhere near the public area I ran outside onto the pavement. Pounding impatiently on the door of the 'Jug and Bottle' I waited until one of the old ladies answered my knock.

After relating my story she banged furiously on the hatch door leading to the bar.

"Tommy! Tommy! Come quick! Carol's in the cellar. There's something wrong with the cat!"

I could hear the message being passed from man to man until it reached Tommy who had reappeared in the bar. Within seconds he had hurtled down to the cellar to comfort Carol who was beside herself with anguish..

"It was probably a rat that did it," he said trying to reassure her.

"B–but why d–dad, why?" she sobbed.

Tom had no answer. Choked with emotion he gently gathered up the pitiful creatures and wrapped them in a cloth while Carol wept.

After moving up to grammar school Carol and I had gradually gone our separate ways. Almost two years older she had begun to outgrow me when she moved to Abercynon 'Clock' school, the local secondary modern. The school had gained its nickname because the cenotaph and clock tower were in a small enclosure at the front of the school. One day I bumped into her, as I was walking up Doctor's Hill, aghast to see that she had changed from a bubbly, round-faced, healthy-looking youngster into a thin, pasty-faced girl with dark circles under her eyes.

"I've been ill, "she told me in a weak voice, "but I'm feeling a lot better now."

"Yew look great!" I lied forcing conviction into my voice.

Unrecognisable, except for the tight, curly hair, her sunken features and lethargic demeanour bore no resemblance to Carol the Thorn. That was the last time I saw her alive. Three months later she died from leukaemia.

The day of her funeral was damp, the sky leaden with black clouds. All the villagers of Abercynon seemed to be crowded on to the road outside the pub. The Thorn was packed with people standing in the entrance hall, up the stairs, under the porch and flowing out over the pavement. Women cried soundlessly while men, shoulders hunched, silently blew their noses remembering Carol, the curly-haired little scamp they used to tease when she scampered behind the bar counter. Not a sound could be heard.

Through the curtains of my grandparents' house I saw the long, black hearse covered in flowers; on the roof, alongside the coffin rails; more filling the foyer with a blaze of colour. As if a pair of hands had gently parted the motionless crowd they moved in silent unison to leave a clear passage in front of the great double doors of the Thorn. Simultaneously afraid and fascinated I watched as the coffin that bore Carol's emaciated body slowly emerged from the doors. I couldn't relate this grim scene to the vivacious girl I had known. A torrent of emotion swept over me; bewilderment, desperate sadness and fear plucked at my soul.

"How could she die; she's too young?" I sighed brushing tears from my eyes. "It's not fair! Only old people died didn't they; not children, not Carol?"

Jesus could perform miracles, I knew. I had read about Him raising people from the dead.

Perhaps Carol would suddenly shout out that she wasn't really dead at all. It would be another miracle, just like Lazarus, and the crowd of mourners would shout with exultation. But there was no miracle, no exclamations of joy, only quiet weeping.

In my imagination I tried to visualise her lying inside the oblong box dressed in her best clothes; serene, released from pain and suffering, but I could not. All I felt was a thrill of selfish fear.

"That could be me," I whispered fingers of terror clutching at my heart.

A bent old lady, with a look of pain and remembered sorrow on her lined face, stepped hesitantly forward leaning on her stick to support her arthritic limbs.

"God keep yew safe in his arms Carol," she whispered.

With trembling, time-worn hands she carefully placed a small bunch of flowers on Carol's coffin before the undertaker closed the door of the hearse.

Silently, the crowd moved back from the hearse: some just stood and watched waiting to walk behind the cortège; others moved towards waiting cars to drive to the cemetery and wait for her arrival. No words were spoken when her parents appeared with a local lad who lodged with them and whom they treated more like a son.

The funeral cars glided silently away and crawled up Abercynon Road. The white-haired old lady still stood alone nervously clutching at the scarf around her neck. People lined both sides of the road past R. T. Jones' shop. Curtains moved aside surreptitiously; old men in the street stopped and doffed their hats inclining their heads in silent supplication. Mothers stood at their front doors and wept openly while drawing their children tightly to them. One whispered,

"Cwtch in to mammy baby. Poor little Carol. It doesn't make sense, does it? Her parents must be goin' through Hell."

"At least she's not sufferin' anymore, is she?" said her neighbour watching the cars roll soundlessly away from the Thorn. The rear of the grieving column of mourners turned slowly onto Abercynon Road leaving emptiness and complete stillness.

For what seemed like hours I didn't move until Nana Smith turned the knob of the front door breaking the spell of poignancy and melancholy that had enveloped me. Not long afterwards Tommy the Thorn and his wife moved away from Abercynon taking their young lodger with them.

Carol's death stirred a restlessness in my spirit that lingered throughout the winter months. Childhood faded as I was caught up in that curious limbo of adolescence. As summer approached spinning dreams on 'Table Rock' melted under the burgeoning teenage culture that rippled outwards from the big cities. The 'season of the long grass' held new, more exciting activities: fashion, swimming in Ponty baths and Rock 'n Roll.

THE BELLY FLOPPERS

We heard the train chugging into the station as we bolted down lower Margaret Street sandals slapping against the stone paving. Racing for the nearest carriage we flung ourselves through the door collapsing in breathless giggles.

"Almost missed it!" I gasped hauling my bag onto the seat.

"Great, we've got a compartment all to ourselves," Anwen enthused. "Let's spread out in case anyone else tries to get in."

Leaning through the window I saw the guard wave his flag at the driver followed by two short blasts on his whistle. The engine groaned as its wheels began to turn hauling us slowly away from the platform. The train wound its way along the track following the black course of the River Taff to Pontypridd.

As we drew into the station heads poked through windows impatient for the train to stop. A rotund porter wheeled a cart full of luggage with passengers hurrying alongside. Crates full of mysterious contents were stacked neatly against the wall emblazoned with labels proclaiming their destination. Unsold newspapers, tied with string, waited for collection. Passengers scurried out of the waiting room anxious to claim a 'good' seat for the journey to Cardiff.

"C'mon, let's get going or we'll miss the start of the session," I urged walking towards the steps that led into the street.

Quickening our pace we bolted down into Taff Street, over the river bridge opposite the New Inn, into the wide, tree-lined avenue of Ynysangharad Memorial Park.

Queues for the 10 o' clock swimming session already stretched along the pavement.

"We're not going to get in," I complained. "Look at the queue!"

Anxiously, we waited as the line filed slowly towards the entrance. We could see the attendant in her little glass-partitioned booth doling out discs dangling from coloured rubber bands.

"Almost there," I nudged Mati.

As we reached the booth the ticket lady shouted,

"We're full for this session.....," My shoulders slumped with disappointment. "but there's room for the last four."

Jubilantly we purchased our tickets, grabbed the bands, and headed into paradise.

The smell of chlorine hit my nostrils as we emerged into the pool area bathed in morning sunlight. The surface of the water glistened, undulating in barely perceptible waves as a swimmer broke the surface carving gently towards the deep end. Separate changing rooms for males and females lined the walls either side of the baths.

"I've got my bathers on under my clothes," I called to the other girls.

"Me too!" they called back.

Leaving our clothes in the bottle-green painted cubicles with their wooden, slat-bench seats we headed for the pool.

Sitting on the edge we tentatively dipped our feet into the 'blue' water.

"It's cold innit?" Mati gasped.

Carefully, I lowered myself into the shallow end that came just above my waist. I dipped my hands in the water and splashed it over my upper body to minimise the shock of the icy water.

"Let's go in together, now!" I yelled lunging forward. "Christopher Columbus, it's freezing!"

"It's great if yew keep movin'," Anwen said teeth chattering like castanets.

Not for us the sultry, indoor pools of latter times with their regulated water temperatures. From May until the end of September we revelled in cold water, in the open air, regardless of the weather.

Followed by the others I swam across the pool to the deep end dodging bodies plummeting from the diving boards. Dog-paddling we clung, spluttering, to the blue-painted wall elated by the sense of freedom and buoyancy of our bodies in the water.

"Let's see how long we can stay under water is it?" Anwen urged.

"I can stay under five minutes," Mati declared.

"Tha's nuts, yew can't stay under that long, yew'll drown," Anwen retorted shooting her sister a scathing glance.

Holding noses we let ourselves sink to the bottom of the pool, eyes open, laughing at the froglike movements of the swimmers' legs or wincing when a foot lunged into our faces. Rising again to the surface, like mermaids, hair spread out floating on the water like fronds of seaweed.

After discussing the possibility of drowning or falling backwards on our heads onto the painted, concrete terrace around the pool we plucked up the courage to go on the lowest diving board. Jumping was forbidden, but very few took heed of this usually losing their nerve to dive at the last moment.

"We'll go off 'first' board then we'll try 'middle' board," I said importantly.

Gradually, our confidence grew until we reached the highest level. I stood waiting for the boy in front to dive off then teetered nervously along the board. Mesmerised, I peered down at the glistening water drawing me; inviting me to fall into its depths. Distant voices reached my ears calling to me.

"Go on, dive yew ninny!" said an impatient voice behind me.

I turned to remonstrate with 'the voice' but lost my balance. Whether I dived or fell is a matter of conjecture.

For a few seconds I flailed the air with my arms then automatically went into a dive position as I rushed headlong to meet the water. Sounds of cheering intermingled with gasps and a resounding 'thwack' that could be heard all over the baths.

"Cor, what a belly-flop! That must've hurt!" said a good-looking, dark-haired boy whose graceful diving we had been admiring throughout the session.

"No, not really. I didn't feel a thing," I choked out.

Stomach stinging, head aching, winded, pride hurting more than anything else I swam carelessly over to the edge and hauled myself out grinning like a Cheshire cat. Giving the boy a scathing glance I walked nonchalantly towards the changing cubicles. Gratefully, I closed the door then doubled up gasping for air.

"Are yew all right?" Anwen called peeping over the door.

"Yeah, but I'm not diving off there again."

"Divin', is that what yew call it?" laughed a gawky girl as she entered the cubicle next door. "Yew could 'ave fooled me," she cackled.

Miserably, I slunk towards the exit wincing with pain and embarrassment at the thought of facing the crowd around the pool. Suitably chastened by my experience I rejoined the others to go back in the baths for the afternoon session comforted by the thought that the morning's spectators had gone home.

We rarely got dressed after a swimming session, just grabbed our clothes, wrapped ourselves in a towel and queued up again to pay for the next session of swimming. We swam under the rays of the scorching, summer sun, under grey, cloudy skies and in the teaming rain. We swam as lightning illuminated the sky jumping out of our skins with fright when thunder rumbled over us. Glinting needles of rain splashed on our up-turned faces, but what did it matter? We were wet anyway. Still we swam oblivious to the fact that we were the only ones left in the pool.

Sometimes, we headed for the bandstand or the sunken 'Harp' garden named after its shape. Tranquil and secluded with formal flower beds, rose bushes, rustic seats set in alcoves around the garden with little paths leading to the entrance. In this quiet spot we ate our sandwiches carefully disposing of our waxed, sandwich paper in the bins. Full and contented we settled back, faces raised to catch the rays of a melting sun, to talk and dream of the future just as we had in the 'long grass'. Later, exhausted by the day's activities, we dragged our way to the station and chugged home, faces glowing with health, knowing that we would be in trouble for staying out so long.

"See yew on Sunday," Anwen called as she ran up the steps to her front door.

"Can't, I'm going to Brecon Sunday afternoon," I replied, "for a picnic by the river."

LILIES AND MINT

Rays of bright, golden light teased my eyelids forcing me into awareness. Enticing Sunday morning smells of frying bacon and black pudding wafted up the stairs, curling their way across the landing urging me out of bed. Billy Cotton, plugging his lunchtime show, shouting from the wireless, "*Wakey! Wakey!*" banished my sleepiness and stirred me into movement. The main source of entertainment the wireless was the focus of contact with the wider world outside the valleys. Roger's voice called at the foot of the stairs,

"It's time to get up and yew've got to get up *now* Mam said or breakfast will be all gone!"

"I'm already up," I replied pulling on my socks as I headed down the stairs.

Breakfast over, my mother put the joint in the oven then settled down to read the morning paper until it was time to wash and prepare the vegetables while the boys and I prepared for Sunday School.

Amid the flurry of activity my mother had been listening to a comedy show that had just finished. Now Wilfred Pickles was urging the audience to '*Have a go Joe*' and instructing his pianist to, "*Give 'em the money Mabel*", over the clatter of pots and pans.

"It's roasting a treat. Just needs a bit more basting. I thought we'd have a change from beef this week," she said looking at the joint of lamb in the oven.

My stomach churned slightly as I watched her scoop up sizzling, liquid fat from the meat tray to pour it over the meat.

"I dwn't want any meat today," I declared thinking about the lambs I'd seen gambolling in the fields on previous Sunday outings.

"What do yew mean yew dwn't want meat? Yew've got to eat

some meat to stay healthy," she retorted, "otherwise yew'll be all pale and anaemic."

"But I dwn't want any…….."

"No 'buts', you're eating some meat and that's *that*. And yew can fetch some mint from Mrs Dennis' garden later on.

'*The Archers*' signature tune brought the conversation to an abrupt end as the gravelly tones of Walter Gabriel filled the room.

"Shwsh now, or I'll miss the best bits like last week. Yew can lay the table if yew like."

The hardships of food rationing were only a fleeting memory of how life had been during the war and for some years afterwards. We ate good, wholesome meals always with some kind of meat. Chops, lamb casserole, sausages with swede and onion gravy, mince, beef stew with suet dumplings, liver and onions. Food fads were unheard of in the 1950s. We ate what was put in front of us, sometimes reluctantly, but mostly with relish. Turning our noses up at sprouts and cabbage was met with,

"They're good for yew. They're full of iron and vitamins!"

For my mother a meal wasn't a 'proper' meal unless it was a cooked dinner with gravy.

On Sundays it was inevitably roast beef, Yorkshire pudding, roast potatoes, roast parsnips and vegetables. In winter dried peas were soaked overnight in a little net bag and served with sprouts and carrots. In summer it was fresh garden peas, dark-green Savoy cabbage, broad beans or whatever vegetables were in season. Jaded with beef we occasionally had lamb or pork that was roasted until the crackling was crisp and served with sharp, apple sauce.

"Yew can fetch some mint now," my mother said as she lifted the lid off a bubbling saucepan of cabbage to check its progress. "Yew can chop it if yew like."

The only thing I liked about lamb was chopping the fresh mint that grew in profusion in our next door neighbour's garden. Mrs Dennis, a pillar of the Congregational Church, answered the door in her Sunday hat.

"Come through and yew can pick it straight away," she said as she ushered me into the kitchen where her daughter, Violet, was chopping mounds of pungent mint.

"It's a smashing smell, really fresh," I said breathing in the odour.

"We've got loads of it this year. I'll have to cut it back or it'll be taking over my lilies. Yew take as much as yew like while I go and change my clothes."

Every year a mass of glowing white, Madonna lilies sprung up in her back garden. At night they shone eerily appearing almost luminous in the black of the night. Looking out of the kitchen window into the gloom we hoped that they would die never to return, but year after year the hated blooms reappeared more lush than the year before.

"I hate those lilies; they remind me of death," my mother shivered.

Although quite beautiful flowers neither my mother nor I could look at them without shuddering.

"They're all right for funerals and cemeteries but not in the back garden," she complained.

"I think they're really creepy in the dark. I can see them glowing from my bedroom window. They give me the shivers," I said.

"I swear, one of these days, I'll go over the wall in the middle of the night and dig the things up," she threatened.

But, of course, she never did because Mrs Dennis loved them. She could often be seen lovingly stroking their luminous, white petals and marvelling at their beauty while we surreptitiously watched wishing they would wilt and wither away.

I washed and chopped the mint, added some vinegar, mixed it lightly and left it to soak just as Jane Metcalfe announced in her cultured voice,

"*The time in Britain is 12 noon. In Germany it's one o' clock.*" before introducing one of our much-loved Sunday programmes, '*Two Way Family Favourites*'.

"I've forgotten to get any drinks," my mother cried. "Can yew pop over to R.T. Jones' shop. It might be still open."

Drinks meant bottles of 'pop', no alcohol. Tizer, a strange

orange-coloured drink, American Cream Soda, ginger beer or Dandelion and Burdock in rubber-stoppered bottles opened with metal push-up levers.

"We like green pop," Michael said.

"Oh, go on then just this once. I said yew couldn't have it again after the way it stained everything. It can't be good for yew," she tutted referring to the lurid, green stains left on the tablecloth and on the fronts of the boys' shirts.

"We'll come to the shop with yew," the boys chorused running after me.

Force of habit made me listen for oncoming traffic but there was no need. Sundays were special days in Wales with few distractions from family life. Closed pubs, open chapels, coach trips to Barry Island, advertised on a blackboard outside Kitts' greengrocer's, or trips motoring in the Gloucestershire countryside. For the weary miners it was a chance to be outside filling their congested lungs with clean, fresh air before being plunged once again into the dark bowels of the earth. In winter they rarely saw the light of day for twilight swiftly followed them as they trudged wearily home after a shift.

Not a sound could be heard except for muted conversation from people returning from chapel or the occasional greeting from neighbours. Wales was still dry on Sundays so the doors of the Thorn Hotel were tightly closed. We crossed the road by Nana Smith's calling greetings to the Bowcott's and the Vickery's, who were soaking up the sun on the benches at the side of their little front gardens, then walked the few yards round the corner to R.Ts., shop at the foot of Abercynon Road where Mrs Stacey, his daughter, was serving.

"Lovely day," remarked Mrs Stacey a fair-haired, pleasant woman with a ready smile.

She eyed the two women who had just come into the shop, scurried to the door and turned the sign to 'closed'.

"Yew're lucky; yew've only just caught me," she said moving back behind the counter. "Half day today. I'll be closing in a few minutes."

We watched as she made an oblong bag from heavy-weight,

dark-blue sugar paper to hold tea ladled from one of the wooden tea chests. She sliced another sheet in half, fashioned it into a cone, filled it with sugar and tightly screwed up the end.

"Why are yew twisting it up like that Mrs Stacey?" Roger asked.

"To stop the sugar falling out all over the floor," she laughed.

Tins of baked beans, soup, peas, corned beef and Spam ranged one wall. A gleaming bacon slicer sat on the counter beside enormous slabs of butter, margarine and cheese.

"Ooh, that looks sharp," I remarked as Mrs Stacey deftly cut through a slab of butter with a cheese wire.

"Sharp enough to slice right through your fingers to the bone," she replied. "Yew can't play around with these things."

Expert slapping with wooden paddles transformed the shapeless lump into a perfect rectangle to be wrapped in greaseproof paper.

"Now what would yew like then?"

"Pop please, green pop," Michael piped.

"Limeade and a bottle of ginger beer please," I added looking round the shop.

On the opposite wall jars of sweets, cigarettes and tobacco. A wooden bench at the foot of the counter held large, open tins of biscuits. Customers helped themselves filling a brown, paper bag with a mix of biscuits from all the tins. Broken biscuits were heaped in a separate tin to be sold at a knock-down price. Each Christmas R.Ts., sold novelties and gifts. Brightly-painted wooden, hand-made replicas of railway engines, gleaming boxed train sets, gaily-painted toddlers' tricycles, carts, pedal cars and cowboy outfits complete with silver-coloured six-shooters.

R.Ts., was a place where the neighbours met to exchange local gossip when they bought their daily fresh bread. Near the door a single, ladder-backed chair provided respite for old ladies to take a rest and chatter while they were being served.

"Oi, did yew 'ear about old Arthur Creases up the road. Died in 'is sleep last night I 'eard," Mrs Rees muttered in a low whisper.

"No! Arthur up by 'The Tump'? " replied Mrs Stacey in shocked tones.

"No, not 'im, tha's not old Arthur. I mean the one up past the woods. The one who always dresses smart; yew know creases in 'is trousers like razor blades."

"Oh, that Arthur. I know who yew mean now."

"Real gentleman he was mind; always raised 'is 'at when 'e passed down the road," Mrs Rees responded shaking her head sadly.

"Is it right yew're sellin' up!" exclaimed Fluff the Barber putting his head round the door.

"Yew're not are yew?" Mrs Rees looked shocked.

"Well, yes and no," Mrs Stacey said. "I couldn't manage a drapers and general stores like we used to. It's been getting harder and harder since my father died."

"Well, 'ave yew sold up or not?" demanded Mrs Rees.

"I've sold the big shop and house to her uncle Donald," she said looking at me, "but I'll still be keeping this one open."

"Oh, well, tha's a relief innit?" she said puffing out her cheeks glad to hear that her chair wasn't in jeopardy.

From then on Mrs Stacey concentrated on fruit, vegetables, bread, cakes, groceries and dairy products while Donald sold mainly confectionary, cigarettes, tinned groceries and a variety of items such as ladies' stockings. At Christmas and Easter elegant boxes of chocolates and giant Easter Eggs decorated with ribbons and little, fluffy, yellow chicks.

"Why do they call him Artie," I asked my mother placing the pop on the table after returning from the shop, "when his name is R.T. Jones?"

"It's just been shortened over the years to R.T., not Artie," she laughed, "the same as 'Use the Oils' in North Street."

"What do they use the oils for?" I asked.

"They dwn't use oils yew silly 'apporth, it's Hughes the Oils: he used to sell paraffin. Everyone thinks it's 'Use the Oils' because some people dwn't sound their aitches. Come on, let's get crackin'. I've got to pack a picnic for our trip to Brecon this afternoon."

I pondered the idiosyncrasies of the valleys and wondered what nickname I would acquire, but it would be many years before I would be known as 'The Duchess'.

CLEOPATRA GLIDING DOWN THE NILE

The street was quiet, just the occasional scrape of a trowel being thrust at weeds in a neighbouring garden and the monotonous drone of a wasp. Outside Nana Smith's house a convoy of family cars stood waiting for the rush of occupants from within. My grandfather's Humber, that had replaced the big, old Austin with running boards, gleaming chrome headlights and fenders, dwarfed Terry's powder-blue bubble car. Behind them an assortment of motorcars filled with hoards of uncles, aunts, cousins, spirit stoves, deckchairs and the multifarious paraphernalia needed for a Sunday afternoon outing.

"Dwn't forget the primus stove," Nana Smith reminded my mother.

"It's already in the boot with the kettle. I've put that metal teapot in as well," she replied.

"Come on, let's get going or it'll be time to come back before we start."

After much coming and going and shifting of seats so that the children had a good view we were off. We travelled in my grandfather's car and, as usual, I sat in front with Nana and Dad Smith.

Our destination was Brecon and a boat trip down the Usk. On arrival we hired an enormous rowing boat big enough for the whole family. We piled into the boat, the men giving orders and the women dragging children and hauling the picnic. To the amusement of bystanders on the river bank we moved unsteadily downstream with the flow of the river.

"Stop moving about Duck or we'll all fall in. Yew know I dwn't really like the water," Nana Smith said nervously using Donald's pet name.

As a small child he used to run around chanting, "I'm Donald

Duck! I'm Donald Duck!" after the Walt Disney character: so much so that she used to call him 'my little duck'; an affectionate nickname only the family was allowed to use.

The boat was keeling over at intervals which brought screams of horror from the women and girls much to the delight of the uncles who were enjoying every minute of it. They spent most of the time arguing about who was most proficient at rowing.

It was warm and peaceful on the river; the water deep and crystal clear. Shoals of tiny fish darted, seemingly without direction, alongside the boat. They brushed against my hand as I trailed it through the water. The banks of the river were covered with trees and shrubs which cast their green reflections on the calm waters. Clusters of gnats suspended over the river buzzed interminably, their sound adding to the lazy atmosphere of the afternoon. Suddenly Donald shouted,

"Row over to the left side. There's a smashing place for a picnic at the top of that rise!"

"No, we can't stop there," Dad Smith retorted, "it's too steep for your mother."

"Oh, 'course we can. Look up to the top; it's perfect!" Donald enthused as he caught at a branch and pulled us towards the bank.

Confusion: oars clattered, stifled mutterings, which I suspect were curses, were hushed by the aunts. The boat rocked and jerked and ploughed bows first into the bank with a violent thud. Scrambling out of the boat carrying kettle, teapot, rugs and a variety of equipment we picked our way up the steep bank. Panting from exertion we reached the crest of the incline breathing huge sighs of relief, deposited our gear and slumped to the ground to regain our composure.

"Now what Duck?"

Donald, a vibrant and larger than life character, with seemingly endless energy and a passion for activity, still stood in the boat chuckling wickedly. Thick-set, good-looking with a wide forehead, straight dark hair slicked back, a deep quiff in the front: quick, knowing, intelligent eyes, a straight Roman nose inherited from my grandfather's family and a smile that flashed constantly as he nervously picked as his nails. Those halcyon days gave no warning of how brief his life would be.

He stood on the boat hands planted firmly on hips and yelled,

"I dwn't think this is a very good spot after all. All back in the boat!"

Nobody thought to challenge his decision as we picked our way down the steep slope and jumped back into the boat. Nobody ever did. He was the natural leader in the family. Nana Smith, a pretty, petite woman with the same dark, watchful eyes as Donald, stretched out and put one foot into the boat. At that moment the vessel moved away from the bank. She screamed as one leg went with the boat with the other remaining on the bank leaving her sprawling dangerously over an expanse of water. Emrys, the smallest of the brothers, with my mother's hazel eyes and build shouted,

"That's not funny Duck. Yew know she's afraid of the water."

Emrys was standing indignantly on the bank with an accusing look on his face. Even in photographs, taken as a soldier on National Service in Malaya, he looked boyish in his long, khaki shorts and big-brimmed bush hat like the kid brother who had dressed up to mimic the older siblings. He was much quieter than the others, more contemplative and thoughtful. Furiously, Dad Smith rushed forward and shouted,

"I'll box your ears for yew Duck! Now pull the boat in before there's a serious accident!"

"It wasn't me Dad, it was Terry. He slipped and his foot pushed against the boat. I always get the fault, dwn't I. Do you really think I'd do a thing like that?" said Donald crestfallen.

His face was a picture of indignation and incredulity.

"Yes, yew would!" Terry spluttered afraid he was going to get the blame.

Nobody would believe that Donald would do anything deliberately, he was too kind-hearted, but he loved a practical joke and this one had gone too far.

Children giggled, aunts and uncles fussed trying to soothe Nana Smith as they pulled the boat back into the side. As it bumped against the bank she fell backwards displaying her long, pink directoire knickers that reached to her knees demurely gathered with lace garters.

"Yew can see Nana's knickers," giggled Barbara's small daughter, who was too young to understand much of what was going on.

"Shwsh now, yew *naughty* girl," Barbara, my aunt, admonished, "before Nana hears yew!"

But she had already heard the 'naughty girl'. Stripped of her dignity, her face aflame, neck covered with red patches of anger and embarrassment she finally embarked and was rowed down the river sitting bolt upright and regal like Cleopatra gliding down the Nile. We averted our eyes as she demurely arranged the folds of her dress. All attempts at reconciliation were temporarily suspended until she gave some indication of thawing her now frozen glare.

Finally, we found a relatively safe place to disembark where the bank sloped gently down to the river. Once on a level, grassy patch above the water there was a flurry of blankets being shaken; tablecloths held at four corners to prevent the breeze blowing them and placed precisely on top of the blanket to provide a smooth, white tablecloth on which to lay the picnic. The primus stove was pumped for the women to have a cup of tea while the men and children cooled off in the River Usk.

It was an idyllic, warm, lazy afternoon. The river was cool and clear reflecting a green light from the surrounding foliage. Long sweeping branches of weeping willow caressed the water as a gentle breeze rippled the silvery surface. Lying indolently on the bank, my eyes closed against a dazzling sun, I watched insects balancing and hopping over the surface of the water. Underneath a seething mass of tiny flecks of liquid silver darting with staccato-like movements amongst the larger fish. Lethargically, I stretched my limbs drowsily aware of the activity around me. At the sound of a loud splash I sat up watching uncles and cousins diving from a small promontory of rock into the cool, green river. At the highest point of an adjacent rock my grandfather stood poised to dive into the sparkling water below.

Around sixty he was still trim and firm, his dark hair slightly greying at the temples. A short man, just five feet six inches tall, with a sturdy, muscular frame and blue eyes with a look more of a centurion than a Welsh man. There was a noble look to his features set off by a straight, Roman nose even more noticeable in profile. With a boyish whoop he dived into the river. As the seconds ticked away we waited for him to surface, but the water remained calm and smooth.

"He's been under a long time," Nana Smith observed in a worried voice.

We looked from one to the other as the seconds ticked away.

"I'm going down to have a look, just in case," Donald shouted to the others. "He might be entangled in weeds or hit his head or something!"

"Per'aps he's unconscious," exclaimed Raymond. "Quick boys, search the river bed!"

At that moment Dad Smith burst out of the water taking in great gasps of air. His face was red with effort and the breath rasped in his throat. My uncles swam around simultaneously relieved and angry like anxious mothers who do not know whether to scold or hug the missing child they have found. They grabbed him under the arms and solicitously started to haul him out of the water. Still too breathless to speak he struggled furiously to fight them off as they tried to drag him towards the bank while he attempted to maintain his position behind a partially submerged log lying near the far bank. Suddenly he spluttered,

"Let go! Leave me alone yew nincompoops; let me get my breath."

"Dad, why did yew have to dive into the water? Yew shouldn't be swimming and diving at your age," Raymond fumed.

Dad Smith drew himself up to his full five feet six inches as best he could still being out of his depth in the water. Stonily, he turned and faced my uncle.

"*Who* do yew think yew *are* saying I'm too old to swim? It's nothing to do with my age! My trunks got caught on this branch. They're ripped right up the back so I can't come out of the water. I need two hands to hold them together or they'll fall off. Now stop your clucking and fetch me a towel!"

Hoots of derision as they doggy-paddled and splashed in the water, coughing and spluttering with the effort of staying afloat whilst rocking with laughter. The aunts on the bank were tittering and shooting each other embarrassed but mischievous glances. Barbara's little one, startled by the commotion, started to cry loudly.

"Keep your distance yew girls," said Dad Smith, "I'm not decent. Well, don't just stand there gawping and laughing. Go and fetch a towel and that spare pair of trunks out of the boot of the car."

Finally, they were recovered. Refusing all assistance he wriggled into them, still in the water, one hand trying to hold a large towel that trailed along the surface of the water.

Later, when the excitement had subsided and we were all on the bank we settled down to eat our picnic. Ham and salmon sandwiches, heavy, home-made fruit cake, tinned peaches and cream, cheese, cream crackers and fresh tomatoes were eaten with relish: washed down with tea made on the ancient primus stove with bottles of Tizer and ginger beer for the children.

At five o' clock, the remnants of the picnic cleared away, children and adults piled into the boat to row upstream to the boathouse. Halfway up the river the uncles started to quarrel about whom should row the boat. Determined that I had a turn at rowing I nagged until Donald said,

"O.K. Yew can row if you fetch the oar."

With that he threw the oar into the river where it rapidly floated downstream towards the weir.

"Go on then, fetch the oar," he laughed knowing I was a strong swimmer.

"Not likely!" I said. "Yew threw it in and yew can fetch it!".

Donald grabbed me and pretended to force me overboard, but I hung on to the sides until my knuckles were white with the strain.

"If she goes in that river Duck yew can look out!" warned Dad Smith. "Stop your nonsense and fetch that oar!"

Finally, he realised that I was not going to budge and the oar was floating dangerously near to the weir. As soon as he had jumped into the water we began to row furiously on one oar whilst children slapped through the water with their hands trying to gain as much momentum as possible.

"Stop it now before there's an accident!" Nana and Dad Smith clucked away disapprovingly convinced that our horseplay would turn into disaster.

"Dwn't worry, he can swim like a fish, yew know that, besides it's only chest deep," Terry laughed. "Look at 'im go!"

Donald was swimming over arm as fast as he could towards the oar.

"Stay away from the weir!" Dad Smith shouted helpless to take any action. "Yew'll be sorry if anything goes wrong," he ranted at his other sons.

On reaching the oar Donald turned round and realised that he had been left behind about two hundred yards downstream. There was nothing for it but to swim to the bank which was now crowded with people sitting in deckchairs or sprawled on blankets. He hauled himself out of the water, raised the huge oar above his head, beat his chest and raced along the bank giving the traditional 'Tarzan' call much to the amusement of those who were watching, in anticipation, for the next episode in this unexpected drama. It was all taken in good fun but I knew that, sooner or later, he would get his own back. His chance came several weeks later on a similar outing.

THE SHOWMAN AND THE TRILBY

The glorious weather had broken towards the middle of August turning the skies leaden and grey. Heavy rain soaked the grass and left trees adorned with necklaces of sparkling rainwater. Separating like beads on a broken string they dripped to the ground to mingle with liquid diamonds threading the grass. Tired of summer Nature was yearning to display her autumn finery before the onset of the first frosts. Miraculously, now the summer was all but over, a bright sun once again floated in an azure sky as if reluctant to depart.

The thought of an Indian summer brought renewed energy and the prospect of at least one more family excursion. Sunday saw the usual paraphernalia being packed into the cars before we set off towards Brecon for another boat trip down the Usk.

"No big boats this time," Dad Smith warned. "I'm not having your mother embarrassed like she was last time. Now did yew hear that Duck?"

Donald sighed, averted his eyes and attempted to look suitably chastened,

"Yes, I heard yew. Do yew think I did it on purpose or what? Anyway the others were to blame as well as me, weren't they?"

"Yes, but yew were up to your tricks, as usual, showing yourself up running up the bank like yew did, and us too. I dwn't want any more of those stupid 'Tarzan' calls!" Dad Smith flung at him as he headed for the door.

An hour into our journey the sky had darkened to a slate-grey sheet of unbroken cloud. I quickly rolled up the car's side window as a splash of rain spattered onto my face and bare arms.

"We can't sit out if it's raining," my mother complained. "We'll have to find somewhere to go to amuse the boys if it keeps up."

"Let's see what it's like when we get there girl instead of moaning about it now," Dad Smith piped up cheerfully.

Capricious as a temperamental diva the weather supported his optimism. Chinks in the clouds parted to reveal a struggling sun that grew in strength lifting our dampened spirits.

By the time we reached Brecon it was a dazzling, hot day. After the fiasco of the previous trip the adults were content to sit on deckchairs on the bank next to the boathouse.

"No boats for yew," my mother declared looking at Roger, "not with an injured arm."

"Dwn't worry, they'll be all right with a pedalo as long as they stay here in the shallows near the bank. I'll keep an eye on them as well," offered the boatman.

After repeated nagging the youngsters were allowed to hire a pedalo and a two-seater canoe.

"Stay near the boathouse and dwn't venture out of sight!" ordered my mother who was nervously eyeing Roger making a beeline for a brightly-painted canoe.

He had broken his wrist while Richard, Barbara's son of the same age, had fractured his arm. Both were in plaster from wrist to elbow.

"Yew heard me, *not* the canoe and that's final!" my mother stated in an adamant tone. "Yew can't paddle a canoe with a broken wrist. Anyway, I dwn't trust yew to stay in the shallows."

"But mam!" Roger wailed.

"No buts, just do as you're told. Now yew and Richard can have a pedalo as long as yew stay in the marked out area. No arguments, do yew hear!"

"Aw, mam please!" wheedled Richard.

"Dwn't mam me; yew heard what I said, no canoes and that's that!" Barbara chimed in with finality.

Both boys sulked knowing that this time their mothers would not yield to cajoling. It was foot power or nothing.

Knowing that this would be too tame for the boys I wondered how long they would last before getting up to some mischief. Michael and Barbara's youngest son, Keith, had a small canoe between them. They were happily paddling backwards and forwards obediently staying in the shallows, close to the bank, neither of them being the adventurous type like the older boys.

"Over here!" Richard called to the younger boys. "Come on, let's change places."

"I dwn't want to change over!" Keith yelled back. "No, I might fall in!"

"Course yew won't. It's easy peasy. Dwn't be such babies, come on over," Roger laughed trying to goad them into the exchange.

After much gesturing and threatening glances the two older boys encouraged them over to the opposite bank still urging them to change places. Wobbling dangerously they frantically struggled to maintain their balance, each of them holding an oar awkwardly with the good hand. Carefully, they lowered themselves into position while my mother and Barbara stood glaring on the opposite bank demanding them to return to the other side and safety. All efforts fell on deaf ears. After much intense discussion as to how they could actually paddle with one hand each they left the sanctuary of the bank and appeared to be managing reasonably well.

At this point a car drove up and out climbed Raymond, my mother's brother. The bachelor in the family he had been with us on the previous 'Tarzan' trip. Good-looking, with the same dark eyes and hair as his brothers, a David Niven moustache and perfect, even white teeth. Much sought after by the local girls he was considered a bit of a heart- throb. With his cronies, all in their mid to late twenties, he had been out to lunch at the Wellington Hotel in Brecon. From his exaggerated attempts at sobriety it was obvious that he had been drinking.

"I hope yew haven't been drinking, especially in the middle of the day?" Nana Smith questioned censoriously.

"Only a little one, tha's all," he replied happily in a vaguely, squiffy voice.

"Well, yew'd better not have been drinking and driving, that's all," she retorted.

Once she had been assured that the driver of the car had not been imbibing she sniffed haughtily and her grunts of dissatisfaction soon subsided.

Donald was standing slightly apart watching the events with a wicked grin on his face. He was up to something.

"Why dwn't you hire a boat Ray?" he said. "Have some fun."

"No, I dwn't think so. We'll be moving on in a few minutes. Besides I'm wearing my best suit."

Grinning benevolently he adjusted the trilby perched on his head to a slightly, rakish angle. Immaculate in a dark-grey suit, white shirt, rather a sober-looking silver-grey tie with smart cufflinks twinkling at his wrists. Unused to drinking in the middle of the day he would never have been persuaded. Contentment resulting from an excellent lunch and the sultry heat, combined with strong ale, fired his enthusiasm.

His friends goaded him on,

"Go on, dwn't be lily-livered. Show us what yew can do Ray. We'd come with yew but there's only a single-handed canoe left. I bet yew can't even paddle a canoe. Well, I dwn't know about yew boys but I think he's all talk."

"Oh yes I can then. I'll show yew how it should be done!" he retorted as he stepped into the canoe Donald had generously hired.

"For goodness sake *act* your age, *both* of yew. You're in your twenties, not little boys, and yew a recently-married man." Nana Smith glared at Donald. "No more nonsense now or I'm not going with yew next weekend. I refuse to be *shown* up like this."

Tentatively, Raymond lowered himself into the craft still wearing his hat, immaculate shirt-cuffs showing beneath the equally immaculate sleeves of his jacket. Sitting bolt up-right, like a businessman at the head of the table in a boardroom meeting, he pushed himself from the bank wobbling slightly from side to side, a smug look on his face.

Suddenly the boys with the injured arms loomed near him. He prodded at their canoe with his paddle but, too late, the canoes crashed together. Lighter in weight, they managed to retain control of their craft but Raymond's canoe overturned. With a loud splash he fell into the river arms and legs akimbo.

There were hoots of laughter from the bank then a deathly hush as he disappeared from sight. The ripples on the surface receded and died leaving the water gleaming and calm.

Nana Smith cried, "Quick, my boy's drowning!"

"Ooh!" said a plump, matronly-looking woman on the bank, "There's his hat."

Still wearing it he rose majestically from the river, weeds adorning his trilby, like Poseidon rising from the sea. He stood chest-deep in the water, his face completely impassive, still immaculate but thoroughly wet. Bystanders on the bank were rolling with mirth, some with hands clasped over their mouths; one man holding his hips while his huge stomach heaved up and down with the effort of laughing; children throwing themselves onto the grass with loud whoops of delight.

Raymond stood there for a few moments; regal, serious and ominously silent. Serenely, he took off his hat, looked at the laughing crowd, bowed as deeply as the water would allow and announced with studied dignity,

"The show's over ladies and gentlemen! Thank yew for the applause!"

Slowly and deliberately he wrung the water out of his sodden hat, put it carefully back on his head, and struggled towards the bank. My grandmother was not laughing.

CARPETS FROM *CAIRDIFF*

"We're going to Dorset and then down to Devon," called my mother as she busied herself in the kitchen the following week. "Donald wants to try camping again, for a long weekend with Nana and Dad, travelling in convoy."

"Oh, no, not in a tent!" I groaned inwardly. "I hate it in a tent!" I remembered my first experience of life in the great outdoors. Another trip to the West country pretending to have a good time in damp, murky fields surrounded by people desperately enjoying themselves. Somehow, the last trip had turned out to be good fun once we had dispensed with the hassle of setting up the tent and subduing my mother's constant complaints. She loved these family outings, but she hated camping and what she mournfully called 'roughing it'. She only suffered what she believed were unnecessary indignities, because Donald took so much pleasure from organising the events.

"Do I have to come?" I moaned. "I'm old enough to stay on my own. Anyway, I'll be going to London with Nia before Christmas."

"Yes, not on your own though; with Aurona May and Ted. You're coming with us so no arguments. Anyway, we'll have to make the most of the fine weather. It's back to school for yew next week so this'll be the last trip this summer," my mother said tartly.

Friday morning dawned with cloudless, blue skies. It was a beautiful day for travelling; warm with a slight, cooling breeze. We loaded the cars with equipment taking care to remember the primus stove. Suddenly my mother appeared and, to our astonishment, put into the car boot two small, rolled-up carpets.

"Why dwn't yew take the kitchen sink?" said my grandfather with exasperation, "Yew've got everything else!"

My mother stuck her nose in the air haughtily.

"I dwn't want people to think we're a lot of 'sionies'[2] from the valleys," she said coining a popular valleys' phrase. Yew know what some of the English are like. They think we live in caves drinking pigeon's milk and saying, 'look yew now'. They can't believe we have smart houses, better than some of theirs. Camping in a tent, for goodness sake! Why does it have to be camping at all?"

"Yew know Donald likes all this outdoors, adventurous stuff. He thinks it's good for the soul."

"Well, it's not good for *my* soul!" she retorted.

"Oh, get in the car, for goodness sake," said my grandfather crossly, "while I'm still sane!"

She gave him a scathing glance sniffing loudly to indicate her disdain.

Finally, we set off gradually leaving the coal tips and the familiar winding gear of the Welsh valleys behind us. At last we caught sight of the Beachley ferry taking on cars for the short trip across the Severn River. This was my favourite part of the trip west. I loved being on the water. Settling comfortably I watched carefully as each car drove slowly towards the boat, up the ramp and on to a turntable.

Attached to the turntable a thick rope snaked away from a metal ring. Once the car was on the turntable a seaman hauled on the rope, rotated it, and positioned the vehicle neatly into a parking space.

"Can I get out on deck to watch the roundabout?"

"It's not a roundabout, it's a turntable. Stay in the car!" my grandfather ordered.

"Well, I can't see anything in here can I?"

"Oh, all right but stay right next to me. No wandering off," he said as he helped me out of the car and threaded his way through the vehicles.

As we made the short voyage across the estuary he explained,

"The waters here are very dangerous. Look, yew can see the undercurrents," he pointed. "Sometimes a huge tidal wave called the Severn Bore travels right along the estuary. I've only seen it once but it's a marvellous sight."

2 Sion is the Welsh equivalent of John

I peered over the edge of the ferry into the murky, brown waters; water so muddy with silt that it looked almost solid.

A gentle bump announced our arrival on the other side. As the ramp slowly lowered car drivers revved up their engines ready to roll off and up the slipway. Impatient honking brought furious looks from the owner of a stalled car. We waited while he rummaged in the boot for the starting handle. Muttering to himself he pushed it in the hole underneath the front of the car and cranked the engine. It stuttered, hung onto life for a few seconds then died.

"Come on mun buttie, we 'aven't got all day!" complained a rough-looking man from the car behind him. "Crank the bloody thing up mun!"

Using all his strength he cranked it round again. Suddenly the engine sputtered into life.

"Keep your foot on the accelerator until I get in Jean. Gently, gently, I said!" he yelled at his wife as the engine roared.

Easing his foot onto the accelerator he carefully lowered himself into the driver's seat. With a last defiant look he slammed the door and clattered off the ferry.

We drove up the ramp at Aust into a foreign country where the pubs opened on Sundays and everybody spoke with a funny accent. Not taking the ferry meant a long, tedious drive round the Severn Estuary into Monmouth and on to Gloucester; a trip that could take a considerable number of hours given the speed of vehicles in those days.

On weekends we often explored the fertile lands of Hereford or the Forest of Dean where we picnicked and played 'hide and seek' in the trees. Fruit farms, fields full of grain and fat cattle came into view as we drove leisurely through the countryside. Fields stretched out before us like a crocheted quilt; colours ranging from bright emerald green to gold and the brilliant yellow of rapeseed flowers. Set amongst the crops slightly undulating fields broken by small copses isolated like an oasis in the middle of a green desert.

Eyes closed I basked in the heat of the sun shining through the windscreen, lulled into drowsiness by the movement of the car. Spotting a grassy lay-by Dad Smith said,

"We'll pull in here for a rest. It's a nice shady place for a brew."

It was a beautiful spot, set just off the road, screened from the highway by a grassy verge covered with trees and wild flowers. I set about my usual task of pumping up the ancient primus stove while the others busied themselves with sandwiches and cakes.

The boys were rolling around in the grass playing cowboys and Indians clearly enjoying the freedom after being confined in the cars for so long.

"I'll be the sheriff. Duck down behind this wagon boys. Bang! Bang!" shouted Roger gleefully.

"Why must yew always be the sheriff? I'm going to be 'im!" Richard asserted dodging imaginary arrows."

"Oh all right, we'll *both* be sheriffs and yew two can be our deputies," Roger conceded. With theatrical intensity Michael and Keith stood to attention, pinned on their badges, and entered the world of make-believe.

Looking around at the happy, animated faces I felt a sense of security, of pleasure and of pain, knowing that it would not always be like this. I shivered slightly feeling a chill breeze that had whipped up unexpectedly as though accompanying my thoughts.

Tiny clouds scudded swiftly across the sky as though they were being swept along by a harassed housewife with her broom. Dark, ominous skies were starting to appear in the West, the direction in which we were heading. We decided to move on as it looked as though a storm was brewing. It was much darker and the brilliant sun was now blocked by heavy, grey clouds.

"Let's pack up before the rain starts," Nana Smith directed. "Come on boys, in the cars before yew get wet."

Large raindrops spattered on the windscreen. All around was a curtain of rain that glinted in the weak shafts of sunlight penetrating the blanket of clouds. We pushed on realising that we would not reach our destination that night. Donald, who was travelling in front, signalled and pulled in to the side of the road. He plunged out of his Dormobile and ran towards us with his coat pulled over his head. Bounding up to the car he stuck his head through the car window grinning, as usual, not at all perturbed by the weather conditions or the bleak prospect of staying in a lay-by all night.

"There's a fog rising," he said. "If it gets worse we might as well pull in and sleep in the car for the night"

He was obviously loving every minute of it: to him it was just another adventure.

"This is your fault again Duck!" said my mother and her sister Barbara, in unison, using his pet name.

"Now what will we do?" wailed my mother. "We can't sleep in the car. We'll be murdered by some tramp!"

"Oh, dwn't be so stupid!" said Dad Smith. The men will take turns to stay awake. It'll be perfectly safe so stop going on. There's nothing else to be done," he said resignedly.

An hour later the fog was so thick we were barely crawling along. Visibility was so bad that with the headlamps on we were faced with a thick, smoky blanket of fog. Without strong lights it was blackness all round. Donald signalled that he was going to pull in. We followed and got up as close to his vehicle as possible feeling a slight bump as the tyres hit some stones. The car rose upwards marginally before settling down.

"The verge is a bit steep here," said Dad Smith peering into the thick, impenetrable, pea-soup fog. "Still we seem to be well off the road, that's the main thing."

Donald dashed up to the car shouting over the pounding of the rain that had started again with a vengeance.

"We'll stay here for a few hours and make an early start as soon as it gets light."

We sat bolt upright all night wriggling and squirming in the restricted space. My legs ached unbearably and I badly wanted to visit the lavatory. Finally, I fell into a fitful sleep and dreamed of faceless bodies chasing me through the fog. I was running towards a light. Voices came to me through the miasma as I struggled to open my eyes, but I couldn't open them. It was as though each time my eyelids parted a searing light pierced my eyes. Distantly, I could hear my mother exclaiming in an agitated voice,

"Wake up dad! Wake up!"

Muscles aching, eyes dulled with fatigue, I sat up and peered out. Shafts of bright sun poured through the car windows bathing everything in early morning light. The sky was once again a clear, sapphire blue. Lush green fields stretched away into the distance. Suddenly, I heard the harsh honking of car horns and muted shouts.

Struggling wearily out of the car I shaded my eyes against the brightness of the morning. Horrified, my mother stood rooted to the spot. Vehicles were moving swiftly around our field, the drivers hooting with great glee. We were perched on top of a large, green mound like parasites clinging to a dog's back.

"My God, we're on a roundabout!" screamed my mother. "Quick dad before the police get us!"

We drove off the roundabout with as much dignity as we could muster. People in cars watching us with huge amusement and delight.

"Good for you! Freedom to park for everyone!" shouted one driver honking repeatedly in support of our unintentional stand on parking rights.

"See!" said my mother sitting rigidly in her seat consumed with embarrassment and indignation. "I knew it! I knew we'd look like a lot of 'sionies' from the valleys! I'm never coming with yew again Duck. Never again!"

Furiously, she wound up the window then sank back into her seat glowering with indignation refusing to respond to his cajoling entreaties.

We had been travelling behind Donald's Dormobile for hours. Every time we stopped at a red traffic light he stuck his head through the window and shouted reassuringly,

"Not much further now! We're almost there! I can smell the sea!"

This was very little comfort since he had been saying the same thing for miles. Suddenly, Michael squealed with delighted,

"The sea! I can see the sea!"

"At last! I thought we'd never get here," Nana Smith declared in a voice weary with fatigue.

It was typical of Donald, driving on and on until everyone was screaming for relief from the motion of four wheels, but he was always forgiven because of his infectious enthusiasm.

Pale, golden sands swept round an arc of sapphire, blue sea. Weymouth beach was alive with holiday-makers making the most of the sunny weather. We drove along the seafront and out of town until we came to a camp site situated in the grounds of a large, old country house set high above the sea affording a magnificent view of the bay. Sighing with relief we piled out of the car glad to be able to stretch our legs after such a long journey.

"I was beginning to wonder if this place really existed," complained my mother wearily as she pulled out sleeping bags and other camping paraphernalia.

It took six of them to haul out the huge, army-surplus bell-tent that my mother had reluctantly bought from a neighbour, Johnny Bartlett, when he had heard we were going camping.

"It'll sleep two families at least, if necessary," he had assured us.

"Yew can see there'll be bags of room in it; more than enough," Donald coaxed knowing that he and his family would be sleeping in his well-equipped Dormobile. "Come on, let's go and take a look at it."

A cursory inspection had revealed that it was in good order throughout and it came complete with a groundsheet. Much to my mother's consternation the deal was done.

Placed in position with the main pole secured to the ground the skeleton of the tent looked enormous.

"Right," said Donald, giving orders as usual, "hold on to the ropes and pull when I tell yew. Right, now heave! Heave!"

Struggling with the weight adults and children strained at the guy-ropes. It was harder and heavier than I thought.

"Oh, for goodness sake put some elbow-grease into it!" yelled Donald. "At this rate we'll still be trying to put it up tomorrow morning!"

Tugging, heaving and puffing we hauled at the ropes and at last the tent began to take some shape as the fabric tightened.

"Right," said Donald, grinning with ill-concealed joy, "pull outwards as far as yew can and secure your pegs."

"Yes sir!" said Betty his dark-haired wife, the dimples in her cheeks deepening as she attempted to conceal a smirk. Arms trembling with the effort she almost lost her grip as she tried to give a mock salute.

Suddenly, there was a new noise amongst the cacophony of sound. It was a dry, tearing noise. As we pulled huge, gaping holes were appearing all over the fabric. One final pull and the tent became a mass of shredded material flapping around in the breeze. Horrified, my mother tried to speak but no sound emerged from her quivering lips; her eyes shone with tears of embarrassment. People around us were giggling and some were openly laughing at our predicament. Betty brought her hand up to her face and stared wide-eyed with disbelief.

"That's it!" said Nana Smith who had said very little during the whole trip. "Another one of your catastrophes again Duck. I've suffered enough humiliation for one day. I'm going home. I've never liked the idea of camping anyway and I'm blowed if I'll sleep in that *thing*!"

Grinning nervously and trying to brush off her embarrassment my mother suddenly disappeared into the boot of the car and began to rummage around frantically. She emerged triumphant and breathless, very red in the face, clasping to her bosom the two lovely rugs she had bought in Cardiff the previous week.

"I'm glad we brought these now," she said, "otherwise they might think we're gypsies."

Dad Smith just gawped at her; a look of complete incredulity stamped on his handsome features.

Furiously, she began shaking imaginary dust from them, looking out of the corner of her eye at the same time to ensure that the audience was still watching.

"I'm so ashamed I could die! This is the very last time I'm going with yew Duck and that's final! Next time I'm going to an hotel. Yew and your hair-brained schemes!" A sob caught in her throat, "We'll never get into an hotel if we haven't booked. What will we do now if it rains?"

It rained – all night it rained: the wind moaned through the trees, along the dry stone walls of the fields and rattled the slates of the old house. We huddled inside our sleeping bags while Dad Smith told us stories about the Great War until all fell quiet.

Out of the blackness a voice said,

"Well, at least they know the Welsh have carpets in their bedrooms."

Stifling a laugh I looked up at the faint chink of light penetrating the top of the tent as my mother's carpets flapped up and down in the wind over the holes they covered to keep us dry. It seemed only minutes later that I became aware of a terrific din. The sounds of crying, giggling, scuffling: the drumming of rain and howling of wind all penetrated my subconscious. Suddenly, I was wrapped in wet darkness.

"Oh no," howled a voice in abject misery, "the tent's collapsed!"

I groaned and let the blackness engulf me.

"This is what it must be like to be dead," I thought, "and in Hell!"

I drifted into blackness. The end of another perfect day.

JELLIED EELS AND PEARLY QUEENS

After bumping up the ramp onto the Beachley ferry the ferryman signalled for Ted to drive on to the turntable. He grabbed the rope and swung the car around to position it safely for our short trip across the Severn Estuary.

"Quick, let's get out 'till we get across!" I urged.

"The water looks muddy. I wouldn't like to fall in there," said my friend Nia warily.

"People have drowned down there in those currents. Look, yew can see the water swirling," I remarked dramatically, remembering what Dad Smith had told me on our last trip across the Severn.

"How deep do yew think it is then?"

"Hundreds and hundreds of feet, I expect."

"Very funny. I bet it's not then. Yew're just trying to scare me," Nia said nervously clutching the rail every time the ferry rolled slightly.

"Dwn't worry, we're almost there now."

Minutes later the boat bumped against the quay on the Aust side. As the ramp slammed onto the concrete slipway cars moved forward ready to climb up the steep slope.

"Newbury first stop then we'll go to see my brother Isaac. He's been very poorly lately. We'll stay there overnight," said Aurona May as the ferry receded into the distance.

"After that we'll be gawin' up to the 'smawk' to see mum," Ted enthused.

A native Londoner he had migrated to Wales after the Second World War and settled permanently.

"Wawn't be too long gettin' there gals."

"We're going to see Buckingham Palace and Trafalgar Square!"

Nia exclaimed excitedly. "I'm glad yew came with us for company."

"Yew won't be going anywhere unsupervised, either of yew," Aurona May said emphatically. "Yew'll stay with us and that's that!"

"I'm going on fourteen!" Nia said indignantly.

"And I'm going on fifteen. I've been to London a few times before."

"Yes, with yewer family. Yewer mother said yew're not to go out on yewer own, and neither are yew Nia. It's not like Abercynon. It's not safe!" she said her expression daring us to argue.

Sullenly, we glowered at the back of her head and contemplated hours dragging behind them for the whole of the trip.

Our spirits lifted when we stopped outside the Railway Inn in Newbury. It had an old-world charm and a cosy dining room with freshly laundered tablecloths and napkins. After a comfortable night, on a deep mattress, we were tempted downstairs by the smell of bacon and toast.

"Smell that!" I said sniffing like one of the Bisto kids.

"Come on, let's get down before it all goes," Nia urged running down the steep stairs.

Full and contented after a huge breakfast of scrambled eggs, bacon, black pudding, sausages, tomatoes and fried bread, followed by toast and marmalade, I sat back in my chair.

"Why do they call it a full English?" I queried sipping at my tea.

"Because that's what they eat for breakfast, innit, silly?" Nia retorted before her mother could answer.

"Well, it's daft! It's exactly the same as a Welsh breakfast."

"Yes, except some people in Wales like to fry Laver bread in the bacon fat," Aurona May observed.

"That's seaweed, it's horrible! I dwn't like that awful black pudding either," I shuddered.

"It's very nutritious so they say. Come on, let's have a look around the town before we go."

After a quick tour of Newbury we headed for Reading to see Isaac: a pitifully thin, dark-haired man, black circles under his eyes and chiselled lines from nose to mouth. When he smiled his gaunt features still retained something of the handsome man he had been before illness struck. An aura of transience clung to him as he offered his pale, delicate hand in greeting.

"So, you're Nia's friend, are yew?" he remarked in a diluted Welsh accent.

"Yes, how do yew do?" I responded shaking a hand that felt cold and clammy.

Inexplicably, I felt uncomfortable as though touching him would be touching death. His dressing gown hung on his emaciated body: translucent skin and fragile skeleton decreed he would not be much longer in our world.

"Why dawn't the girls go out into the garden for a bit while we talk to Isaac," Ted suggested.

Thankful to escape the cloying atmosphere of his sick room Nia and I escaped into the garden and fresh air until it was time to depart. Blue sky and bright sunshine soon lifted our spirits as we reached the outskirts of London and headed for the sights.

Previous visits to London, with my family, had always been concentrated on tourist areas such as Westminster Abbey, Trafalgar Square, and the museums. Dougie Davies, our teacher in Carnetown Primary School, had also organised an educational sight-seeing excursion in my last year in the school. As the coach approached Buckingham Palace we could see the guardsmen in their scarlet tunics.

"They're not real soldiers," remarked a bespectacled girl with fat pigtails reaching to her waist, "just dummies for decoration. They're not movin' a muscle."

"Oh, yes they are then, look!" screamed Melvyn.

"They're changing the guard," informed Dougie as the soldiers stamped to attention ready to march off.

Children stood up craning their necks to see the guardsmen in their busbies.

"Calm down now and sit in your seats before there's an accident," warned Emlyn Jones, one of the staff."

"But sir!"

"We've passed them now so settle down," he ordered firmly as we headed for the embankment. "We'll be going on the river soon. Yew'll enjoy that."

Slowly, our boat furrowed its way through the water taking us down river to Kingston-on-Thames. Children clamoured to get near the rails to watch the ramp being hauled away.

"Away from the side, please," ordered Dougie, "and sit on the benches."

Always indifferent to orders Danny, already on his way to becoming a legend, hung his upper body over the side trying to touch the water.

"What have I told yew?" Dougie fumed grabbing him by the scruff of the neck. "Now get over there before I give yew a thick ear. Do yew hear me my lad?"

"But sir, mun!"

"Yew'll have my hand against your backside in a minute if yew keep arguing with me! Now get over there and *stay* there!"

Danny slunk off and threw himself on the seat swinging his legs with frustration.

"Spoilsport!" he whispered vehemently as the boat slid away from the bank to begin its journey.

As we moved downstream Dougie pointed to various forms of wild-life that lived on the river. Suddenly, the chatter was broken by a shrill cry.

"Look, a kingfisher!" Dougie pointed.

Every face turned in the direction of the bank trying to focus on what he could see.

"Sir! Sir! I can see it sir!" cried an excited child. "Oh, innit beautiful sir?"

Suddenly, in a flash of greenish-blue and orange-brown the bird dived into the river reappearing with a fish.

"Watch carefully," Dougie instructed.

As the kingfisher returned to his perch he threw the fish into the air, caught it and swallowed it whole, drawing a corporate gasp of wonder from its admiring audience.

"Do yew think it'll do it again sir?" queried a plump, freckle-faced lad.

"That's how they survive lad, by fishing for food. Sometimes, if the fish is too big to swallow the kingfisher will bang it against a stone to soften it up."

"Gosh, tha's fantastic innit sir?"

Tired out, on the return journey children settled comfortably to chatter amongst themselves. The sun poured its rays over the cool waters; a dazzling display of sun and shadows that hurt my eyes. Lush greenery, a sense of tranquillity and the soothing motion of the craft soon lulled me into a dream-like state. Smoothly, we glided through the water the bows furrowing little troughs either side of the boat. Behind my closed eyes I felt something vaguely wet land on my cheek.

"Aw no, it's rainin," complained Little Dai as the heavens opened and poured down on us as we disembarked.

Scurrying like ants disturbed by an overturned stone we scampered for the shelter of nearby trees.

Suddenly, Dougie said,

"Where's Brian?"

"I saw him sitting with Ian on the boat," Mr. Jones assured him, " and I counted him as he got off."

"Well, he's not here now. We'd better take another head count."

Frantically, Dougie made another roll call but it was obvious that Brian had disappeared. The coach driver waved us into the 'bus stating emphatically that he had a schedule to follow.

"Never mind about your schedule; there's a child missing," Mr. Jones barked angrily.

"Stay here with Miss Thomas and dwn't move an inch!" ordered Dougie. Mr. Jones and I are going to look for him.

As they weaved in and out of the crowd of tourists lingering on the jetty Emlyn Jones shouted,

"There he is, on the boat! Hey stop!"

Too late, the boat disappeared round a bend in the river with Brian waving hysterically from the rail.

"Wait 'till I get my hands on him; he's going to be a very sorry little boy!" seethed Dougie. After a hurried discussion the staff called the police who decided to drive down to the next port of call to bring Brian back.

Overhead the sky was molten lead creased with shafts of silver light that lit up the driving rain. For the rest of the afternoon it poured, abated, then poured again until we were soaked and miserable. Fractious children wandered round the Serpentine splashing through puddles that seeped through our sodden shoes leaving our feet cold and uncomfortable. With a few hours to wait Dougie waved us on to the coach for our journey home leaving Mr. Jones behind to deal with the errant Brian who had sneaked back on the boat to 'spend a penny'.

After lunch we drove from Trafalgar Square along Oxford Street then on towards the British Museum. Nia and I eyed each other nervously. The newspapers were always full of stories about gangsters in London particularly in the East End. British crime films featured Spivs, murderers and gang fights. Everybody had heard of the mass murderer Reginald Christie who had been hanged in Pentonville Prison in 1953.

"That murderer Christie lived in London," I said apprehensively.

"That was in Nottin' 'ill," Ted said over his shoulder. "We're not gawin' anywhere near there. We're gawin' right awver north of Bloomsbury first. It's where all the writers used to hang out."

Shuddering, we consoled ourselves with the thought that the chirpy Tommy Steele was an East Ender and he looked friendly enough.

Just like Londoners thought that all Welsh people dressed in tall, black hats, lived in tiny, dark cottages dotted along the hillsides under the slag heaps and proclaimed, "look yew now!" at the end of every sentence (a phrase I have never actually heard in Wales) so we mistakenly believed that all Londoners were Spivs or rough, tough undesirables who robbed or murdered at the blink of an eye.

"They talk a bit funny though dwn't they?" said Nia.

"I know, they can't say three only 'free' and they use some kind of slang words like 'norf' and souf'," I giggled.

"Shwsh or Ted will hear us," chortled Nia stuffing her fist into her mouth to conceal her laughter.

"This is it!" Ted exclaimed as we pulled up outside a large guest house, its peeling front door evidence of years of neglect.

"Come on then. Let's gaw inside."

Hesitantly, we trailed into the hallway noting the shabby, frayed carpet and garish, artificial flowers constructed from blue, crêpe paper. Ted rang the desk bell with the palm of his hand.

"Gaw on, it's not that bad," he said looking at Aurona May for support.

"Couldn't yew find anything better than this dump?" she whispered.

The desk clerk, a shifty-looking man with dirty, greasy-hair, shoved two sets of keys at Ted.

"Second floor, rooms seven and eight. Anything else sir?" he said perfunctorily turning his back to us.

"Well, let's hope this is the worst bit of the place," Aurona May fumed as we headed for the threadbare stairs.

"Pardon," apologised a plump, middle-aged woman chattering animatedly in rapid French as she squeezed by on her way downstairs.

On our way up we passed a young, black man on the stairs. Smiling broadly, revealing very white teeth, he greeted us in accented English.

"Good afternoon."

We shrank back against the wall afraid to move. Flustered, we mumbled an acknowledgement,

"Er, yes, er, afternoon," and waited for him to pass.

"They're all foreigners," I whispered uncertainly.

His smile turned to a grimace of annoyance as he continued down the stairs leaving us feeling vulnerable and anxious. We were comforted only by the knowledge that Aurona May and Ted's room was next door to ours.

Tentatively, we ventured into our room looking round at the stark, ugly furnishings with trepidation.

"Look at that sink, it's filthy," I shuddered eyeing the chipped, murky-looking wash-hand basin.

On one wall a gas fire set in a black, cast-iron grate, surrounded by dark-green tiles. Under the window a gas stove alongside a

290

plywood cupboard painted a garish green that clashed violently with the cracked fawn and brown linoleum on the floor.

"It's terrible *and* I can smell gas! We'll be gassed to death in our sleep or murdered!" Nia shrieked. We'll ask Ted to see if it lights."

"Yeah, and then we'll all be blown up if it's leaking," I retorted.

Set against the side wall was a wardrobe with one of its doors hanging on a rusty hinge. I pulled open the door complaining,

"What a stink!" as a damp, musty smell hit my nostrils.

Suddenly, the door creaked and crashed to the floor revealing dozens of tangled, wire coat-hangers suspended on a rickety rail.

"Well, *I'm* not hanging my clothes in *there!*" I declared. "Yew never know what yew'll catch!"

"The bed doesn't look very nice either, does it?" Nia said miserably pulling back the faded, candlewick bedspread. "Well, at least the sheets are clean. I'll be glad to get out of here."

"Well, I suppose we'd better have a wash, at least," I said straining to turn on the big, brass tap.

For a few seconds nothing happened then the pipes began to gurgle and tremble. A blast of dirty water suddenly gushed from the rumbling tap turning the sink a rusty brown.

"That's it, we can't even have a wash!" I cried.

Eventually, the water cleared allowing us a perfunctory rinse of our faces and hands before we ventured downstairs to find Aurona May looking equally perturbed.

"Didn't yew check on this place before yew booked?" she asked angrily marching out of the front door.

After picking up Ted's mother, who had moved out of the East End after her house had been blown apart by a bomb in the blitz, we headed once again for the sights. A sweet, silver-haired old lady with pale, blue eyes like Ted and the same peculiar accent.

"Look," Ted pointed as we drove past St. Martin's in the Field, "there's the Pearly King and Queen."

"Where? Where's the Queen?" I said looking at the tail end of the parade.

"Not *the* Queen. They're called the Pearly King and Queen

because they have mother-of-pearl buttons sewn all over their clothes. It's a big honour in the East End."

"The paride's awver naw," his mother remarked giving a final wave at the disappearing backs of the marchers.

"Never mind, we'll gaw out for a real treat liyter on."

Ted took us to a traditional pie and mash shop near Tower Bridge for our special treat. We studied the 'everything with chips' menu but before we had chance to order Ted said,

"Naw, let me order for ya; a real East End dish."

"What is it?" we chorused.

"The sime as they're eatin' awver there," he grinned gleefully.

To our horror diners on the next table were eating chopped up bits of greyish-coloured snakes covered in a slimy film.

"Yuk! What are those snake things?" I choked.

"Jellied eels!" exclaimed Ted rubbing his hands together.

I shuddered convinced that the 'snakes' were moving around amongst the peas and mash looking for a hiding place.

Jellied eels all rawnd then?" Ted beamed expectantly.

"No thanks," the three of us said quickly opting for steak and kidney pudding.

Ted consumed the jellied eels relishing the opportunity of eating something he had been deprived of since living in Wales. Wincing, we looked away trying not to show our disgust, stomachs churning with every mouthful he swallowed.

Later that night we returned to the guest house. Once inside the room Nia and I locked the door then used all our strength to push a grubby armchair against it firmly lodging it under the handle. I sniffed the air.

"We'd better open the window just in case we're gassed in our sleep," I declared anxiously.

The windows, their catches encrusted with layers of thick paint, resisted all attempts to open them. Thankfully, the sash let in a two-inch gap of fresh air near the top of the rickety frame.

"Well, at least nobody can get in," I remarked.

We hauled another chair, placed it under the window, and perched our overnight cases precariously on top.

"That's it," Nia breathed a sigh of relief.

"If anyone tries to break in the cases will fall and we'll hear them," she said sounding more confident than I felt.

On our arrival we had heard the owner talking about a young girl who had been murdered in the vicinity of the guest house. Too frightened to sleep we dozed between patches of wakefulness jumping awake at the slightest sound.

Breakfast the next morning was completely inedible. Tense and bleary-eyed I stared at the small shot glass of squash posing as fresh orange juice. Aurona May pulled a face,

"I can't eat *that* Ted, it's disgustin'."

Half a cold, fried egg, cemented to the plate with fat that had congealed into a grey-white splodge, sat forlornly on the blue-speckled Formica table. Stuck to the side of the plate a half-slice of insipid, wafer-thin sliced bread.

"Yuk, I can't eat that mess!" I declared.

How I longed for a slice of Nana Smith's fresh batch, a Swansea loaf with thick Shir Gar butter or a door-step of brown, whole-meal with thick strawberry jam.

Nia and I looked at each other then at Aurona May who had a face like thunder.

"Humph! This is the first and *last* time I'll stay in a place like this. What *were* yew thinkin' of?"

"Well, how was I to knaw. It wasn't like this last time I was 'ere."

"Well, next time we stay in the West End and yew can go and see yewer mother by tube!"

She glared at Ted who looked sheepish for the rest of the day, but all was forgotten when we returned to Newbury and stayed again at the Railway Inn.

That night we lay in our twin beds giggling hysterically about our trip to 'The Smoke'. Snuggled in crisp, white sheets I wriggled my head on the feather pillows luxuriating in their softness.

"Won't be long for Christmas now," Nia said. "I'd like a new duffle-coat, bright red. I've seen 'em in the shops," she sighed.

Suddenly, she shot up in the bed.

"What about the chickens?" she exclaimed.

"What about 'em?" I replied.

"They bought 'em to fatten up for Christmas dinner didn't they?"

"Yeah, but dwn't worry, they won't kill 'em, not now," I replied.

Drifting into sleep I remembered how we'd bought the cute little chicks in Pontypridd market.

CHRISTMAS CHICKS

In the 1950s Pontypridd was a bustling, market town where shoppers ambled and jostled their way into John Collier's, Woolworth's, Marks and Spencer, furniture shops, clothes shops, shoe shops, grocers and butchers. As we walked down Taff Street weak shafts of sunlight played across a fine drizzle reflecting watery, rainbow colours. Within seconds the rain intensified to glittering, silver needles that bounced off the pavement. Umbrellas bloomed like flowering cacti after a good watering obliterating the pavement ahead.

"Shall we go to Haines' first?" Aurona May asked my mother. "I want to get some new hand towels."

"Yes, I dwn't mind. I've been wanting to get a couple of cushions for ages, but I want to pop in Leslie's Stores after that. I saw a *lovely* three-piece suite there last time I was down."

Inside Haines' curtains were displayed on the walls. Sheets, pillow-cases and towels were stacked in neat piles on shelves behind the counter.

"Thank you. Will there be anything else?" asked the grey-haired sales assistant as my mother handed over the money for the cushions.

"Er, I dwn't think so. No, no thank you."

I watched as the woman put the money into a fat cylinder and pushed it into a metal tube that ran up the wall into the room above. With a loud 'whoosh' of air it was sucked up to the office returning within minutes with change and a receipt.

Outside the rain had stopped leaving shallow puddles that soon evaporated under a warm sun leaving the pavements clean and dry. Crowds of people, from surrounding towns and villages, descended on Pontypridd every Wednesday and Saturday: from Abercynon, Aberdare, Porth, Penrhiwceiber, Tonypandy, Llantrisant and Merthyr Tydfil. They flocked to the indoor market to buy meat, fruit, vegetables and flowers: fresh fish, Laver bread, mussels and cockles from the Mumbles in Swansea.

"I couldn't eat that Laver bread, could yew?" my mother remarked screwing up her nose with disgust. "I tried it once but I couldn't stomach it."

"It's supposed to be lovely cooked in bacon fat, but I dwn't fancy it myself. Ycha fi!" Aurona May replied.

They moved leisurely from stall to stall stopping to admire china ornaments, brass wall-plates and decorative fenders while Nia and I pored over second-hand books and 78s". A myriad of stalls creating a clamorous, cornucopia of studded dog collars, bird cages, brightly-coloured wools, knitting needles, patterns, baby clothes, costume jewellery, watches; hand-made chocolates, humbugs, aniseed balls and striped, soft-centred 'loshins'. At the side entrance an engraver worked quietly over a silver bracelet in his little glass booth.

Outside stallholders plied their wares tempting onlookers to part with their money for brightly-coloured towels or a length of curtain material. Bales of velvet, silk, net, taffeta and cotton, in all colours of the rainbow, lying in neat rows or standing behind the stall like faceless sentinels. A glib salesman enticing bystanders as he threw rolls of fabric that opened and spilled over the stall in a vibrant burst of colour.

"I'll tell yew what I'll do, but just for yew mind," he grinned at a stout woman in a brown, felt hat and sturdy shoes.

"I wasn't born yesterday," she retaliated.

"I can see yew're an intelligent woman missus. Tell yew what, if yew buy a whole bale I'll throw in a pair of bath towels, but only 'cause I like those big, blue eyes. Can't say fairer than that now, can I?"

"Aw, go on with yew," she simpered melting under his attention.

On the stall opposite baskets of crockery were thrown up in the air to the gasps of women who feared they would smash to smithereens. Deftly catching it, without breaking a single cup, the marketeer shouted,

"Aw, come on ladies mun! A complete dinner service. Not two pounds, not thirty shillings. To you one guinea."

Shaking their heads the women edged away but not before they heard,

"Do yew want 'em for nothing? Fifteen shillings then, ten bob, 7s 6d, five shillings and that's my final offer!"

Hurried rummaging for purses lost in the contents of full shopping bags. Mutters of frustration in case they lost their chance. Sighs of self-satisfaction as they triumphantly walked off with their bargains.

Inside the market stood two cramped cafés with small, square tables covered in patterned oilcloth and wooden, ladder-backed, kitchen chairs. They plied a roaring trade from passers' by tempted inside by the enticing smell of crusty, home-made steak and kidney pie. Cheap, wholesome meals filled the menu: fat faggots and peas, crisp, battered plaice and chips with slices of bread and butter followed by generous slices of steaming apple tart and custard.

Tucked away discreetly, along the side wall of the indoor market, were the second-hand, clothes stalls where they bought and sold garments. Children eagerly pulled their parents towards the rabbits, tortoises, kittens and puppies that gazed soulfully from their little wired cages. Tropical fish swam in tanks of water through swaying fronds of sea ferns and shells. Excited boys and girls clung tenaciously to containers with a single, lonely goldfish peering bug-eyed through the glass globe.

Yellow, fluffy chicks huddled together in open, wooden crates waiting to be bought and raised for Christmas.

"Let's buy some chicks!" Nia exclaimed attempting to stroke the squirming birds.

"Yes, we could have two each for company. We'd feed them ourselves, wouldn't we?" I said looking at Nia for support.

"Don't be so silly! Yew can't keep chicks in the house. They're not pets. Where would we keep them?" my mother laughed.

"Well, we could keep them in the back garden, couldn't we?" Suddenly Aurona May said,

"Do yew know, that's not such a bad idea. I've just rented that allotment to grow vegetables in; the one right across from the lane behind my house. We could keep them there and fatten 'em up for Christmas dinner."

"Oh, I dwn't know......it'd be a lot of potch feeding them every day, wouldn't it?"

"Yew can't eat chicks!" I protested.

"Well, they won't be chicks by Christmas will they? Anyway what do yew think yew usually eat?" retorted Aurona May.

They bought two chicks each and carried them home on the 'bus in a cardboard box with little breathing holes pierced in the sides. Ted built a wooden, chicken coop in Aurona May's allotment extending it into a small wire-enclosed run. Chicken wire was placed discreetly under the privet hedge to stop them getting out into the lane.

Every day my mother and Aurona went to the allotment to feed the chicks. Sitting on the rustic seat, sipping cups of tea, they commented daily on their growth or worried about a perceived limp.

"Do yew think that one looks a bit quiet today? She's not moving around much."

"Yes, she's all right; look, there she goes," Aurona May replied as the growing chick scampered across to the others, head darting from side to side.

One by one the chicks acquired names and became so tame they pecked for food from our hands.

"Come on Ginny, there's a good girl," my mother coaxed holding out some corn, "and yew Bella. Come on, chick, chick."

"I'm glad we bought them now," Aurona May smiled as she sat on the bench drinking a glass of ginger beer.

"Me too, they've been really funny at times," replied my mother raising her face to the sun in an attempt to acquire a tan. "Still we'd better not get too attached."

As the months wore on my mother and Aurona stopped talking

about fattened chickens and Christmas dinner. Instead they laughed at the antics and peculiarities of the birds that had become pets. Slaughtering them had never really been a considered option just a vague, romantic notion of raising their own stock. A few weeks before Christmas they ordered their seasonal poultry from Woodley's butchers, as usual. However, fate was about to strike a cruel blow to the chicken-lovers. The owner of the allotment decided he wanted it back.

As Christmas approached both women put on a brave face avoiding the fact that the chickens would have to be killed. Aurona May tried to sound matter of fact, but she didn't convince anyone.

"Well, that's what we bought them for yew know. I wish we hadn't bought them now though."

My mother lamented,

"It's terrible, poor little things. Well, one thing's for sure, we can't do it, can we?"

The problem was *how* it was to be done and who *would* do it.

A cursory exploration of local slaughtering talent produced nothing. Not even the butchers were prepared to kill the birds.

"If they're dead I can pluck 'em, skin 'em or carve 'em," said Jones the Meat, "but I'm not killing 'em."

Nobody had the stomach to kill living creatures. Finally, Dad Smith persuaded a local farmer to carry out the dreadful deed the day before Christmas Eve, but he insisted on doing it on-site. We speculated on how he would carry out the killings and hoped it would be as painless as possible.

"Don't worry cariad, they won't feel a thing," promised Guto the Farm as he sauntered off to the allotment, unaware that we were trailing in his wake curious and scared for the birds.

He rigged up a taut, wire line, caught the chickens by their feet, and strung them up squawking and struggling for freedom.

"Go back home!" my mother ordered seeing me coming through the allotment door.

Hastily, I closed it behind me then stared through a gap in the hedge to see what was happening. Transfixed with horror my mother stood staring at the poor creatures. When she saw the sharp blade poised ready to strike she turned to run into the lane. Too late! Guto the Farm had slit the throat of the first chicken rapidly silencing the other three as he proceeded along the line.

Reaching our kitchen she sank onto a chair her chest heaving from running, waves of nausea washing over her as she visualised the macabre act. Guto appeared with two of the dead birds hanging from a piece of string and presented them to her.

"Good fresh, healthy birds there missus." He glanced knowingly at me. "Yew can help yewer mother to pluck 'em. I've no time for pluckin' but I'll show yew how to do it."

I couldn't look as he explained the rudiments of chicken-plucking whilst exposing patches of pink 'goose-flesh'.

After he had gone we stared at the poor, mutilated bodies trying to muster enough courage to pick at the feathers. For some obscure reason he hadn't decapitated them. The heads hung backwards in nightmarish fashion revealing the bloody contents of their throats.

Tears running down her face my mother plucked, sobbed, plucked and sobbed her way through the task while I tackled the other one. As I attempted to extract the first feather the chicken gurgled and jerked in my hands. We both screamed,

"It's still alive! Oh, my God, it's still alive!"

She ran across the road and dragged Dad Smith over to our house crying incoherently about dead birds coming back to life. When he saw the chicken he smothered a smirk and explained that sometimes nerves made them jump as if they were still alive.

"They'll stop after a while, just keep on pluckin'."

"No, it's no good, I can't do it; my stomach's churning. They're not just any old birds are they? They were eating corn out of my hand yesterday," she sobbed.

Dad Smith finished off the plucking assisted by Terry who gleefully waggled the chicken's dead head at me through the kitchen window.

"Now, stop that!" Dad Smith chided. "They're upset enough as it is."

"How would yew like it if someone cut your throat and took all your skin off?" I cried as my mother retired to the kitchen too nauseous to watch the desecration of the birds.

After much sighing and sympathetic glances Ginny and Bella were finally dressed, stuffed and put in the oven. Tiny chipolatas were placed carefully around the bird like an Egyptian Pharaoh carrying gifts into the next world. We couldn't bear to look at them, so naked, turning into a crisp, golden brown. Periodically, my mother checked their progress closing her eyes as she speared them with a fork or basted their plump bodies with spoonfuls of fat that had gathered in the bottom of the meat tray.

Festive decorations, Christmas music and laughter from the wireless made us feel marginally more cheerful as we consumed the soup while the birds rested on a large, oval, meat dish waiting to be served. The first incision started Roger and Michael snivelling.

"They've been murdered haven't they? Ginny and Bella's been murdered!" Roger wailed.

"Dwn't be so silly!" my mother cried tears welling up in her eyes as she pushed her plate away. "How can it be Ginny and Bella when yew were with me when I ordered the meat from Woodley's?"

"Well, I dwn't want any."

"Nor me," Michael chimed in.

"I couldn't eat it any of it either," I said.

Biting my lower lip I hung my head morosely contemplating my lap. Nobody ate any Christmas dinner but Tammy, our Pembrokeshire corgi, gulped down every delicious morsel.

WAS IT TWITS OR TWEETS?

Dreams we had spun in the 'long grass' were fading like a half-forgotten memory as I stirred into consciousness on Table Rock startled by the sounds of wildlife scurrying in the undergrowth. The air still hung warm and heady, birds chirruped in the surrounding trees, butterflies danced amongst the wild flowers. Tranquillity and stillness covered me like a comforting blanket against the real world in the streets below urging me to drift once again through time and space to a far distant summer.

Bill Hayley and his Comets, worn out from constant playing while we gyrated to the music, groaned incoherently from the amplifier as the gramophone slowed down. Between flailing arms and legs I rushed over, grabbed the handle and wound it up.

"C'mon, yew stupid machine, speed up!" I implored.

"Wind it a bit harder," Anwen urged. "I was just gettin' in full swing then."

Frantically, I wound faster and faster gripping the metal handle so tightly that it left angry grooves on the palms of my hands.

"*We're go-o-o-nna r-o-o-ck arou-ou-ou-nd the cl-o-o-ock ton-i-i-i-ght,*" promised Bill in a drunken voice.

Suddenly, the handle caught and wouldn't budge. Exasperated, I gave it a mighty wrench falling backwards on to the sofa as the lever came away.

"*Now* look what yew've made me do!" I complained as the needle jumped and careered crazily over the 78". It's all scratched now and I've only got a few Rock 'n Roll ones left and most of those are ruined. I'll just have to ask Terry to mend it for the time being. We can't use the proper record player 'cause it's broken down. I'll have to wait 'till Christmas now before I get a new one."

"What shall we do now then?"

"Let's go up the 'long grass' for a bit, is it?" I asked.

"Yeah, but not for long. I thought we could go to the 'flicks' tonight. There's a new Elvis film in 'The Hall'.

Snow-white clouds scudded over the crest of Cefn Glas blown by a mischievous breeze that pleasantly fanned our faces and ruffled our hair. The mountain was alive with the sounds of nature. Wind berry bushes, scattered in dense patches, had taken hold of the verdant hillside. Our favourite climbing tree spread its foliage to shade us from the sun as we laboured up the path to the 'long grass'. Lying back on the warm stone we talked, but it was different talk, not the dreams of our childhood. Anwen stretched and sighed,

"I'll be leavin' school in a few weeks and straight into work. Won't have much time for the mountain then. Mind yew it 'asn't been the same this year."

"Well, we've been to Ponty a lot, and down Joe's listening to the juke box."

"We'll go down Sunday night, if yew like, when the crowd's there, is it?"

"Yeah, we could call in for a Vimto Saturday night as well on the way to the Empress."

"Come on, let's make our way back down now," Anwen said sounding bored.

Within weeks she had moved into the adult world of work and her own pay packet. As the months passed and Christmas loomed I began to spend more time with Nia drooling over the latest 'pop' records.

Most records were bought from Fred Faye's in Taff Street, near the ornamental fountain in Pontypridd, a favourite haunt of Tommy Woodward later the world famous Tom Jones.

"When we go to Ponty I want to pop in Faye's to get some sheet music or a song book ready for Christmas," my mother informed me as we knocked on Aurona May's door.

Nia and her mother appeared at the door muffled in scarves and heavy coats.

"We're ready. We should catch the next Red & White in about ten minutes," Aurona said, "then we'll have time to do a bit of shoppin' before having something to eat."

We trudged up Thurston Street to wait for the 'bus on 'Top of the Hill' breathing out white, cold vapour like angry dragons as we stamped our feet to keep warm.

"Here it comes," I said as the bull-nosed vehicle came round the corner.

The 'bus lurched to a halt throwing passengers, standing in the aisle, forward in a domino effect.

"Standin' room only ladies or yew can wait for the next 'bus."

Hanging on to the overhead rails we bounced and swayed the few miles to Pontypridd staggering against other passengers every time the 'bus stopped and started again. We alighted behind the Town Hall, made our way across Gelliwasted Road down the hill into Taff Street to meet the crowds.

It started to rain; a light drizzle that chilled the bones as it gradually seeped through clothes. Bundled in long coats and zip-up bootees middle-aged women carted brown, paper carrier bags, with flimsy string handles, bursting with Christmas shopping. Some arm in arm with their men folk; others marching ahead while their errant husbands trailed behind blowing out cigarette smoke with pained expressions on their faces. Young mothers pushed 'prams' their babies muffled inside padded 'siren' suits. People jostled along the crowded pavements stopping to gaze in shop windows or greet friends. Passers by stepped into the road to make progress down the street towards Market Square and Woolworth's.

The store was so crowded it was impossible to move more than a few inches at a time. I strained to edge nearer to a display of colouring books and crayons, but my arms were firmly pinned at my sides by dozens of pressing bodies. Claustrophobia gripped me with a burning desire to get out into the air. My mother was two bodies in front wedged against the counter.

"I'm going over there by the door. I can't breathe in here, it's too crowded," I called over her head.

She pushed her way through the mass of bodies breathing a sigh of relief as she felt fresh air from the door that was rapidly opening and closing as people came and went. Minutes later Aurona May and Nia came jostling through the crowd.

"Never again, it's pandemonium in here. Let's get out before I faint off."

We threaded our way through the outdoor market examining the bales of material, slippers perched on upturned shoe boxes, handbags, pots, pans and carpets hanging like tapestries from the back wall of the stalls. Inside, the smell of fresh fish, meat, faggots and peas, freshly baked bread and cakes intermingled with the earthy smell of vegetables and the strange odours of the pet stalls.

"It's just as crowded. Let's go and have a cup of tea in Princes' café and a custard slice," urged my mother.

Downstairs was packed with steaming bodies, taking refuge from the rain and bustle outside, so we decided to have a cooked lunch upstairs instead. Gratefully, I deposited the Christmas presents I'd bought by the side of my chair and studied the menu deciding on roast pork followed by apple pie and custard washed down with a cup of steaming tea. Fortified by the hot food we reluctantly vacated our seats under the watchful eye of those waiting for tables.

"Up to Fred Faye's then is it?" queried my mother as we emerged onto the pavement.

"Yes, did I tell yew Silas is comin' home from America?" Aurona May asked as they entered the shop.

"Is that the one who had the accident?"

"Yes...." her voice trailed off as she tried to remember what she wanted. "There's a record I want to get Pam for Christmas, but I'm blowed if I can remember what it's called."

Neither of them was well informed about teenage 'pop' music and never seemed to know what title had been recorded by a particular artiste.

Faye's was crowded with teenagers listening to the latest number one. We edged nearer as the crowd thinned around the counter waiting our turn to be served. Very tentatively Aurona May ventured,

"I'd like a record but I'm not sure of the exact title. It's something to do with 'believing, we believe, make believe' or something like that, I think."

She gazed over Fred Faye's head, brow furrowed with concentration, trying hard to remember the title. Suddenly, she blurted triumphantly,

"I've got it! 'Only Make Believe' by, er Connie, Conrad, no Conway, that was it. Conway Twotty, Twutty or Twatty. Something like that, wasn't it?" she said innocently turning to my mother for confirmation.

Fred Faye tried his best to cover up a smirk while some of the customers in the shop sniggered behind their hands.

"I think you mean Conway *Twitty* madam," he said politely, turning away from the counter.

A man, avidly studying a song book, smothered a guffaw, leered then turned to face the stand of sheet music.

"What's he laughing at?" I quizzed.

Puzzled and indignant at his rudeness we looked back at the man who was still laughing his head off. Looking flustered Aurona May snapped angrily,

"Just put it down to his ignorance!"

Completely unaware of why they were the source of amusement they headed for the door noses in the air. Aurona's dark eyes glittered with fury while my mother looked embarrassed and bemused, her eyelashes fluttering rapidly as they always did when she felt unsure of herself.

When Aurona told Ted what had happened he smothered a laugh of embarrassment unable to offer an explanation. Days later, after Ted had finally educated Aurona, she related the explanation for her gaffe to my mother. Squirming with humiliation they vowed never to go in Fred Faye's again. The following week they walked down Taff Street, on the opposite side of the road, shielded by the fountain. Darting in to the indoor market Aurona May declared,

"Well, anyway, how was I to know with a *stupid* name like *Tweety*?"

CARY GRANTS UNDERSHORTS

Aurona May had another brother besides Isaac and Silas. Jeremiah, a bachelor brother who lived with her family all his life. Jeremiah was a miner and strictly a creature of habit. Every morning he rose at the same time and left for work at exactly the same time every day. After his shift he arrived home, bathed, shaved, ate his dinner and retired to bed. At exactly 8 'o clock every evening he met his two bachelor friends, all in their late fifties, and went off to the local pub for two pints of beer. The three friends dressed immaculately in similar vein; tweed sports jacket, slacks, always a shirt and tie plus a 'Dai' cap. Every night he left the pub at dead on ten o' clock closing time calling,

"G'night then boys. See yew tomorrow then."

"Aye, g'night Jeremiah."

Whistling, he made his way home and directly to bed to repeat the exercise every day until he retired. One day Jeremiah was taken ill, went to bed and was dead within weeks. To me it seemed like a wasted life based on habit and routine. Once the routine was broken by retirement his life ceased to have any meaning.

Aurona May's other brother, Silas, was the black sheep of the family, but he had *such* tales to tell. As a young man he had emigrated to the United States and taken American citizenship, but he had a dual passport. During a stint in New York City he was hit and pinioned between two, yellow taxi cabs crushing most of the bones in his body. Compensation for his injuries reputedly amounted to a quarter of a million U.S. dollars, a huge amount of money for the times. After his recovery he embarked on fast living and managed to meet and socialise with a number of Hollywood film stars.

Enraptured, we listened avidly as he told us stories about his colourful life and the places he had visited in 'the States'. Niagara

Falls, Beverly Hills, San Francisco; places we had only seen in films.

"Marlene Dietrich. What a gal! Always la-ast down the stairs," he related laughingly.

"She'd arrive la-ast at the top of the most o-opulent staircase in the hotel so she could make a gra-and entrance."

My mother and Aurona listened with rapt attention as he talked about Stewart Granger, Cary Grant and other well-known film stars he was supposed to have met.

Prudish shock and disbelief sprang into their eyes when Silas, a hard-drinking womaniser, described his alleged drinking binges with Errol Flynn, whom he adored, and regarded as a soul-mate. No-one knew how much was fact or fiction, but he swore that his stories were true.

"It can't be true. I bet yew can take all that with a pinch of salt Aurona. He's playing us for fools, I'm sure. Look at him winking," my mother laughed but they still listened eyes wide with astonishment.

Silas narrated how he had spent all night drinking with the legendary Flynn in the boiler room of one of New York's most prestigious hotels. Nia and I were not supposed to be listening, but we strained our ears and listened behind the door of the living room looking at each other in amazement.

One titbit of interest was that he knew that Cary Grant allegedly only wore the new-style, nylon, boxer shorts which had not yet reached the valleys. One day he pulled out cellophane packets containing what appeared to be knee-length swimming trunks; one brand-new pair of pale blue and another pale lemon.

"Ca-ary gave me these," he said with a mischievous smile. "Yeah, one Christmas in Be-everly Hills," he drawled in his vaguely Welsh American accent.

Everybody was fascinated ogling what were supposed to be Cary Grant's under-shorts. What a giggle and what naïvety. They tentatively touched the hem of the screen idol's unmentionables and burst into fits of giggles.

"They're bra-and new," he said. "Never bin worn. They're what ya call drip-dry in the States. Wouldn't wear 'em maself – too baggy and uncomfortable. They'll make great swimmin' trunks though."

"Oh, I dwn't know," said my mother when he offered them to her for my step-father. "I dwn't like the idea of him wearing shorts that belonged to somebody else."

"Don't ya worry," said Silas, "I told ya, they're absolootely bra-and new. Look, here's the receipt and the price tag is still on 'em."

Leonard wasn't happy but, not wanting to offend, he very reluctantly took them when Silas shoved them at him. Bought from a famous New York department store they were pushed into the back of a drawer with the price tag still on them. Thrilled by the very name of the city I conjured up vivid pictures of skyscrapers, yellow cabs, gangsters and movie stars.

Months later, on another excursion to Hay-on-Wye, my mother grabbed the shorts from the back of the drawer and said to Leonard,

"Yew can try these on today. Go for a swim like the other men. Dwn't worry they were brand new in the packet. Besides, I've unpacked them and washed in disinfectant *twice*."

Leonard hated the water and began to protest but she cut him short.

"You're always the same. Well, this time we're all going to have a dip and that's that!"

In those days the River Wye was as clear as crystal. Every Sunday saw bathers at any point where they could swim in the cool waters. The usual crowd of uncles and aunts were on the trip. The men solidly built, of medium height and darkly handsome. Terry, Donald, Emrys, Raymond and Dad Smith were all happily swimming in the depths of the river while the giggling women were dipping their toes at the edge of the water.

My mother and Barbara, her sister, both blonde, small-boned, pretty and petite sat chattering and laughing on the grassy bank. Nana Smith was sitting on a deckchair watching the children from behind her sunglasses while I swam out to join my uncles who were more like older brothers to me. As usual Donald started to clown around ducking my head under the water. I was prone to severe nose-bleeds which left me pale and washed out. Unfortunately, holding my head under the water started off a nose-bleed.

"For goodness sake Duck!" remonstrated Emrys. "Leave the girl alone. Yew've started her nose bleeding now!"

"That's your fault again," I grizzled at Donald.

My grandparents chided him for his stupidity while I scrambled out of the water holding my nose.

"Hold your head back and sit quietly. Pinch your nose and try not to swallow any blood," said my mother. "Pass me that bottle of cold pop and I'll hold it against the back of your neck."

All this time the young men had been swimming trying to see who could go the deepest and stay under water the longest.

"How long has Terry been under?" queried Vera his blonde, blue-eyed fiancé.

"Too long I think, come on!" urged Donald to the other boys.

Frantically, they dived into the water and disappeared beneath the calm surface, for what seemed to be an eternity, as we all watched anxiously from the bank. Suddenly, four heads broke the surface at the same time bringing Terry, coughing and spluttering, to the surface.

"We got him just in time," said Raymond. "He was tangled in a piece of barbed wire that some idiots must have thrown in. If I get my hands on them!"

Nana Smith fussed, chastised and threatened her boys about their horseplay.

"It'll all end in tears one of these days if you're not more careful. I shudder just to think what might have happened."

Eventually, everybody settled down and fell quiet for a while relaxing before tea but decidedly more subdued. The feeling didn't last and before long a tennis ball was produced then a cricket bat and some hurriedly-fashioned, makeshift stumps. We were the only people in this particular spot, a favourite of ours for this very reason, so we could play freely beside the river until the picnic was ready. After satisfying our hunger and resting for a while we started to pack away the remnants of the picnic into the boots of the cars.

Though evening was approaching an iridescent sun still shone fiercely without a cloud to break the cerulean sky. The thought of sitting in a hot car sent us back to the water's edge for a quick paddle before journeying home.

"Len yew haven't been in the water yet!" my mother exclaimed.

"Doesn't matter," he cried nonchalantly, "another time. I dwn't really want to go in anyway."

"Oh, come on, be a sport Leonard," said Nancy, Emrys' wife. "Yew've sat on the side all day."

Roger, Michael and Barbara's boys took up the chant.

"Come on! In the water! In the water!"

"Come on," said my mother with a smirk, "show Nancy and Betty the swimming trunks Silas gave yew. Yew'll never believe it Nance. Cary Grant, you know *the* Cary Grant the film star bought them for Silas, Aurona May's brother, or so he claims."

By this time he had dipped his toe into the river but hesitated about going any deeper. After much ridiculing and joking Leonard finally let himself into the water.

"Oh, good god, its freezin'!" he moaned jumping upwards as the chill got to him.

He stood knee-deep in water resplendent in Cary Grant's Christmas present to Silas. Everybody stopped talking and stared at him. My mother and Vera stood with their hands over their mouths averting their eyes. Nancy and Betty were giggling hysterically while Nana Smith's expression was transfixed in horror.

"Ycha fi!" she said putting the tea-towel over her eyes. "Disgusting! Do something about him please."

Leonard just grinned inanely not realising his predicament. With that Dad Smith shouted at me,

"Get in the car now and dwn't yew dare look my girl! Do yew hear me!"

The men and boys were encircling Leonard with towels like Spartacus' soldiers protecting him with their shields. The almost tragic day had turned to comedy. On contact with the water Cary Grant's present was now completely transparent. It was to be whispered about with hilarity and embarrassment for many years to come when the 'season of the long grass' was a distant memory hovering like a butterfly that fluttered in and out of my thoughts: pushed aside while I danced to the heady music of the saxophone.

TANGO IF YEW MUST

Sid Davey, the owner of the Empress Ballroom, stood in the foyer eyeing the prospective dancers as they surged through the doors: a quiet, diminutive man in a well-worn suit and grey, button-up cardigan. By his side stood Slogger Jones, the bouncer, ready to prevent any troublemakers from entering the hall. Beetle-browed, broad shouldered, receding hairline and perpetual green-grey sports jacket and flannels worn by the majority of miners during their leisure hours.

He smiled benignly at the sight of the village's 'Teddy Boy Trio', but Slogger's eyes glinted under his bushy eyebrows. The boys swaggered along in their long coats and velvet collars, tight drainpipe trousers and crêpe-soled shoes. As they spotted a group of girls they fiddled with their string ties and smoothed back the brilliantined sides of their Tony Curtis hairstyles.

"There'd better not be any trouble from yew lot tonight," Slogger warned, "or yew'll be out on yewer neck."

"Aye, arright Slog….."

Slogger glared menacingly at Ricky in his bright, blue suit daring him to continue.

"I mean Mr. Slog….er….sorry….Jones," he winked at the others as he made his way to the boys' stairs making sure Slogger couldn't see him.

The boys stairs ascended to the dance hall from the left of the ticket booth with the girls' stairs to the right. Anyone rash enough to use the wrong entrance would be escorted back into the ballroom and pointed in the right direction.

Inside the lights dimmed, the mirror balls gleamed and sparkled as they caught the light shooting brilliant, rainbow shades over the dancers; freckling the floor with patches of colour. Boys stood around the hall, hands stuffed in pockets, eyeing the girls as they danced by. Heads in the air, feigning disinterest, we tripped past trying not to catch the eye of anyone we particularly fancied. Girls never danced face to face but stood, side by side, with their arms around each other's waists, as if they were marching a Military Two Step. Quicksteps, foxtrots and the waltz were all danced in this peculiar fashion around the edge of the floor.

The usual crowd of girls demurely lined the walls occasionally glancing in the direction of the boys doing the same thing from the opposite side of the room. Anwen and Mati suddenly emerged from the shadows at the far end of the hall and rushed across the floor.

"Haven't seen yew for ages. C'mon. let's dance!"

"Dwn't look now," Anwen hissed a few minutes later, "but I think those boys over there are going to 'tap' us."

"Which two?" I said through the side of my mouth trying to appear nonchalant.

"The blond one in the grey suit and the one next to 'im. Keep dancin'; they're comin' over now."

Eyes straight ahead we danced on waiting for the light touch on the shoulder, but the boys had skirted past and 'tapped' the girls behind us. Sounding miffed, Anwen cocked her nose in the air and declared,

"Well, I didn't like the look of 'im anyway."

"Neither did I. Did yew see his acne?"

"Oh no," I mouthed as I spotted a dumpy lad moving towards us, "it's that Ronnie with the slimy grin. I'm not dancing with him. C'mon, let's sit down, quick!"

As we were about to leave the floor Phil, the bandleader, announced,

"It's a Coronation Tango folks. If yew must dance then *tango* please."

Breathing a sigh of relief we stayed on the floor watching the two boys retreat to the shadowy edges of the hall.

Phil, the epitome of elegance and romance in his dinner jacket, caressed his saxophone under the spotlight as the others plucked their strings and blew their brass. Eyes sparkling with merriment Dick Gibbs, the percussionist, who owned a shoe shop in Cilfynydd, banged the cymbals, tinkled the glockenspiel or stroked the drums. Jovial, stocky and moustached he beat the rhythm of every dance with happy abandon. Latin American numbers saw Dick on his feet shaking the maracas; smiling broadly as he swayed to the rumba and bounced to the beat of the samba.

Only the good dancers danced 'properly' swaying and dipping dramatically to the music of '*Jealousy*'; swept along on a tide of fantasy with some hot-blooded Latino while others, dancing with male partners, swayed in the middle of the circling throng. Slogger surreptitiously eyed the smooching couples in the middle then pounced.

"That's enough of that yew two. Let's see some daylight between yew or yew're off the floor."

"Oops, there's going to be trouble. Let's sit down," I remarked as a gangly youth cut in on a couple in the inner circle who were 'going steady '.

"Get lost!" glowered a tall, dark-haired boy menacingly.

"I'm 'tapping yew arright!" retorted the foolhardy youth.

Grabbing him by the lapels the 'boyfriend' snarled,

"Oh, yew are, are yew? Well, this is *my* girl an' she only dances with *me*, get it!"

Heated words and gestures until Slogger miraculously appeared from nowhere to defuse passions.

Finely tuned to spotting trouble nobody argued with Slogger. Dragging them apart by the scruff of the neck he shook them like rats forcing them to shake hands. Only the foolhardy or uninitiated dared to start a disturbance. He moved amongst the dancers like a cat, silent and smooth as quicksilver, or lurked in the shadows ready to pounce. Within minutes the culprits found themselves unceremoniously ejected and permanently barred from the delights of Phil Hopkins and his band.

Halfway through the evening the musicians took a break but not the dancers. They danced on as the vinyl spun.

"C'mon girls, let's bop," Anwen said enthusiastically as the crowd moved onto the floor.

Boys with long sideburns gyrated to the sounds of '*Jailhouse Rock*'. Pony-tailed girls in billowing, multi-layered net petticoats, soaked all night in sugar water to make them stiff, threw themselves into the jive. In black, velvet ballerina shoes, topped by shocking-pink or lime-green socks, they mouthed '*Stupid Cupid*' along with Connie Francis as they bopped until they were breathless.

"Yew can feel the floor movin' when yew bounce. It's great innit!" Mati called as she twirled.

A very grand establishment for a small village like Abercynon, the Empress boasted the finest dance floor in South Wales fêted for its smooth, shiny surface and sprung joist floor.

"Oh, the band's coming back in," I moaned. "Just when I was getting going too. I could dance on this floor all night, couldn't yew?"

"Yeah, it's great," Anwen beamed.

"We might as well go for a drink now, as soon as this record's finished."

Having a drink meant going into a refreshment area at the side of the stage where Mrs Davey served tea, crisps, chocolate, pop and sandwiches. Alcohol was strictly forbidden. Shoulders squared Slogger eyed the boys for any signs of concealed, illicit drink poised ready to propel the reprobate firmly through the doors.

On Saturday nights, after the pubs closed at 10 o' clock, the Empress filled to capacity with all ages from fifteen to sixty plus. Sometimes mothers, fathers and even grandparents appeared to enjoy the last hour of dancing until 11 o' clock when the band played '*The Last Waltz*' followed by '*Hen Wlad Fy Nhadau*' and '*God Save the Queen*'.

"Let's get our coats before the crowd gets there," Anwen urged rushing to the cloakroom.

"The other girls are waitin' outside for us with the boys," I replied. "We're all walking up together, but I think Paul wants to walk me home."

Shuffling impatiently, hands in pockets, the boys greeted us.

"Where've yew been for goodness sake. We've been out 'ere ages waiting for yew."

Laughing, talking, walking hand in hand, the crowd drifted up Margaret Street or across to Glancynon.

"Oh, *great!*" I exclaimed spotting my uncle Raymond sauntering behind us at a discreet distance. "Trust him to be here again. He'll be watching us all the way home now, as usual!"

We laboured up Doctor's Hill with Raymond still trailing behind. As we past John Evans' shop he marched briskly past calling,

"Goodnight all."

"G'night," we chanted.

"He's gorgeous in 'e." Anwen sighed gazing after him as he disappeared into the brightly lit hall of my grandparents' house.

"He's at least going on thirty yew know," I declared indignantly.

"I dwn't care. I wiped my face in the towel 'e used when I went in yewer gran's bathroom yesterday," she sighed.

"Aw dwn't be so stupid! Anyway, yew'd better not let Nana Smith hear yew talking like that or it'll be the last time yew go in her house."

"Dwn't care, I'll never wash my face again."

He'll be watching me through the window, yew can bet, and Terry as well," I groaned.

"See yew next Saturday. Dwn't forget the fair's comin' to the basin," she called as she disappeared through her gate.

Lingering under the street lamp outside my house Paul and I chatted amiably for a few minutes. Tentatively, he put his arm round my waist leaning forward to give me a peck on the cheek then thought better of it.

"Goodnight then," he sighed noting my nervous glances.

Across the road, in Nana Smith's, the lights suddenly dimmed.

"Dwn't look now," I grinned, "but I think we're being watched."

Revealed by the light of the street lamp Nana Smith's curtains twitched surreptitiously in the shadows while two dark shapes moved barely perceptibly in the gloom.

THE BALLROOM AND THE BASIN

It was high summer when the showmen rolled their travelling fair into the Basin. An important part of Welsh history the Basin was the shipping point for barges from Aberdare and Merthyr. In the 1950s water from the Glamorganshire Canal, built in the eighteenth century to ship coal and timber to Cardiff, could still be seen from the bridge in Glancynon. Richard Trevithick's famous steam engine, the first to run on rails from Penydarren to the Basin, heralded the demise of the canal. In later years a plaque to commemorate this historic event was erected at the entrance to the Basin while the boiler plate was salvaged and housed in the Kensington Patent Museum in London.

"The fair's in the Basin!" Anwen cried as she bounced into the kitchen. "Let's go over and take a look, is it?"

"I'd rather go when it's dark; it's more fun when it's lit up," I replied.

During the day the fair ran gently, revolving roundabouts with giant chickens, snorting horses, sports cars and bicycles for young children.

"P'raps we could go tonight if we come out of the dance early enough. There's a rumour going round that a nightingale was heard there last night. Half Abercynon's going over to hear it. My mother's taking the boys for a treat so I've got to meet her outside the dance about a quarter to nine."

After the Saturday night dance at the Empress people trouped to the fair set up in the Basin. Screeching dodgems, gaudily-painted carousels, gaily-painted swing-boats, their occupants screaming in mock terror, eyes shut tight or looking pale and sickly from the motion of the swing plunging downwards.

"C'mon let's 'ave a go on *something*," Anwen cried. "What about the chairoplanes?"

I eyed the little chairs suspended on chains that swung out and higher into the air the faster it moved.

"I want a go on that," Roger cried tugging at my mother's skirt.

"Absolutely not and that's my final word, especially after what happened to that poor girl last time the fair was here," my mother retorted referring to the child who had plunged to the ground from the highest point when one of the chairs broke loose from its moorings.

Queues moved slowly outside the fortune-teller's tent, girls giggling as they clung to the arms of young men who scuffed their feet and feigned nonchalance. Others nervous and fidgety already worrying about the fate that awaited them. A poster pinned to the booth declared in garish, red letters,

'Madame Laila – Clairvoyant – Fortune Teller To The Stars'.

Anwen pushed towards the queue dragging me with her.

"I've always wanted my fortune told," she squealed with delight. "I wonder who I'll marry."

Feeling decidedly nervous I retorted,

"Aw, it's a load of old rubbish. *I'm* not going in. Yew'll have to go in on your own. Yew can tell me all about it when yew come out."

Seeing my mother watching the boys on the roundabout I ran over relieved to be rid of my apprehension.

"I've changed my mind," Anwen laughed running up behind me. "Come on, let's go on the dodgems!"

Evening wrapped the fair in a festive cloak of myriad colours. At night the atmosphere was magical; bright, fairy lights, a cacophony of sounds and the tantalising smell of candyfloss that floated on the warm summer air. Smells different from seaside fairgrounds: pungent odours of engine oil mingled with sweet-smelling grass, fried onions and trampled earth. 'Rock and Roll' music blared as dodgem cars ground around the circuit with shouts from the showman of,

"No bumpin'!" which were completely ignored by the majority of drivers.

Colliding with a loud thump their occupants laughed and called to people in the other cars. Another shout,

"Car number three, 'oive warned ya once already," he snarled in a strange accent.

Multiple thuds signalled a pile-up with drivers pressing down on the accelerator frantically spinning the wheel to disentangle the cars. Our 'dodgem' was jammed against the edge by four others preventing any movement. A beefy showman jumped from car to car onto the back bumper holding on to the metal pole at the rear. Freeing the cars he guided the dodgem to the side muttering furiously at the errant occupants.

"Last warning for ya now or ye'll be off."

For a short time, chastened and subdued, they drove sedately around before seeking out their friends to collide again with whoops of joyous laughter. A horn blared signalling the end of the ride.

"I didn't even have a proper drive," I complained as we squeezed out of the car and headed for the gallopers.

Still frustrated with my impeded progress on the dodgems I climbed onto my favourite carousel.

"Hold on toight now!" warned the showman. "Here we go!"

Slowly, the carousel gathered speed until we were flying to the rhythm of the organ music. Faster and faster we rode as the showman moved among the horses giving instructions.

"Keep ya legs in me darlin' and hold the reins with both hands," he advised as he drew up the reins and placed them in the woman's hands.

"And that's enough of them shenanigans from ya laddies or ye'll be off the ride now," he bellowed at two boys pushing and shoving each other from side to side.

His voice faded as I surrendered to the sensuous thrill of the ride.

Galloping horses, gaudily-painted, carved flowing manes, kicking heels and red, flaring nostrils. Fathers holding toddlers in front as they cantered into the air. Mothers watching excited children as they followed the ride towards the sky. Sitting high astride a magnificent wooden steed, eyes closed, soaring up; up towards the night sky. Gentle and beguiling they moved gracefully up and down, up and down, to the rhythm of the mechanical, organ music. Hair streaming like strands of silk through slow-moving water, summer's heady breath on my face, I rode over sand dunes, over prairies and through cool mountain springs. Imagination fed an ever-changing vista that rolled out before me like illustrations in a book. Below me smiling faces, voices shrill with pleasure and exhilaration.

Men at shooting galleries and darts' stalls, young courting couples taking aim at the coconut shy; others throwing rubber loops over cheap prizes set on wooden blocks. Children squealing with delight as they tried to capture a plastic duck with a wire hoop on the end of a pole as it swam aimlessly, round and round, through a channel of never-ending water. Pennies dropping to activate a mechanical claw that foraged amongst a clutter of furry, miniature bears and squeaky toys. A colourful myriad of dolls, fancy mirrors, teddy bears and trinkets, that glittered in the reflected light, lined the walls at the back of the stalls.

Back on firm ground I moved amongst the throng drinking in the atmosphere as my friends chattered at my side.

"I've got a shilling left so I'm goin' to 'ave a go on the coconut shy," Anwen declared running towards the stall.

"Well yew'd better be quick 'cause the fair's closin' down now," Mati remarked looking at a nearby stall where a peroxide blonde, with a cigarette dangling from her lips, was pulling down a canvas canopy over the front of the stall.

"It can't be closing yet, it's too early," I complained as my mother called,

"We'd better make a move or the boys will be half asleep by the time we get home."

"We won't, we won't. Can't we stay a little bit longer?" they cried.

But the music had already stopped suddenly exposing the babble of conversation as people slowly wandered past the dying stalls dragging reluctant children whose hearts had leaped at the magic of the fair.

Silver stars twinkled in the velvet, midnight-blue sky above the fairytale scene below encapsulating the unreality of the moment; an atmosphere charged with a vibrancy that would leave a longing and restlessness in the hearts of our quiet village. When the last ride closed we slowly and reluctantly wound our way home looking over our shoulders as the lights of the fair closed down, one by one, and the Basin was left in darkness until another summer. Another season beckoned as the 'long grass' faded and slipped away lying forgotten in the recesses of my memory until it called me back again.

RETURN TO THE LONG GRASS

I shielded my eyes against a pale, watery sun that shone from a diluted firmament of blue. Fuzzy, elongated clouds drifted wraith-like across the heavens like dissipating plumes of smoke. A distant, deep-throated rumble heralded a passing jet on its journey to America leaving a trail of vapour across the sky. From the streets below a cacophony of harsh, traffic noise beat like discordant drums on the warm summer air, continuous and unrelenting. Meg, my mother's Staffordshire Bull Terrier, bounded ahead past the derelict shambles of Brown's slaughter house onto Cemetery Road that led to Table Rock in the heart of the 'long grass'.

"Stay Meg!" I ordered as I crested the hill.

The road still undulated to the gates of the cemetery, but as my eyes travelled the distance I saw that the black, cast iron gates had disappeared, the path running alongside cordoned off with wire. The road that once snaked up the mountain past Horse Rock and on to Van Pouke's farm completely obliterated by an avalanche of massive stones and rocks: the trusty steed that had carried us across the prairie smashed and buried beneath tons of rubble.

"The short-cut!" I remembered feeling excitement rising in my chest. I picked over the stones by the stile at the top end of Bateman's Field. "The path through the trees should be just here." I thought feeling increasingly disoriented as I was confronted by an unfamiliar landscape.

Trees either side closed their branches over the steep tunnel of embedded stones that once led us to the 'long grass'. Climbing over decades of weather-beaten rocks and fallen branches I clambered upwards towards the light forcing its way through the foliage in the near distance. Dank earth smells filled my nostrils as I moved deeper into the woods. A chill blanket of darkness covered the narrow clearing impeding my progress. Gradually, the light grew in intensity until I emerged, puffing and gasping, onto a patch of land over-looking the valley.

Far below the River Cynon, once black with coal dust, ran crystal clear like a ribbon of silver running through the valley: the surrounding hills still covered with oak, silver birch, thick blankets of fern and seasonal heather below a back-drop of dark-green pine trees. All round me coarse, yellowing grass grew calf deep unfettered by the feet of walkers or children at play. Rough shrubs, weeds and wild flowers fought for supremacy amongst the ant hills and stones. An occasional wind berry bush survived amongst orphan trees that had flourished plunging their roots deep into the earth for sustenance. Nature had embraced the 'long grass' and kept it for her own.

A sense of sadness enveloped my soul as I searched for Table Rock amongst the trees that had sprung up and covered the clearing where we once romped in the lush grass. The farm road had all but disappeared, reduced to a narrow, stone-strewn path. The view over the valley was partially obscured by tall trees. Below, the earth was blackened by fire, tree trunks wrenched from the ground to flatten the land for re-planting. All round lay the charred remains of branches that snapped and crackled underfoot. I kicked forlornly at the grass pushing aside ferns and branches in my search. Then I saw it, set like an unpolished, grey jewel, amongst trailing fronds of grass and rambling bushes.

My heart leapt with anticipation as I ran towards it, but the magical place of my childhood had melted into the past. Instead, an insignificant, flat rock patched with lichen, stray weeds growing from weather-worn crevices. Feeling empty and disappointed I sat down heavily on Table Rock closing my eyes against the glaring sun. Meg settled on the grass, eyes drooping, until she fell asleep occasionally twitching from the depths of her canine dreams. Weariness of spirit overcame me as I lay back, sharp edges of rock pressing painfully against my skin. Sighing, I ran my hands over the stone and felt myself drifting; spinning slowly through time back to the magical 'season of the long grass'.

Through the swirling kaleidoscope of time faces appeared and disappeared like wraiths of mist rising from a river in the early morning. Anwen and Mati lying on Table Rock making music with blades of grass; laughing inside our den of golden, long grass. Groups of picnickers sitting on snowy, white tablecloths while children foraged for wind berries. Snatches of muted conversation crowded into my memory.

"Well, did yew 'ere about Mrs Cardwell, yew know the one I mean, all airs and graces."

"Oh aye, I know who yew mean, yew'd swear butter wouldn't melt!"

"That's the one, well by all accounts........."

The voice drifted away as I remembered dipping our toes into the icy waters of the stream on Ghylfach-y-Ryd. The clink of horses' hooves as they skirted Table Rock. Sunny, summer mornings with my mother's clear, soprano voice singing, '*O Mio Babbino Caro*', as Tammy howled in doggy pleasure. Nana Howells' finely-cut features; blue eyes smiling and sad as she helped me sort the button tin in Milton Villa. Bending over the stove muttering,

"Drat, I've caught it just in time," as she rescued the home-made jam simmering on the stove.

Clinging to her wind-blown skirts as she held me close on the rocks in Ogmore. The thwack of tennis balls on the pine end. The breeze blowing up the sand in Barry Island as the sweet smells of candy floss floated on the evening air.

Dad Smith taking me to watch the blacksmith shoeing the horses swam before my eyes. Riding down to the farm beyond the village on the back of Duke, the big grey stallion, his voice ringing in my ears as he sang to a blushing Nana Smith,

> "*When I was a boy from the mountains and you were a girl from the hills,*
> *We would meet in the valley 'neath the old pine tree alone with the whip o' wills,*
> *We would meet there when school days were over,*

We would both say the same things again,
When I was boy from the mountains and you were a girl from the
hills."

Images as fresh as when we spun our dreams on Table Rock danced tantalisingly across my memory. Enchantment resonated in the air like tinkling bells on a snowy winter's night echoing another time. Past and present fused into an eddying miasma of thought connecting the mind and spirit. Table Rock stood like a sentinel guarding Time watchful of the passing years, but memories of childhood never die. It is here and now, past and present. When the present becomes the future it will drift into the past once again for they are as one entity commingled with the spirits of those who share our destiny. This is the magic of 'The Season of the Long Grass'.

When I Was A Boy From The Mountains
Words and Music by Young and Brown
© 1932 EMI United Partnership Ltd, London WC2H 0QY (Publishing) and Alfred Publishing Co, USA (Print)
Administered in Europe by Faber Music Ltd